Firing and Flying for the Field Artillery in Korea

By

Kincheon H (Bert) Bailey

This book is a work of non-fiction.

First published by AuthorHouse 08/27/04

ISBN: 1-4184-6969-6 (e-book)
ISBN: 1-4184-5280-7 (Paperback)
ISBN: 1-4184-5279-3 (Dusk Jacket)

Library of Congress Control Number: 2003094185

This book is printed on acid free paper.

Printed in the United States of America
Bloomington, IN

ACKNOWLEDGMENTS

Although well versed in grammar and other aspects of the English language, thanks to my formal high school and college training, I needed help in the latest development and intricacies of the modern computer. As an electrical engineer skilled with the use of the slide rule, vacuum tubes and early solid state devices, I retired prior to mastering today's higher level computerese. Not to worry, two computer gurus assisted me in "disking" my book, my oldest daughter, Mrs Linda Bailey Hux in Louisburg NC, and one of my top electronics students, Clement Matthews, Class of 1980 of Wake Technical Communty College in Raleigh where I taught electronics engineering technology for 25 years. Before I could erupt in violent temper tantrums, these two brilliant scholars rushed upon the scene and calmly pushed the right buttons so I could recompose myself and continue with my book. Both Linda and Clem were my "sina qua non". Full quieting was made possible by my son-in-law, Bob Brodd, an astute professional computer guru.

Of course, the "Little Woman", Tommye Lou, my better half, suffered in dedicated silence as I ignored the inevitable plumbing, automotive, yardwork and other problems associated with most, if not all, homesteads, while I devoted almost all my hours to "The Book". She was, in all aspects, an understanding, devoted wife..

The time and effort put in by LtGen Sidney Berry in his reply to my request for his thoughts on the Korean War are deeply appreciated. His outstanding service while in the 35th Infantry and his high regard for the field artillery support he received strongly reflect the camaraderie that existed between his Cacti and the Redlegs who gave him their all in direct support.

I am also obliged to express my appreciation to the Field Artillery School at Fort Sill in Indian Territory, whose training methods as presented in all their formal classes and in FM 6-40 Field Artillery Gunnery insure that the American field artillerymen are the best trained field artilleryman in the Universe.

FOREWORD

One of the several reasons I wrote this book was my realization that history, as related by several historians, is but one man's idea of what took place in the past. I was astounded to see on a TV historical presentation that two different groups of archaeologists, one British and one German as I recall, believe two different things, one, the Trojan War as presented in many school texts and library offerings, is factually correct and there are evidences of such war. Two, the other group(I forget which is which) states just as positively that there was no Trojan War and that it was a fabrication passed on from generation to generation by bards strumming their musical instruments while singing about a war never fought.

Wars never fought or forgotten? What's the difference in recorded history? There are those today who blithely term the Korean War, the Forgotten War, or the Korean Conflict. Assigned to the 2d Armored Division in Germany in 1954, I, along with other newly assigned officers who had fought in Korea, were not warmly received at first. Again, we were unctuously reminded our battles were of the Korean CONFLICT. However, when the STARS AND STRIPES printed some of the actions we new arrivals had participated in and medals won, the attitude of fellow officers who rode the WAR out in the Occupation of Germany changed perceptively.

These thoughts and attitudes bothered me. I fought in this WAR for 16 months and knew from personal experience both that the war was REAL and that, for many reasons it will never be forgotten.

We lost 33,000 KIA in the first year of this war and, in 7 years of the VN War, their KIAs numbered the same. In Korea the ubiquitous Field Artillery fired more projectiles than ALL THOSE FIRED in WWII! The Korean War was never forgotten and never will be. "Nuff said.

Having spent my time in Korea with the same battalion, the 64th FA Bn, I became well acquainted with all the men with whom I worked. FOs came and went but I got to know them well, also, But the cannoneers, FDC crews, the motor maintenance and commo sections, mess personnel, and those in supply, Sv Btry ammo handlers, and all the rest,—I became keenly aware of their dedication, hard work, and attention to the details required by their MOS. Few knew these heroes better than I ; so I feel qualified to describe their everyday performance, and how such contributed to our success in Korea. I could not fail but note that all members of my battery possessed attitudes that played a major part in their ability to survive and help the rest of us do the same. First, they had an undying love of God and Country,. Second, most had strong family ties that sustained them thru the more harrowing episodes of our fight. Third, all firmly believed that discipline was, simply put, the habit of intelligent obedience.

That we did not win the war in Korea was not the fault of any of the American or other UN soldiers who fought there. Given the opportunity by political power on the home front to win, our military will, as sustained by its aforementioned philosophical beliefs, successfuly defend our great country no matter how violently tactics, strategy, weapons systems, battle or AREA fields, and other aspects of the military domain, change. And there can be no doubt that the Great Architect of the Universe is on the side of the greatest democracy in the world and its sanguine future.

The FIELD ARTILLERY JOURNAL

MAR.-APR. 1950

A BOUQUET

In the Jan.-Feb. 1950 issue of the Armored Cavalry Journal, Garrett Underhill reviews at some length Colonel Louis B. Ely's book, THE RED ARMY TODAY. The two paragraphs below are extracted from this review.

It's high time we heard from the Artillery, too. The only thing wrong with our Artillery during the war was its public relations. Our Artillery was so good that it didn't have to whip up interest. Few know that the boys out at Sill by the mid-1930s had worked out tactics and technique which stood up to the test of war as did the T & T of no other arm of any Army. Our Artillery, though teaching one of war's most complex arts, did a marvelous job of training too.

25th Infantry Division Band in Japan

Major Herman Smith

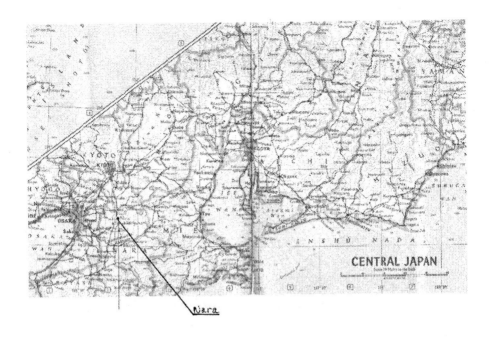

Nara

CENTRAL JAPAN

CHAPTER ONE

Japan to Korea

Not having joined the 64th FA Bn until late August 1950, I knew nothing about how the battalion got to Korea. Since this book is about the Field Artillery in general and the 64th in particular, I needed complete information about the preparation for, as well the participation in combat of the battalion. Luckily, I learned about HERODOTUS II who kept a daily log or journal of the activities of the 64th with remarkable clarity, objectiveness and accuracy. This superb journalist was Major Herman Smith, our battalion executive officer. He, incidentally, maintained a similar type journal for every day of combat in which he fought in WWII,1942-1945. Unfortunately, as we shall read later, the good major broke his elbow fighting in Korea, and was evacuated to Japan on 27Nov50. Thereafter, my effort in writing this book was concentrated more on the actions of my own unit, "A" Battery of the 64th.

With(now colonel) Smith's OK via e-mail, I will start this effort with his complete log just as he recorded it, inserting comments of my own at appropriate intervals. In this way, I feel you, the reader, can get a good grasp of field artillery operations at both the firing battery level as well as that of the the battalion.

MAJOR HERMAN SMITH'S LOG OF THE

THE 64TH FIELD ARTILLERY BATTALION IN KOREA

3 JULY 1950

Bn alerted for rail movement to KYUSHU w/35th RCT

4 JULY 1950

0200 Bn started loading in NARA; entrained on 4 trains for CAMP HAKATA, KYUSHU. We cleared NARA at 1255 leaving Capt Block and a 6 man cleanup detachment behind.

5 JULY 1950

Unloaded at CAMP HAKATA; Bn closed 1435, remainder of day spent in getting oriented on our new mission. Bn occupied the 52nd FA Bn area.

6 JULY 1950

Day spent in organizing for occupying and administering the 24th DA zone of responsibility. At 1830 received coded orders for immediate movement to KOIZUMI, HONSHU (North of TOKYO). Loading officer, Lt Cole immediately dispatched to obtain necessary trains.

7 JULY 1950

Trains departed CAMP HAKATA at 0300, 0500, 0730 and 1000 by Btry in order A, HQ, B, Sv. Bn Commander and Lt Nyval to fly up later in the day.

8 JULY 1950

Bn less Sv Btry closed in CAMP ZAMA, HONSHU (West of YOKOHAMA) at 2305. Lt Col Hogan transferred to 25th D/A, VOCG. Maj Smith, Exec Off assumed cmd. (author's note: See map of Japan on page x.)

9 JULY 1950

Sv Btry closed CAMP ZAMA at 0300. Bn attached to 1st Cav D/A. Day spent in drawing TO&E shortages and maintenance of equipment, especially vehicles.

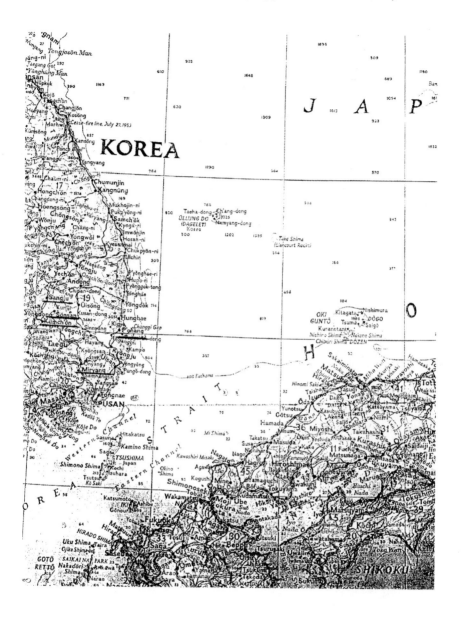

10 JULY 1950

Lt Ross sent to CAMP DRAKE as Bn Ln Off with 1st Cav D/A. Major Braatz (S-3) and Sgt Francis sent to 1st Cav Div G-3 as Bn embarkation team.

11 JULY 1950

Preparing for amphibious landing. Bn Co at Camp Drake for conference with Gen Palmer, CG 1st Cav D/A. Bn replaced L-4 aircraft.

12 JULY 1950

1400 Bn marched by motor convoy in the order A, B, Hq, Sv to CAMP OPPOMA, HONSHU. Bn closed in bivuoac area at Oppoma Ordnance Center at 1925, marched 47 miles.

13 JULY 1950

Bn started loading on LSTs 742, 795 and the Japanese LST Mara Maru. Bn has 1 1/2 basic load of arty ammo with an additional 3600 rds underdecked on LST 795.

14 JULY 1950

Completed the loading. One man per vehicle remained aboard ship; Lt Griffin on LST 742, Lt Cook on LST 795 and Lt Duncan on the Mara Maru. 1640 Bn departed by bus convoy, along with the 82nd FA Bn for CAMP DRAKE, HONSHU. Closed in Camp Drake at 1920; travelled 47 miles. Bn billeted in barracks.

15 JULY 1950 Awaiting call to board ship for movement to KOREA.

16 JULY 1950

No change.

17 JULY 1950

Bn entrucked at 0700 for 2nd Trans. Med Port, YOKOHAMA, HONSHU. Closed at 1100; travelled 40 miles. Loaded on USNS Gen E. D. Patrick at 1130; sailed as part of 1st Cav Div (Inf) at 1830 for KOREA. This was the 2nd lift.

18 JULY -21 JULY 1950

Enroute to KOREA in convoy with USNS Shanks, Ainsworth and one destroyer. Convoy put to sea in order to miss two typhoons. The crossing was quite rough.

22JULY 1950

1600 arrived POHANG DONG, KOREA beach. 1830, Bn less Sv Btry debarked by LSU and unloaded in the POHANG port. 2010 Bn entrucked and moved to Airport vicinity POHANG DONG. Travelled 7 miles. Billeted in old Jap barracks. Lt Col Hogan assumed command upon debarkation.

23 JULY 1950 (author: See Map of Korea/Japan on page 3)

0415, Bn's vehicles arrived in area. 0600 Sv Btry debarked and closed in area at 0750. 1200, Gen Allen, Asst CG 1st Cav Div visited the CP. At 1230 Bn CO and Lt Nyval flew to 8th Army Hq. 1825 Lt Col Hardman, 8th Army G-3 Sec arrived and notified Bn Exec that our Ln plane and pilot would remain behind, for use by the Navy and C Btry 159th FA, when the Bn left this area. Lt Reece was selected to remain and fly the requested missions.

24 JULY 1950

0300 S-3 and advance party left. 0600 Bn moved out under the Exec Off in the order A, Hq, B, Sv and closed in KUMCHON after marching 113.9 miles. At 1330 D/A CG met advance party 10 miles S of SANGJU (1114-1505) and ordered Bn into rendezvous area at KUMCHON. At 1920 Bn moved out under Exec in order B, A, Hq,

5

Sv for SANGJU. At 2135, 5 miles S of SANGJU Bn was met by S-3 and D/A Asst S-3, Capt Moran, and ordered into rendezvous area 3 miles back toward KUMCHON (1111.8-1496.5). Bn marched into SANGJU, turned around and marched to selected point only to find area impassable. At 2235 Bn marched 2 miles further South and went into rendezvous N and E of OKSAN-DONG. Bn closed at 2330. Marched 156 miles for the day.

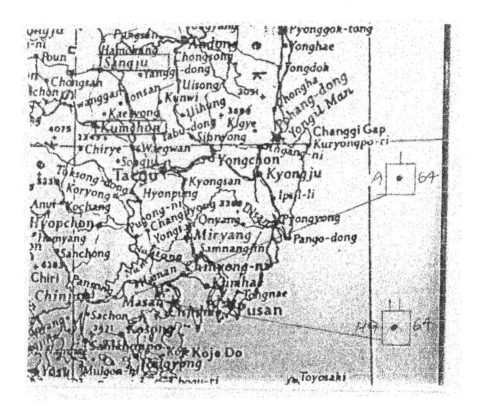

25 JULY 1950

1000 Bn Co and BC parties left for posn area reconnaisance N of SANGJU 1100 Bn moved out under Exec in order B, A, Hq with Sv Btry remaining in present posn. At 1135 Exec Off rcvd radio msg from Bn S-2 to disperse the Bn Vicinity of SAMGKI (1114-1505) as enemy planes had been strafing N of SANGJU. 1210 Bn was dispersed in SANGJU. 1410 B Btry moved out of SANGJU and at 1505 closed in posn at (1108.9-1512.1) Capt Sherman arrvd and assigned as Asst S-3, Lts Roper and Osborne to A Btry and Lt Sexton to B Btry. 1450 A and Hq Btrys moved out of SANGJU. Hq Btry closing in posn vicinity of (1112.8-1510.0) at 1600. A Btry closed in position vicinity (1114.4-1516.2) at 1735. No ammo expended. Hq btry outposts report hearing enemy activity; however our patrols failed to reveal any enemy. Our mission is DS 35th Inf.

26 JULY 1950

0130 Bn Exec Off, S-2 and 10 men made patrol for the enemy reported by Hq Btry outposts. Patrol contacted no enemy. 1100 B Btry registered by Air OP. 1115 A Btry registered by air OP. 1130 received msg from D/A to paint white identification stars on all vehicles. At 1800, as a result of phone msg from 35th Inf, Bn Exec left on posn area reconn to the South and West. 1850 Bn Co and BC parties left for D/A Hq in SANGJU. 2225 Bn moved out under S-3 in order A, B, Hq. Our mission now GS 159th FA Bn who are in DS 24th Inf. Bn Co 159 gave us mission of GS 2nd Bn 24th Inf. Expended 146 rds.

27 JULY 1950

0130 Bn closed in area NAKSO-RI (1100.7-1502.8). Marched 19 miles. Expended 350 rds. (Total to date 596)

28 JULY 1950

1340 A Btry displaced to rear at (1101.2-1502.1). 1500 B Btry displaced to rear at (1102.2-1501.8). Bn CP at (1100.7-1502.8) did not move. Sv Btry displaced forward to SANGJU from posn near OKSAN DONG. Displacement of firing btrys was necessary to enable us to fire defensive fires for the 24th Inf which had pulled back all along the line. Bn had Capt DaPrado as Ln Off with 2nd Bn 24th Inf. and Lts Duncan and Griffin as FOs. The 2nd Bn was defending to the North and protecting the North flank of the Rgt. From E Co. on the right there was a gap of 8000 yds to E/35th to the NE. Contact between the two has not been made. Bn laid on CA 5700 to protect the N half of the sector. Defensive fires were shot in to protect the 2nd Bn. Radio communication with the LnO and FOs was nearly non-existant due to the mountain type terrain. Wire communication was maintained however. Expended 1558 rds. (Total to date 2154).

29 JULY 1950

0600 Lt Sheets relieved Lt Duncan as FO. Lts Bell and Osbourne sent out as addditional FOs to 2nd Bn 24th Inf. Lts Sexton and Ross returned to SANGJU as air observers for the Bn. During the morning Approx 900 rds were fired on RJs, villages and suspected enemy areas (all unobserved fires). Large stocks of ammo were on hand in SANGJU (1114-1505) and in view of the possible loss of the town, ammo expenditures were high rather than having to destroy unfired ammo later. At 1900 MG and small arms fire was received by 2nd Bn 24th from the front, flanks and rear; the enemy having moved in behind on both flanks of the 2nd Bn thru the draws. Light arty and mortar fire was brought to bear on our posns as far to the rear as the foremost Arty Btry posn. We delivered defensive fires on all sides of the 2nd Bn 24th and searched the draws leading into the Inf. posn from the flanks. Lt Bell furnished valuable observation and fire when the enemy was first discovered. At 1030 observers were sent out to the high ground on both flanks of the 64th to observe against flanking attacks down the road. No enemy was observed. A large volume of Arty fire, using VT fuze was delivered against the enemy and by 2130 it appeared that the attack had stopped although scattered MG fire continued until 2230. Approx 150 enemy dead were caused by the Arty. Expended 1391 rds. (Total to date 3473)

30 JULY 1950

0630 Enemy Arty and mortar fire began falling on the Inf posns and on each side of the N S road as far back as (1100.8-1502.6) right in front and on the right flank of our C. P.. One rd landed within 5 yds of Lt Ross and Pvt Gillman, who were on a Bn flank OP; two other rounds bracketed them for range. A heavy volume of Arty fire against the envelopment of the 2nd Bn 24th Inf was to no avail and the Inf began drifting to the South from their defensive positions. 0900 Lt Bell and his FO party were driven from their OP by mortar and MG fire. PFC Peter Janettas was seriously wounded and had to be left behind on the OP. Lt Sheets and Pvt Bates A Btry were wounded and PFC McQuitty carried them down the hill under fire and evacuated them. 1000 Bn now reverts to DS 35th RCT. Bn Exec Off left on reconn for new posn area. 35th Inf will take up a defensive posn S and W of SANGJU. 1040 Btrys moved out under the S-3 in the order of Hq - the FDC, A, and B. 1150, Bn in rendezvous S of SANGJU at (1113.1-1501.2). Small arms fire was being received in the Bn area prior to the Btrys moving out for our new mission. On the N and W the enemy occupied the high ground looking down on the 24th Inf and its supporting Arty; 159th and 64th FA Bns. Direct fire at ranges of 1000 yds or less was used by C Btry 159 which was in position 200 yds S of our Bn CP. A gap of 3000 yds between the 3rd Bn 24th Inf, in the center defending to the West and the 2nd Bn defending to the North made possible the rapid advance South by the enemy just prior to 1100. At 1600 Bn closed in posn area (1111.2-1494.5) and prepared defensive positions. Marched 14 miles. Received 4 new officers and made changes in assignments: Capt Anderson to BC Hq Btry; Lt McGrady to Comm O; Lt Chastain Ln Pilot; Lt Barron to Sv Btry Motor Officer; Capt Stockton to Ln O; Lt Chapman to Tns Comdr; and Lt Campbell to B Btry. Expended 853 rds. (Total to date 4326 rds)

31 JULY 1950

0710 registered A Btry. 1300 displaced B Btry to (1108.5-1496.7). 1600 received order by phone from D/A to prepare to move S and E. SANGJU was to be evacuated by Div. Div would use the road SANGJU, OKSAN DONG, and SOUSAN. This order interrupted the displacement of A Btry to their forward posn. 1825 Bn Co and BC parties moved out on reconn. 1900 Bn moved out under the S-3 in order A, Hq, Sv, B. Bn Exec remained behind to get Sv and B Btrys on the road hurriedly as the entire Div would soon be on the road. Sv and B Btrys got sandwiched in the Div column behind the 25th QM Co. 2030 Bn closed in posn at (1115.3-1486.0). Marched 12 miles. No registration was obtained because the Inf was still far to the West and the Div and 6th ROK Div were using the SANGJU, OKSAN DONG, SOUSAN road. Fearing an enemy thrust North from CHUMCHON; Lt McFerron, B Btry Exec was ordered to remain at the RJ as an observer until relieved by Lt Roper, A Btry. Observation was held on the highway to the South and on the area to the West but no enemy attack materialized, nor was any activity observed. No Arty fire was received. Expended 45 rds (Total to date 4371 rds).

1 AUG 50

The day was spent in getting 3 FOs in position to observe and establishing communications with them. 1100 Bn registered A and B Btrys. Bn also registered A Btry 90th FA which was attatched. No enemy contact during the period. Expended 11 rds. (Total to date 4382)

2 AUG 50

0001 Bn alerted to move, sent quartering party of 2 Off and 2 EM to CP 35th Inf. 0030 Bn ordered to move as soon as road was clear. 0130 Bn Co and BC parties, less B party, leave on reconn to South. 0430 Bn moved out under Exec in order A, Hq, Sv; B Btry remained behind with the covering force. 0800 B Btry moved out. 1500 Bn less B Btry closed in rendezvoux area in MIRYANG (1174-1393).

Travelled 94 miles. 1635 sent message to CG D/A requesting information re POL, Rations. 2200 B Btry closed at MIRYANG. No ammo expended.

3 AUG 50

1000 Bn Co and BC parties left on posn area reconn. 1030 Bn moved out under exec Off in order A, Hq, B, Sv. 1630 Bn closed CHUNG-NI (1151.5-1363.5). Marched 52 miles. 1715 Hq Btry field range fire unit exploded setting a trailer on fire. Quick thinking on the part of the drivers averted a serious disaster as the entire Bn was jammed into a school yard in parade ground formation. The fire was extinguished with only minor damage to items of personal equipment. 2100 Bn Co and BC parties left on recon for posns vic CHUMGAM-NI (1134.5-1364.8). 2330 Bn Exec rcvd msg from Bn Co for the Bn to remain in place over nite and have the Bn less Sv Btry halted at N edge of CHUMGAM-NIat 0630 4Aug. No ammo expended.

4 AUG 50

0500 Bn moved out under Exec in order A, B, Hq. 0830 Bn closed in posn's occupied by 11th and 13th FA Bns (24th Inf Div). Btry occupying B/13 FA posn (1134.3-1365.5) and A Btry in A/11 FA posn at (1133.3-1364.3). Bn CP at (1133.9-1364.7). Marched 14 miles. Bn took over missions of 13th FA Bn who were in DS 19th Inf. Bn attached to 35th RCT with C/90th FA Bn attached. 35th to relieve 19th Infantry. Enemy activity was observed in all sectors throughout the day and targets of opportunity were taken under fire. 3 FOs were out; Lts Campbell, Roper & Osbourne. Bn expended 281 rds. (Total to date 4663). Capt Stockton was Ln Off with 2nd Bn 35th Inf.

5 AUG 50

0001 1st Plat, A Btry 25th AAAW and C Btry 90th FA Bn attached as of 1200 4 Aug. The AAA platoon was split between our A & B Btrys and C Btry of the 90th. 35th Inf now in defensive positions to the W and N; 2nd Bn in contact. The terrain in this area is extremely rugged and mountainous and this unit is handicapped by our maps as the URYONG sheet 6819I 1/50,000 is uncontoured. It is extremely difficult to direct the Air OP and fighter strikes and to obtain accurate coordinate location from such a map. 0730 Lt Swenson and TACP arrived at our CP to handle all air requests and strikes for the 35th RCT. Expended 565 rds. (Total to date 5228). Also expended 43 rds of 155mm by C/90th FA Bn.

6 AUG 50

0700 Lt Cook, Hq Btry sent out as FO to E Co 35th who were outposting the river line to our N. 35th was in contact in all sectors. Bn fired observed fires on targets of opportunity. 1315 Sv Btry displaced forward to vicinity of CHUMGAM-NI (1134.7-1364.4) in a dry stream bed. 1330 B Btry displaced to (1133.1-1363.2). Bn fired observed fires on tgts of opportunity. Pvt Stevens, Hq Btry member of Ln party with 2nd Bn 35, was wounded and evacuated; he died of wounds later in the day. Expended 346 rds. (Total to date 5574) Expended 328 rds of 155mm How, C/90th FA Bn.

7 AUG 50

0001 35th RCT will attack at 1000 7 Aug; arty will fire a 20 min preparation. 0940 fired a 20 min prep for attack of 2nd Bn 35th Inf. 1100 attack of 35th progressing slowly - difficult going over the mountainous terrain. Heat exhaustion is prevalent among the Inf. Bn supported the attack, planned & fired defensive concentrations and observed fires on tgts of opportunity. Our Air OPs are invaluable. Lts Duncan and Bourassa are our Bn observers. They are doing an outstanding job. 1600 displaced C Btry 90th FA Bn to posn vicinity (1132.7-1362.7). Expended 972 rds. (Total to date 6546) Expended 407 rds 155mm How, C/90th.

8 AUG 50

0001 Supporting attack of 35th Inf. Resistance very slight. Inf has captured several truck loads of abandoned equipment, including MGs, mortars and ammo - also two 1/4 trucks of 27th Inf. 1430 FO Lts. Campbell, Roper and Osbourne were relieved and Lts Sexton and

Griffin from B Btry, Lt Ross from Hq Btry and Lt Chapman from Sv Btry were sent out as FOs. Capt Metcalfe, BC B Btry, relieved Capt Stockton as Ln Off with the 2nd Bn 35th. Capt Anderson was relieved as CO Hq Btry and sent out as Ln Off to lst Bn 35th Inf. Capt Stockton was assigned as CO Hq Btry: he was not aggressive enough as Ln Off. 1400 A Btry displaced forward through the gap to (1130.9-1157.8); approx 6 miles. Bn continued to support the 35th RCT. Expended 94 rds (Total to date 6640)

9 AUG 50

0815 FDC displaced by echelon to (1131.7-1360.4) with the remainder of Hq Btry remaining in old posn. FDC is located on the edge of a steep mountain road - room only for 5 or 6 vehicles. Radio communication by FM radio very difficult and sporadic due to the ruggedness of the terrain and line of sight characteristic of the radios. 1000, a radio relay station was established in the pass over the mountain; this helped immeasurably. Wire communications forward was exceptionally hard to maintain due to tanks and the extreme narrowness of the mountain road. Wire crews worked around the clock in an attempt to keep wire in. Feeding of the FDC crew posed a problem for Hq Btry as they were located 5 miles to the rear and had no hot food containers. The water point is located 9.5 miles to the rear of A Btry - water in their vicinity is contaminated with dead N. Koreans. 1000, an advance ASP established at CHUMGAN-NI RTO. 1015, Lt Cook, HQ FO with 2nd Bn 35th Inf, was injured in action when a tank on which he was riding fell through a bridge at (1125.7-1355.7). 1100, M/Sgt Guill, Hq Btry, was sent up to 2nd Bn Ln O to replace Lt Cook as FO. Very little enemy activity noted during the period, however our Air OP observed and adjusted on targets of opportunity. Bn expended 322 rds (total to date 6962). Expended 147 rds 155mm How, C/90.

10 AUG 50

At 1040, radio communication and fire coordination established with Backfire (555th FA Bn supporting 5th RCT on our left or South Flank). 1045 notified 555 FA Bn by radio that we could assist their attack vicinity (1134.5-1349.0) with the fire of 2 Btrys. 1130, coordinated with 555 by radio relay through our plane on "No Fire Lines" for each Bn. 2100, C Btry 90th FA Bn displaced forward to (1130.85-1157.25). 2300, C/90th laid and ready to fire on CA 4700. Bn expended 378 rds (total to date 7340) Expended 92 rds 155mm How, C/90

11 AUG 50

0130, Phone call from DA 3 that units working with Wilson (5th RCT) will not fire N of 1354.5 and it is requested that units N of 54 not fire S of 1354.5. Units not supporting Wilson will not fire into the following zones: (1124-1356) (1124-1353) to (1137.5-1344.5) E to (1144-1345) NW to (1138-1354) W to (1129-1354) NW to (1125-1356). 1540, B Btry displaced forward to (1122.23-1355.8) 1700 B Btry laid on CA 4400 and ready to fire. 1745, Bn CP located at (1126.7-1355.8). 1750, A Btry displaced forward to (1123.3-1355.8) 1750, Pvt Iberra, Hq Btry shot and killed 3 S Korean civilians. Bn Exec Off took his weapon and placed him under arrest. Capt Stockton, BC Hq Btry, investigated the shooting. 1750, Bn now given an additional mission of supporting the 3rd Bn, 5th Inf which has contacted the 35th and are now vicinity (1120.0-1353.5). 1855, A Btry laid on CA 6100 and ready to fire. 1930, Capt Anderson and 3 FOs sent to 3rd Bn 5th Inf. 2215, two red flares reported by our forward elements. Defensive fires were shot in for the 35th and 3rd Bn 5th. Bn expended 663 rds (total to date 8003). Expended 30 rds 155mm How, C/90.

12 AUG 50

0730, Capt Stockton took Pvt Iberra to the rear and turned him over to Div Provost Marshal. The Div JA assisted in drawing up the charges against Pvt Iberra. 0800, Our Ln plane Air OP reported increased enemy activity to our S & E along MSR of 5th RCT. 1130, Col Dick, DA Exec Off arrived CP area and notified Bn Co that part of the 90th FA and 555 FA Bns had been over-run by the enemy. 1145, Col Sandeen, Maj Evans and Capt Hill, 90th FA Bn arrived in the area and informed the Bn Co of their losses. 1200, Our Air OP ordered on surveillance of the area PO GAM NI. Activity noted but we are unable to get clearance to fire as the disposition of friendly forces in that area is unknown. 1230, Bn Survey sect occupied and organized an OP 800 yds S of our CP (1126.8-1355.0) and overlooking the MSR of the 5th RCT. 1455, two CID agents arrived at the CP to investigate the case against Pvt Iberra. 35th in light contact. 1500, Sv Btry displaced to (1130.2-1356.4) 2000, Sv Btry displaced forward to (1124.8-1356.7). Defensive concentrations were fired in for our supported units. Bn expended 558 rds (total to date 8561). Expended 205 rds 155mm How C/90.

13 AUG 50

0700, Ammo train of 555 FA Bn arrived in Bn CP area and were fed by Hq Btry. They have been attempting to get thru to their Bn but have been unable to make it. Contacted their Bn by radio and were instructed to find posn near 64th and remain there. 0815, Maj Brooks, CO 555 FA Bn arrived at CP, requested fires of this Bn and air strikes in area around PO GAM NI. Bn fired missions thru 555 Air OP. 0950, Bn fired on friendly troops; 2nd Bn 5th Inf (1131.5-1350.5). This fire was requested by, adjusted by, and reported by 555 Air OP. Fires were cleared by Col Ordway, CO 5th Inf. 1145, B Btry displaced to rear (1124.3-1356.5) by platoon. Move made necessary to obtain better coverage for our supported troops. 1330, per phone call S-3, 35th RCT; our mission has been changed. There will be a general withdrawal behind the line NAM-GANG River-HAMAN and on S. 35th Inf to form a defensive line. 5th RCT to move immediately followed by 35th RCT. 64th FA Bn with C/90th attached to furnish continuous support to cover the withdrawal. 1345, Btry A given march order and ordered to proceed E thru the pass and occupy C Btry 90th FA old posn area at (1132.7-1362.7) and report when laid and ready to fire. 1450 A Btry started to displace and moved into a gap into the column of 1st Bn 5th Inf. Sv Btry was alerted to displace E thru the pass and occupy their old posn at (1156.9-1358.9) in the vicinity of MASAN. 1535, Sv Btry displaced by infiltration. 1610, A Btry reported as in posn and ready to fire. 1620, Bn Commo established radio relay station in the pass to our E between the FDC and A Btry. Hq Btrys non-essential vehicles displaced by infiltration to old posn area in CHUMGAM-NI (1133.9-1364.8). 1700, Bn Exec Off, Asst S-3, 1/2 of FDC, Surv Sect and a wire truck left on reconn for posns E and N of HAMAN from which to support the 35th Inf in their new posns. Bn Co, S-3, with 1/2 of the FDC remained in posn. 1915, a friendly tank fired on a MG emplacement of C Btry 90th FA Bn destroying the gun and wounding the crew. 2040, B Btry displaced E thru the pass to posn area in a dry stream bed at (1134.4-1365.5) 2200, C Btry 90th displaced E thru the pass to posn at (1146.1-1365.9). 2200, Hq Btry, 1/2 FDC arrived in rendezvoux area at (1149.3-1364.9). Bn expended 538 rds (total to date 9099). C/90 expended 219 rds 155mm How rds.

14 AUG 50

0310, C/90th in posn at (1146.1-1365.9), one platoon laid on CA 5200 and the second plat on 6200. 0550, B Btry displaced from dry stream bed to RTO CHUMGAM-NI (1134.2-1365.3). Move necessary due to very hard rain storm and flash flood that flooded the creek. 0830, 1st Bn 35th Inf cleared the pass moving E. 1300, Capt Metcalfe, LnO with the 2nd Bn 35 arrived at the CP with their dispositions. 1355, A Btry displaced rearward to posns vicinity KONAN and SASO (1142.75-1367.0) for the 1st Plat and (1143.7-1366.0) for the 2nd plat. 1645, Hq Btry closed in CP area vic CHUNG-NI (1151.5-1364.8). 1700, A Btry in posns and laid on CA 4800 and registered. 1730, messenger from Capt Anderson, LnO with 1st Bn 35th arrived CP with their dispositions. 1750, B Btry started to displace to the rear. 1955, Bn Co arrived at new CP. 2040, B Btry closed in two platoon posns at (1152.7-1367.9) and (1151.8-1369.7) laid and ready to fire on CA 6000 and 6400. 2135, new TACP, with Lt Quanbeck in charge, arrived at CP and relieved Lt Swensen and his TACP. The Bn is scattered over a wide area with A and B Btrys each occupying two platoon positions. This was necessary in order to accomplish our mission of supporting the 35th RCT. Bn expended 53 rds (total to date 10,152).

15 AUG 50

Very quiet day. Bn remains in position in support of 35th RCT. Registered for corrections and checked all defensive concentrations. Expended 79 rds (total to date 10131). Expended 28 rds 155mm How C/90.

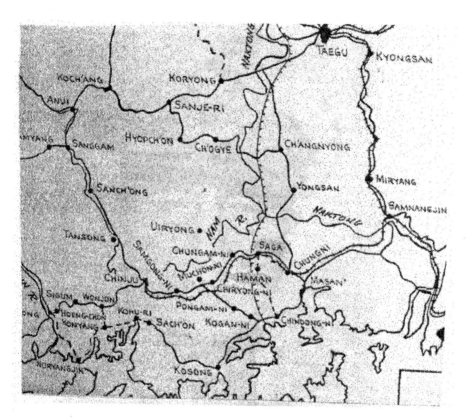

AUTHOR'S INSERTON:

"SEQUENCE OF EVENTS IN THE FAR EAST THEATRE THUS FAR 1950 26 June Emergency Session of UN Security Council decides to aid South Korea 27 June President TRUMAN shifts 7th Fleet to FORMOSA Strait 4 July US troops first meet NKVA just north of OSAN and are forced to retreat 8 July General MacArthur given command of UN Forces Aug-Sep General WALKER's EIGHTH ARMY holds PUSAN PERIMETER against North Koreans

16 AUG 50

Very quiet, little activity. Registered, checked defensive fires and fired harassing fires during the night. Expended 45 rds (total to date 10276)

17 AUG 50

There is a gap of 6 miles between the 25th Inf Div and elements of the 24th Inf Div. to the N. Ln plane reports that the road thru the pass at (31.3-59.7) repaired and evidence of vehicular use. Attack expected from direction CHUNGAM-NI. 1510, one platoon of A Btry displaced to (1144.2-1370.85). 1600, 2nd Lt Jensen arrived at the CP. He is the advance officer for C Btry 537th FA Bn, redesignated C Btry 64th FA Bn. Expended 102 rds (total to date 103,78)

18 AUG 50

0615, A/35th attacked on 3 sides and driven from their posn. 0800, Ln plane and Tac Air report tanks and Inf. vic CHUNGAM-NI. One tank destroyed by arty fire. 1035, B/35th Inf jumped off in attack to retake high ground at (36.1-67.3). 1125, B/35th Inf retook the objective - 40 enemy dead and 1 prisoner. Arty fired preparation for the attack. 1600, Bn Co registered with VT on a ford at (41.2-83.9) concentration to be on call. 2055 NK crossing river at (41.2-83.9). B Btry fired 24 rds VT - boats sunk, enemy killed. Fired harassing and interdiction missions throughout the nite on roads and into CHUNGAM-NI. During the day several air strikes were directed by our TACP with good results observed. Expended 774 rds (total to date 11152). Expended 86 rds 155mm how, C/90th.

19 AUG 50

Fired on a few tgts of opportunity during the morning with minor activity in the 1st Bn sector and none in the 2nd Bn. 1510, adjusted on a column of 15 trucks at (30.7-71.5) - destroyed 10 trucks. 1830, A/29th and C/35 jumped off to gain high ground along (36-64) and

(36-65) with Bn firing a short preparation. 1900, A/29th and C/35th on intermediate obj. 2130, ordered by DA to place bulk of harassing fires in CHUNGAM-NI area and S to the Rgt Bdry. It is felt by DA that the principal build-up is developing in that area. 2200, A/29th and C/35th withdrew to the high ground N of the road. Withdrawal covered by Arty fire. Expended 554 rds (total to date 11606). Expended 303 rds 155mm, C/90th.

20 AUG 50

0315, silenced 2 med Arty and 3 light Arty pieces by getting 2 observer azmiths and then searching the area by fire. Approx location (32.3-62.6). Had 2 air strikes during the day on massed personnel. Bn Exec Off relieved Capt Anderson as LnO with lst Bn 35th at 1600 on the 19th Aug. Capt Anderson sent back for 3 days rest. Fired 7 observed missions on massed personnel with excellent results. 1650, destroyed enemy arty piece at (35.0-70.6). 1655 Ln 1 reports that refugees say that the enemy has withdrawn 3 miles to the W because of arty fire and air action. No activity in 1/35 sector since about 1130. It is felt that the combined arty and air activity have averted an attack for tomorrow. Fired moderate harassing fires during the nite. Expended 969 rds (total to date 12575). Expended 402 rds of 155mm how, C/90th.

21 AUG 50

0800, No enemy attk this morning. It is believed that the greatest enemy strength in this sector has sideslipped to the S, possibly for an attk on the 24 th RCT. 1300, Leopard (35th) reports that a penetration has been made at (40-57) on the 24th and 5th RCTs boundaries, has broken thru the S Korean police holding that sector. 1/29 has been alerted for possible movement to the S. 1700, laid 2 howitzers of C/90th FA on CA 4200 to reinforce the fires of the 159th FA Bn. Fired in reinforcing fires for the 159th and moderate harassing fires during the nite. Bn expended 268 rds (total to date 128430). C/90th expended 237 rds 155mm how.

22 AUG 50

0730, A/35th, the reserve Company, was pushed off their posn at 0400 this morning but have regained their posn. This was our first report of this action. The arty did not fire. Div plans to use the 1st Marine Brigade in the Div. sector on EUSAK order. 1250, from Sgt Guill, FO with A/29th; he informs us that a PW has been captured who stated that his unit, originally of 500 troops now has about 100 due to arty fire and air action and that their weapons and ammo are low. 1900, Bn CO, Lt Col Hogan, awarded the BSM in ceremonies at 35th Rct CP. 1900, Tac air hit what now appears to have been an ammo dump in HOMI-DONG (32.6-77.0) Flames went 500 ft in air. 2200, fired on a column of trucks with head lights on - results unknown - lights went out. Fired harassing and interdiction fires during the night. Bn expended 527 rds (total to date 13,370). C/90 expended 153 rds 155mm.

23 AUG 50

Many scattered groups of enemy noticed during the day. No real profitable arty tgts. Fired some fires to reinforce 159 FA Bn. Gen Collins, C/S was in the Div area throughout the day. 1430, Bn Exec Off left for PUSAN to escort C Btry 64th FA Bn to this area. 2310 Exec Off returned from PUSAN with msg that Btry delayed 2-3 days due to bad wx. They are coming on USNS POPE, ETA probably 25 Aug. A Btry now in one consolidated posn at (42.3-66.7). Fired interdiction and harassing missions during the night. Capt Anderson now Ln 1. Bn expended 515 rds (total to date 13,865). C/90th expended 320 rds155mm.

24 AUG 50

0330 Ammo truck from C/90th caught fire along MASAN road and blew up destroying 75 complete rds of 155mm ammo. The cause was unknown, however sabotage is suspected. 0825, Ln plane reports evidence of armored activity during the night as there are many tracks in the area of CHUNGAM-NI. 0830, DA-2 notified us that the 8th FA Bn had a direct hit on their FDC, CP killing 6 and injuring four. 1030,

Bn Co and BC B Btry went on reconn for posn for B Btry. C Btry will occupy B's present position when they arrive. 1400, B Btry displaced to (46.88-73.28). In posn and registered at 1625. Fired many missions on concentrations of troops, vehicles and arty with excellent results - destroyed 1 arty piece, 4 vehicles and many casualties were noted. Had a difficult time obtaining any TAC air as they have been diverted to the zones of the 5th RCT and 24th RCT. M/Sgt Guill appointed 2nd Lt. Bn expended 2004 rds (total to date 15869). C/90 expended 716 rds155mm.

25 AUG 50

0700, Ln plane adjusted on and destroyed 4 arty pieces along road at (34.5-65.1). 1030, all arty ordered to C/F as enemy was observed waving a white flag at (37.4-64.6). The attempt at surrendering was a ruse -when the arty C/F the enemy immediately attacked. 1500, C/90th FA ordered to displace one how forward to posn at (42.3-66.7) so that we can interdict URYONG (25.5-71.7) and its river crossing. 1735, have 2 90mm M-26 tanks in posn at (42.3-66.7), direction of fire 5050. They will be used to interdict URYONG. 1850, registered C/90's forward piece by Air OP. Attempted to register the 90mm tank guns but could not observe any of the rds fired - they have no WP smoke rds. Had to fire them using map data corrected and we had no 90mm range tables. 1900, received notification that the 7th NK Div was massing in URYONG (26-72) for an attack tonight. 2030, have a platoon of 3 76mm tanks now in posn at (41.8-67.0). We are going to use them on harassing missions. Had a lot of trouble getting them layed and ready to fire. 2110, was notified that we were limited to 50 rds per 105mm per day, 155mm was unlimited, effective at 0001 25 Aug. 2135, cancelled all harassing fire except 50 rds, on order of CO 1/35 on account of our ammo restriction. Expended 1852 rds (total to date 17,721). C/90th expended 641 rds.

26 AUG 50

0015-0415 Spent laying and adjusting 76mm tanks on CHUNGAM-NI. 0655, an unidentified Russian Tupelov, 4 motor bomber passed over our CP flying an Easterly course. An underwater sand-bagged bridge has been located at (38.7-73.4). This bridge was hit by air at 1720. Sent one EM from B Btry to the Div Rest Camp. Our quota is one EM. 1730, Lts Seely, Hart and Ceravsky arrived at the CP from PUSAN. They are the FOs from our new C Battery. Lt Hart temporarily sent to B Btry and Lt Ceravsky temporarily sent to A Btry until their Btry arrives. Lt Seely to go out as FO in the morning; to relieve Lt Guill at C/29th. Had difficulty during the day getting air strikes - diverted to areas of 5th and 24 RCTs. Bn expended 355 rds (total to date 18,076). C/90 expended 1024 rds.

27 AUG 50

0105, Noises of enemy vehicles and troops were heard in front of 1/35. 0600, fired some harassing and interdiction missions during the night. Excellent results were reported from the interdiction fires. 0600, an unidentified multi-motored plane was over the area flying a N-S course. 0900, DA CG visited CP and FDC ; requested that we conserve our ammo by decreasing our harassing missions and using fewer volleys during fire for effect and to hit the lucrative tgts. 0930, CG left to visit one of our OPs in the 1/35 area. 1015, Lt Brown, C/90 FO with B/35 directed an air strike on tanks, troops and vehicles. Three tanks were knocked out, one vehicle destroyed and fires and explosions were started. Bn CO spent most of the day with the tanks and C/90 roving gun. Had several air strikes during the day with excellent results reported on troops, ammo dumps, vehicles and tanks. 2145, our 1/35 reported several fire fights with infiltrating enemy patrols but every thing under control. Lt Guill, FO with C/29, was relieved by Lt Seely, C/64, at 1000. Bn expended 345 rds (total to date 18,421 rds). C/90 expended 207 rds.

28 AUG 50

0515, reported by Ln 1 that two enemy patrols were probing our defenses in 1/35 sector. Several trip flares were set off. 0600, fired harassing fires and interdiction missions during the nite; used 76mm and 90mm tanks on some of these missions. 1150, ammo reports now due as of 1200 daily instead of 1700. 1245, Bn started big fires in village at (41.1-80.6); possibly POL or ammo - one vehicle destroyed.

1400, Lt Bailey joined and assigned to A Btry. 1430 Pvt Miller, A Btry FO party, returned and went to the Div. Recreation Center. 1535, FO with G/35th observed moving haystacks at (37.4-74.5); fired on, burned several and dispersed the personnel. 1645, our Air OP observed 2 vehicles and an arty piece at (35-75). Mission given to TAC air but never acted upon -missed the tgt. 1900, PW rpts 7th NK Div going to attack in boundary between 1/35 and 2/35 at 0001 29th Aug. Inf began calling for all sorts of defensive fires and fires on suspected areas. 2048, Leopard 5, Col Doen arrived at CP with directions that we fire at (35.1-70.1) and (35.8-71.1). Also notified us that Leopard 6, Col Fisher directs that we take under fire all tgts reported to us and that he would answer and be responsible for all ammo expenditures above our daily allotment. 2210, DA S-3 notified us that we were authorized an additional 300 rds tonight for harassing missions. 2230, DA S-3 notified us that we would lose the 76mm tanks and that the remaining 90mm would not fire. 2315 prepared to fire illuminating shell from C/90 roving gun on (35-67) at 2400. Bn Expended 213 rds as of 1200 (total to date 18,634). Lt Ceravsky, C/64, sent to 1/29 to familiarize himself with their counter attack plans and be prepared to go with them as an FO using a party formed in A Btry. C/90 expended 114 rds of 155mm.

29 AUG 50

0001, fired 10 rds 155mm illuminating shell vic (35-67). No activity observed. 0015, an unidentified single engine plane dropped a flare over (48-65). 0155, notified that a PW reports that the 7th NK Div CP at (31.6-70.6). Fired on by C/90 roving gun, results unknown and un-observed. Fired harassing and interdiction fires during the nite. 0650, LnO 1 reported that C/24 had been attacked during the nite and were still under fire. 1110, fired two volleys VT at troops vic RTO in CHUNGAM-NI causing approx 20-25 dead. Confirmed by an Inf. patrol. 1445, Lt Goodman, Adjutant, evacuated for appendicitis. 2350, fired illuminating shell but no activity was observed. Bn was vaccinated for small pox and must be repeated at 6 week intervals.

TRUE EXTRACT COPY OF UNNUMBERED MEMO 35th RCT, dtd 25 AUG 50 The march discipline of the 64th FA Bn and its attached units is the best in the RCT. All others are unmentionable. Lt

Chapman, ammo train commander, was appointed Bn PX Officer and directed to use the Hq Fund to establish a Mobile PX that could visit each Btry daily and to stock up on soft drinks, cookies, candies, snacks and magazines with some cigarettes and tobaccos. Bn Expended 439 rds (total to date 19,073). C/90 expended 460 rds 155mm.

30 AUG 50

0001-0500, fired interdiction and harassing fires. 1045, dropped leaflets on a group of approx 900 refugees and later adjusted fire short of them to drive them W back across the river. Fired several observed missions on personnel; used both air and ground observation with excellent results. It was estimated that on one tgt there were 90% casualties on a group of 50-85 NK enemy. 1400, Col Dick, DA Exec Off visited the CP and told us about C/24 losing their positions this morning. 1700-2000, checked in defensive concentrations and registered for corrections. 2010, Capt Waddell, BC C Btry, and Lt Gramlich, Btry Exec Off arrived from PUSAN. Were given Bn FM radio frequencies and declination constant for their aiming circles and M-2 compasses. 2030, Lt Goodman, Bn Adj, called from the Div Clearing Co saying that he was OK and that he would pick up the Bn payroll tomorrow. Expended 890 rds (total to date 19,963). C/90 expended 518 rds 155mm.

31 AUG 50

0001-0500, Spent in firing harassing and interdiction missions. Relaid one how. of C/90 to interdict the RR tunnel S W of CHUNGAM-NI. 1000, Capt Waddell, C/64 was shown the posn that he was to occupy with his Btry when it arrives here from PUSAN. WOJG Mullahey, 64th Pers. Off, arrived in the area to pay the troops. 1030, Lt Goodman, Bn Adj returned to duty from the hosp. 1300, Bn Co, Lt Kranbeck TACP Off and Capt Bornhouser visited B/35 FO Lt Beverly of C/90. 1355, Capt Waddell and Lt Gramlich left for PUSAN and C Btry. 1800, PFC McQuitty was presented the Silver Star Medal for heroism W of SANGJU by Gen Barth CG DA at a ceremony at DA Hq. 2110, 1/35 reports that they are having enemy patrol activity in their sector and that their general posn area is being shelled by small caliber arty. 2330, arty fire in front of 35th RCT now becoming more intense. FOs reported azimuths to flashes. Bn firing close in defensive fires on call and counterbattery fires. There is an acute shortage of WP ammo. There was heavy patrol activity during the day. C/29 patrol ran into an enemy company asleep in their fox holes but were beaten off by the co. of enemy. Capt Anderson reassigned from Ln O to command of A Btry. Capt Bornhouser relieved of A Btry and assigned as Ln O. Bn expended 462 rds (total to date 20,425 rds). C/90 expended 210 rds 155mm. AUTHOR's COMMENTS: Now that Major Smith has recorded my entry into the ranks of the 64th FA Bn, I will retrograde a bit to explain my preparation for visiting the "Land of the Morning Calm." I departed Washington National Airport on 15Aug and wound up in Alaska where I was grounded for aircraft's requiring maintenance. After several days of playing pool at the O-Club, and already longing for my wife's companionship, I said: "The heck with this. There's a war on!" So I grabbed a flight on the first plane headed west. After an uneventful takeoff, the pilots tried a straight-in approach through a pea-soup fog to the one and only strip in Shemya, Alaska. (See map). As we descended thru the fog, we broke out at about 50 feet, lined up PERPENDICULAR to the runway!

On the go-around, with us passengers sweating with the pilots, they made a successful landing. No KIAs yet! We all spent the night in a barracks at the other end of the runway. Shemya is a very small island with the operations shack at one end of runway and barracks at the other. Running back and forth creates a metropolis effect. Yet duty there has to be boring and maddening for active men, especially flyboys.

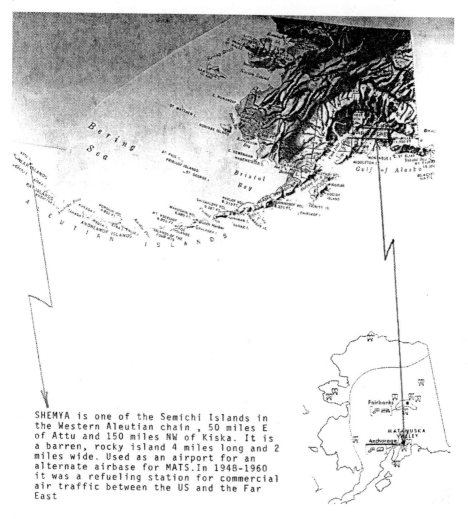

SHEMYA is one of the Semichi Islands in
the Western Aleutian chain , 50 miles E
of Attu and 150 miles NW of Kiska. It is
a barren, rocky island 4 miles long and 2
miles wide. Used as an airport for an
alternate airbase for MATS.In 1948-1960
it was a refueling station for commercial
air traffic between the US and the Far
East

During WWII, a later acquaintance of mine, Major Deadwyler, had command of a 90mm battery there. To reduce suicides, he set up service practise, firing at 55-gal drums bobbing in the ocean. Good initiative and he was seldom visited by the brass. But ever-present USAF pilots took a dim view of 90mm-ers flying across the runway when they tried to land. So, it was back to exciting ping-pong, horseshoes and swimming with the sharks in the cold Bering Sea. The next day, we finally landed in the southern part of Honsu, Japan, at the old WWII Repple-depple at Camp Drake near Tokyo. We stripped down to the essentials,——duffle bag, musette bag, and weapon. Trunk lockers, banjos, tennis rackets, my brand new box of cigars,——all were picked up and placed in storage "for the duration".(In WWII this meant four years!) In Aug 50, the Army was short caliber .45 pistols, so all we officers were issued M1 rifles. (Plebe year all over again!) Finally shipped out to Pusan, Korea, with eventual assignment to the 25th Infantry "Tropic Lightning "Division's 64th FA Battalion, 105mm towed. Catching rides on various vehicles, I got to where its Service Battery was located. Tagging the foot of the 64th Motor Officer, Lt Richard Cole who was lying beneath a prime mover, I asked if he knew where Bn Hq was. He rose up, brushed himself off and volunteered to jeep me there while welcoming me to the Land of the Morning Calm. From frequent contacts with Lt Cole(soon Captain) I realized he was an outstanding officer and very capable Motor Officer. We ran across each other later at Fort Sill where he, again most helpful, helped me with my Chevrolet problems. After Richard led me to Masan, I dismounted and entered the revetted CP of the 64th FA Bn. LtCol Arthur H Hogan, USMA '31, assigned me as Recon O of Btry "A". Drawing myself up to my full height, I informed the colonel I had hoped for a flying slot since I was wearing L-Pilot wings. His reply: "We have two of them already. Report to "A" Btry". I saluted, about faced and posted. The BC of "A", Capt Sam Bornhouser, briefed me on the essentials and I wandered about the perimeter. The next day, Col Hogan phoned Bornhouser and told him to make me btry XO. Apparently, Col Hogan reviewed my record more closely, noting I had spent a year with school troops at TAS (The Artillery School) where one learns all about firing on the ranges and running a firing battery. Firing almost every day and many nights with the 96th FA Bn during all of 1948, I fired 105 hows, 155 hows, both towed and SP as well as 4.5 guns. These guns were all assigned to "C" btry of which I was the exec! This assignment did not go over too well with the current XO, Lt Roper but I went to work improving guns that were not too well maintained, digging in ammo pits, checking the lay of each piece to insure all were parallel, checking commo both at the guns and at FDC plus bn. The btry exec is responsible for EVERYTHING having to do with the howitzers. The BC watches over all else, i. e. mess hall, motor pool, btry hq, btry commo, assignment of FOs, and other matters not directly related to the howitzer sections. I very soon became aware of the "Nara Syndrome." When I volunteered for combat in July '50, I was flying for the 2d Armd Cavalry Regt at Ft Meade, Md. I was shipped out as an individual replacement to the 64th. All other officers in the 64th at the time I joined had been stationed in the town of Nara. All I heard, day and night: "Wuz you in Nara?" When "C" Btry joined the 64th, all these people had trained together as a battery in the 537th FA Bn in the ZI. They, for one, had their own "Nara", somewhere at Colorado as I recall. But, one thing most all had in common,—we were all trained at Fort Sill, Oklahoma. (See "NARA gang" remnants on the next page.) Like Major Smith, one big problem I encountered was the difficulty of reading the maps issued. Completely foreign to the maps typically provided Army troops, with coloring distinguishing vegetation, streams and ground areas and readable contour lines; the maps we had to use in Korea were colorless and used hard-to-interpolate hachures. Many times, to insure the safety of all troops, we fired on a pin-pointed location, obtained registration corrections and backplotted to obtain usable coordinates for our gun position. Eventually and not too soon, we received usable maps and more accurate survey data. Our "A" Btry was most fortunate in having an oustanding Chief of Firing Btry, M/Sgt Germanus P Kotzur, who soon advanced to the rank of First Sergeant, when his predecessor, William Parker was evacuated for medical problems incurred during WWII. Today, now Cmd Sgt Major Kotzur and I communicate at times. Retired in Colorado, he is not in the best of health as eventually becomes the fate of us all. The howitzer section chiefs, all top leaders, were M/Sgt Rufus Cole from Chapel Hill, NC, Cpl Arnold from Michigan, Cpl Cecil Meares from Richmond, Va, S/Sgt Mitchell from Asheville, NC, Sgt Hammer from Brooklyn, NY, and Sgt Cummins from Kentucky. (See next page for the layout of the btry).

On 1 Sep my cannoneers excitedly pointed out some movement in bushes about 100 feet up the high hill to our left rear. My cannoneers went to whom they thought was our best rifle shot, me. Call it soldier respect or regard for their officers' abilities, a good mark for good discipline or whatever. Obligingly, I scanned the woods with my M13 binoculars and seeing suspicious activity, I propped my leg against the FDC 3/4T, and taking careful aim, sqeezed off a round from my M1. Seeing violent movement, I emptied my clip. When a small group scrambled up the hill to investigate, their curiosity aroused but yet on full alert, they returned a short time later, saying they found the spot where where NK soldiers had been; a small mirror, broken probably by my rifle shots, was hurriedly left behind in several pools of blood. (The broken mirror is shown on the following 2d page.) We all came to the same conclusion, since some had seen flashes of reflected light in that vicinity earlier in the day, that these NKs had been transmitting CW (Morse Code), identifying exact locations of our howitzers. This, we shall see, turned out to be an accurate assessment of the situation. In the FDC, as with the chiefs of howitzer sections, I had topnotch people. All had gotten their start as

cannoneers, i.e. S/Sgt Francis of Charlotte, NC, Cpl McDonald from Boston, MA and a gung-ho Nisei corporal, all of whom did most of the plotting to insure accurate adjustments and FFE(fire-for-effect). Working in the FDC is tedious, demanding work. Only seriously dedicat ed men can "cut the mustard."

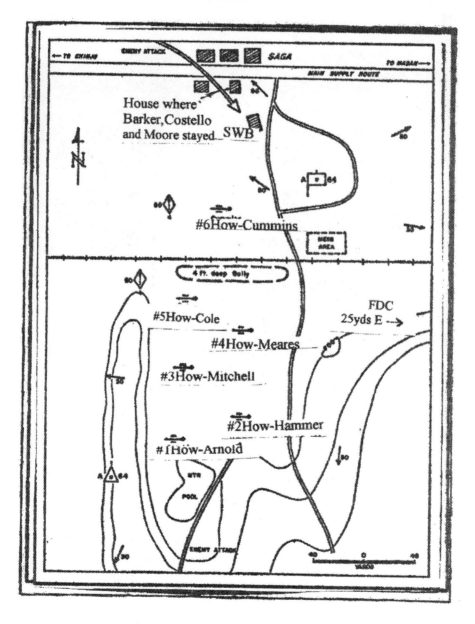

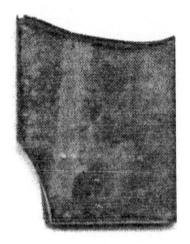

Cannoneers can usually rest a while between rounds or missions but in the FDC, much work must be done AFTER the mission is complete, e.g. replot targets, correct GFT\GST settings, maintain an accurate record of ammo expenditures to know when more need to be requisitioned. All these chores are the key to the very survival of the firing battery. Besides the yeoman efforts of our firing battery, outstanding defense by our supported 35th Infantry "Cacti" helped us to keep our guns. The "Cacti", the true, unpublicized heroes of Guadalcanal, who never retreated except under order, enabled the 64th to move, intact, into new firing positions. Such stability was vital as we headed North to the Yalu. A strange event occurred in the FDC one night. Someone, out of the blue, transmitted over our battery's fire channel: "FIRE ON COORDINATES 45612312! "When we checked these coordinates (exact numbers long forgotten today), they plotted on one of our doughboy positions. When I queried the transmitter "Who is this?", I got the reply: "RATTLESNAKE SIX". When Bn FDC could not identify this callsign, I then knew the call was fictitious. For one thing, the voice sounded foreign, a nasty enemy. We did not fire this mission on our own troops. No way Jose! As suspected, on the evening of 2 Sep, our battery was hit with a furious mortar barrage. As I ran about the gun sections checking to see that all cannoneers were under cover, Chief of Firing Battery Germanus Kotzur called out: "Take care of yourself, lieutenant! The men are OK. Don't get yourself killed." This is the old timer NCO looking out for his occasionally brash junior officers. Another reminder to me of the close feelings existing always between top NCOs and their leaders. In the middle of this barrage, one gun pit received several hand grenades. It was Sgt Mitchell's crew. After crouching and getting cramped in the narrow confines of the pit, ole Tarheel hillbilly Sgt Mitchell jumped up and started flinging grenades right back, shouting: "You SOBs, we got some of those, too!" His crew quickly grabbed their chief back. Combat does get frustrating at times and our grizzled Tarheel reacted in haste. Luckily he survived. But the episode did provoke typical GI mirth when it was all over. As it turned out, the mortars inflicted little damage. We realized, however, aware that our enemy ammo supply was always scant, the attack forewarned of a more deadly attack to undoubtedly ensue, —— — and soon! Sgt Mitchell was an astute NCO. Having trained myself

33

to require boreighting of all pieces right after they were layed, Sgt Mitchell reminded me that the guns could be boresighted anytime. He was correct because what the exec does in "laying the battery" is render the SIGHTS on the pieces parallel. Tubes should, at all times, be parallel to their panoramic sights M12A1. At times, however, such as when the C/S does not remove this sight from its mount when March Order is given, the mounting screws of the sight may loosen when travelling over rough roads, causing excessive skewness of the sight from the axis of the tube.

NOW BACK TO HERODOTUS:

1 Sept 50

0015 Reports from all Ln Os indicate a slight lessening of enemy arty activity. Bn was used on counter-battery. 0030 A full scale attack has begun on the front of the 35th RCT, however it seems to be all along the front. Bn Called on to fire on all defensive concentrations. 0315 Lt Seely, C/64, FO with C/29 was wounded and evacuated. 0600 Bn still firing defensive fires. All wire communication with Ln Os and FOs out. Wire crews were out all nite. Communications were maintained by radio. Pvt Fair, Hq Btry, manning our radio relay station 18, was instrumental in maintaining satisfactory communications and in keeping simultaneous fire missions straight between all FOs, Ln Os and the Bn FDC. His outstanding performance of duty enabled this Bn in the accomplishment of its mission. 0650 An air drop of ammo was made by Ln plane to B/35, who retained their position. 0700-1200 Bn was continuously firing observed missions. Of particular note were two air missions. One was an estimated 4 companies of NKs attempting to cross the river to the N at (34-73). VT fuze was used and approx one Co. of NKs escaped. These were taken care of by the Air Force, who strafed them. Another mission at (35.0-71.5) destroyed 2 vehicles, one ammo dump and caused approx 200 enemy casualties. The air observer quoted, "we caught them with their pants down and it was murder." VT fuze was used in effect against the personnel. 1030 Two platoons of G/35 were completely surrounded by the enemy. Bn controlled a close in air strike completely around their posn. Sgt Stampley, Hq Btry, FO with G/35 lost all communications with the Bn and his Ln O. He spent the day directing the fire of the Inf. mortars. 1215 The 3rd Bn 35th is to be committed to wipe out all infiltrating enemy in the rear of the 1st Bn 35th. Capt Rutherford, BC Hq Btry, sent out as Ln O and Lt Ceravsky, C/64 was sent out as an FO to the 3/35th. 1300 B Btry 8th FA Bn attached, given a position area at (1145.75-1372.60). 1430 Air dropped, by Ln plane, two sets of radio batteries to G/FO, Sgt Stampley. 1610 Lt Petkov and new TACP arrived and releaved Lt Kronbeck and his TACP. 1610 Displaced C/90 roving gun to the rear of the position with remainder of C/90 at (1151.11_1363.98). 1700

B/8 in posn, laid on CA 4800 and ready to fire. 1700 Air drop by Ln plane of medical supplies and ammo to two platoons of G/35. Sgt Stampley was with these two platoons. 1310 The FO party with, Lt Milleren A/64, who was with E/35 came in minus the Lt who was last seen by them at 0430. This party had their jeep, radio, and BC scope destroyed by enemy fire. 1835 Road cut behind B/64 and B/8 by a NK patrol. A wire crew from B/8 had 2 men killed by this patrol. 1930 B/8th FA displaced to the rear and occupied posn at (1148.53-1374.08). Bn continued firing observed missions until dark, then fired 3 counter battery missions and close in defensive fires. 2010 Ln O#2 reported that all of his FOs were OK and that he had talked to them. 2100 C/90 displaced by platoon to posn at (1151.1-1363.98). Closed in posn at 2335. 64th remained in posn in support of 35th RCT. Bn expended 2302 rds of 105mm (total to date 22,727). Expended 830 rds of 155mm C/90th.

2 SEPT 50

0001-0600 Bn fired harassing and interdiction missions in front of 35th RCT. Two counter battery missions were fired, the guns were neutralized and one direct hit was observed. 0600 The 77th Eng were pushed off of the high ground (1142.0-1365.5) South of A btry, by an estimated 250 NKs. 0610 A Btry reported arty fire falling 400-500 yds short of their Btry posn. 0650 A Btry has one platoon ready for direct fire and the Btry is now drawn into a tight perimeter. 0750 E/35 being attacked and were about to be overrun. FO, Lt Milleren, A/64, called for fire on his own posn in order to repel the attack. 0815 Two tanks and some Inf have been sent by Leopard Blue (3/35) to help defend A Btry's posn. 0825 Attack on E/35 has been repulsed. Lt Milleren OK. 0830-1400 Fired observed fires using both air and ground observation on concentrations of NK troops with excellent effect. 1410 C/64 arrived in area, went into posn at (1149.55-13721.48), laid on CA 5000. 1550 FO B, Lt Beverly, C/90, adjusted on and destroyed a SP gun at (35.5)-66.5). 1600 Sgt Stampley, Hq Btry FO with G/35, was relieved by Lt Griffin, B/64. 1600-2000 Fired on several concentrations of enemy troops, killing a minimum of 200 of them. 2020 Received a delayed report from DA-3 from Scotch-2

(8th Army) that there are 1000 NK troops at (1151-1365). This location is 100-200 yds from our CP. Investigated and found no NKs.

2030 FO B, Lt Beverly, C/90 adjusted on two SP guns, destroying one and neutralized the other, probably damaging it. 2050 FO C, Lt Guill, B/64, fired on the SP gun and neutralized it. 2140 FO B, Lt Beverly, C/90 fired on and neutralized an arty piece. 2200 FO B reported a convoy with lights coming thru the pass at (31.5-60.0) Tgt was beyond our maximum range but we assigned A/64 some interdiction concentrations on the road S W of CHUNGAM-NI to be fired every half hour. Reported this to TAC Air. We understand that their B-26s had a field night on convoys W of the pass. 2200-2400 Fired harassing and interdiction fires for 35th RCT. Sometime during the period 1930-2140 the roads leading to A/64 and B/64 were cut by the enemy and blocked. Pvt Williams, Sv Btry, was wounded when attempting to get to A Btry with ammo. Pvt Martin, B/64, a wireman was killed by the block near B Btry. We have decentralized our FDC. Capt Metcalfe, Ln O with 2/35 has 1/2 half of the FDC and B/8, B/64 and C/64 on his firing chart. All of these batteries can be massed. A Btry fires have been placed at the disposal of Capt Barnhouser, Ln O with 1/35. Bn retained control of C/90 and used them in a reinforcing role. Bn expended 1341 rds (total to date 24,068). Expended 567 rds 155mm with C/90th.

3 SEPT 50

A dark and foggy night. 0001-0230 Continued firing of harassing and interdiction and some close in defensive fires. 0240 Heavy fighting on all fronts. A Btry recd counter battery, mortar and small arms fire. 0330 A Btry reports 2 howitzers out of action as result of mortar fire and that the enemy is within their perimeter. 0410 Fired C/90 in defense of A/64. The fires were placed directly in front and on their left. 0445 A Btry back in action with 2 howitzers in defense of 35th. 0655 A Btry has 5 howitzers in action. The NK infiltrators had written something on the tubes of two of the pieces. Visibility now limited by a heavy fog. 0820 A Btry suffered 7 killed: Sgt Rawls, Sgt Pursely, PFCs Carrol, Rowatt, Snouffer; PVTs Fletcher and C. Wallace. Injured and evacuated; CPLs Benton, Morgan and Bauter; PFCs Ashford, Schick, Fagan, R Campbell, Hood, Barker, F

Campbell and PVT Riggs. Their 2 ½ ton maint truck burned, four 2 1/2s were immobilized because of damaged radiators and flat tires, also one 3/4 ton and one 1/4 ton truck. 0820 Ln plane still cannot observe due to dense ground fog. 0830 Bn Co left for A Btry posn area. Lt Bailey and M/SGT Kotzer were the back-bone of A Btry's defense.

AUTHOR'S NOTE. To avoid interrupting the continuity of the Bn Log, a detailed account of "A" Btry's actions on 2-3Sep will be rendered after the Bn Log entry for 5Sep.

BACK TO BN LOG:
0910 A Btry casualties arrived at 35th collecting Co and were quizzed by the Bn Exec Off. 1035 Lion Blue (3/27) in process of clearing the MSR and high ground along it of infiltrating NK forces. This road has been cut and blocked by small arms fire 3 times this morning. 1244 Received from DA S-1, we would receive 100 ROK soldiers for use in How Btrys as replacements.1600 Our radio relay station reported that they get MG fire every time that they attempt to get out of their holes. 1735 B/8th displaced to rear posn at (1150.4-1371.38). 1900 B/8th laid on CA 5000 and ready to fire. 1900 Capt Cole, Bn Motor Off, reported that A Btry's vehicles have been repaired or replaced and that they are ready for any movement ordered. 1905 Ln0#1, Capt Bornhouser, requested an air strike on (1143-1372). The enemy are launching an attack on the 1/35th. Bn Exec Off requested of DA-5 and Leopard 6 additional defensive troops to cover A and B Btrys 64th. A Btry has I & R platoon consisting of 1 Off and 23 men. B has Capt Ashley and 30 men. We feel that this is inadequate. We were notified that we would get no further assistance as there was none available. 2147 Leghorn (159 FA Bn) requested clearance to fire on (41.0-66.0). Clearance was not obtained due to the lack of information as to the perimeter of Lumber A (A/65th Eng). 2200-2400 Interdiction and harassing fires by C/90 and tgt assignment for A, B, C 64th and B/8th. Continuous attempt to get information on Lion White (2/27th) for Lightning 6. All during A Btrys attack this morning we had good telephone communications and complete progress reports from the Btry. Bn expended 1343 rds (total to date 25,416). C/90 expended 155 rds of 155mm.

4 SEPT 50

0140 Ln O#1 received report from Lion White as to his location and that his ammo was low and unable to resupply. He may be reached thru Leopard Red to Blue to Lion White. 0215 Ln O#2 reported that a Sv Btry truck loaded with small arms ammo and grenades missed B Btry's turn off and was stuck approx 1000 yds beyond there and left by the driver. 0615 Fired on a convoy of vehicles and troops N of CHUNGAM-NI (34.37-65.3). Results unknown but the fire was reported to be on the tgt. Several fires were noted. 0915 Ln O#2 reported that Lion White requested an air drop of ammo, medical supplies and a Doctor. Forwarded this request to Lightning. 1030 100 ROK soldiers received by the Bn sent 33 to A Btry, 33 to B Btry and 34 to C Btry. 1040 Bn Co & DA CG left for B/64 posn area. 1200 Ln O#2 reported that B/64 was under small arms fire from an estimated Co of NK and that C/64 and B/8 were firing in their support. 1345 B Btry Exec, Lt Bell, reported 3 men killed by mortar fire; SGT Jones, CPL Beveridge and PFC Greenup. Two men were wounded; SGT Rushe and PFC Duggan. 1400 Two tanks and 3 M-39s now in support of B Btry. Attack has broken up and B now firing in its own defense. 1405 A Btry fired on two tanks and enemy troops; one tank destroyed and 32 enemy killed. 1420 B Btry started to displace to rear posn at (1150.2-1371.74). 1558 Lt Hoffman, Radar Off, A Btry, 1st FA Obsn Bn reported his location at (1151.42-1364.606) and covering three sectors CA 3700, CA 5195 and CA 405, all of which we forwarded to DA. Bn fired several concentrations on enemy troops and enemy Arty in the period 1600 to sundown with excellent results: destroyed an enemy gun, one tank, an ammo dump and caused an estimated 200-225 casualties. 2025 B/64 closed in posn at (1150.2-1371.74) and laid on CA 5600. Displacement was made under difficult conditions; narrow muddy roads, 25 AAAW vehicular failures and the proximity of the enemy. They had to rebuild the road in two different places. 2100-2400 Fired harassing and interdiction and on call defensive fires. Bn expended 1584 rds (total to date 27,300). C/90 expended 159 rds 155mm.

5 SEPT 50

0001-0300 Fired usual harassing and interdiction missions and one close in defensive fire. 0340 Fired on a bridge that the enemy was constructing at (40.8-76.8), dispersed the enemy and later fired harassing fire on it. 0530 DA requests that we notify them before moving any of C/90as they may need one platoon to support the troops to our S. 0700 visibility extremely limited - dense ground fog. 0915 Fired on enemy attacking C/35. Attack repelled and casualties noted. 1000-1100 Fired on two concentrations of enemy troops near (45.5-69.8). Killed 220 and levelled one of the villages. 1145 Leopard 5 recalled the I & R Platoon from A Btry's perimeter. 1158 Bn Co called, notified FDC that the road to B & C Btrys was blocked by enemy fire at CHIRWON (51-70). The enemy also occupied the high ground to the N and E, also 200 NKs at (49.8-70.5) 2000 yds from our FDC. Turned 1 plat of C/90 to cover this threat. 1200 Bn Exec Off and Lt Oxendine, Exec C/90 left for SAGA (1141.5-1366.9) to reconnoiter for a posn to emplace a roving 155mm How. 1500 Displaced 1 How C/90 to posn at (1141.3-1366.95) to be used to interdict the pass and as a roving gun. 1715 Displaced 1 Plat C/90 forward to posn in the loop (46.3-65.7). 1725 C/90 had one piece in their rear plat blow up from a premature, damaging another How and injuring only 4 men. 1850 Sv Btry ammo train will leave for B and C Btrys as soon as road block N of Leopard CP has been cleared. 2115 Road block broken by tanks and Inf - road now clear. 2115 C/90 received 2 new Howitzers - now in posn and ready to fire. 2210 C/90 forward Pltn in posn, laid and ready to fire. 2215 Sv Btry ammo plat arrived at B and C Btrys posn area with 1200 rds ammo. Bn expended 2463 rds (total to date 29,763 rds). C/90 expended 483 rds 155mm. The following EM were wounded in action: SGT Mansker, Kilbi, Wallace, Stickler and Dougan.

AUTHOR'S ELABORATION ON ACTION IN "A" BTRY POSITION ON 2-3SEP:

On the night of 2-3 Sep, the NKs launched a company-sized attack against "A" Btry. Anticipating such attack, I spent the night in the FDC dugout, along with the FDC Chief, Sgt Francis, chart op Cpl

McDonald and LtRoper who was sweating out a possible attack. As stated in the bn log, heavy rain clouds were hovering over the battery area, absorbing the sound of any small arms firing in the vicinity. What faint clatter we heard was attributed to routine protective firing at the MLR (Main Line of Resistance). When a steady fire builds up to a crescendo, dig in and get ready for an attack. We at the battery heard no such heavy fire and so were not expecting an attack at this time. At about 0245 hours, battalion phoned and asked why the battery was not firing. I told Lt Roper to run down and check out the gun positions. Roper, cowering, did not make a move. I ran quickly to the guns to see, first-hand what the trouble was. North Koreans had overrun three howitzer sections and M/Sgt Cole was crouching with his 2d howitzer section. waiting for an attack on his section. The NKs had sneaked in behind our Cacti and were after our battery. That is why we heard no heavy firing on the MLR, our usual alert that an attack was imminent. The NKs had thrown hand grenades into M/Sgt Hammer's gun emplacement, igniting unfired powder charges placed in the section's ammo pit, causing an eerie glow about the left flank of the gun area. I could see enemy jumping about M/Sgt Hammer's pit as well as Cpl Arnold's, the left flank piece of the battery. Because of all these hazards, no cannoneer wanted to reach for the telephone posted atop the parapet of each gun pit. This explains why my FDC got no word of the situation developing so rapidly. Action was building up fast. I leaped into the gun pit of Section #3 and directed the C/S Cpl Cecil Meares of Richmond, Va, to have his crew fire at the enemy with their sidearms as I was doing with my rifle. I helped the C/S and gunner load projos with Fuze Time M54 set at 2.0 seconds. I dared not prepare the standard Fuze Quick. If such projo skipped over the hill directly in front of our battery or missed it entirely, it could slam into our own doughs holding the MLR. The Fz Time round exploded just beyond the NKs. Feverishly, we cut time fuzes to 1.0 and 0.5 seconds. Still missing, so we cut our fuze to 0.0. seconds! In theory, such time would cause the projo to explode in the tube. However, I did remember, in the heat of the action, that an interrupter pin in fuze M54 prevents the fuze from arming until clearing the tube, when it then flies out. The 0.0 second round exploded 50 feet from the gun tube, breaking up the attack on the howitzer sections. C/FB Kotzur helped C/S's Cole and Cummings on either side of the RR tracks to maintain control of their crews. About this time Sgt Francis at FDC shouted: "Do you want some 155s dumped on the attackers?" Our Bn CO, Col Arthur H Hogan, was at the 90th FA Bn FDC, our general support bn and he was helping prepare direct support for "A" Btry. I replied to Sgt Francis: "Yes, put some rounds on the hill in front of the hows." Few artillerymen have ever fired on any of their own occupied gun positions! But Col Hogan, on the road night and day, it seemed to us, knew the precise location of each of his batteries; he was helping plot each battery. This knowledge insured that exact coordinates were plotted for safe, accurate fire. When Sgt Francis shouted out to me at the guns: "ON THE WAY!", those rounds came whistling in right on the hill plotted which was a little more than 50 yards from our howitzers. I gave the command: "RIGHT 50, DROP 50, FIRE FOR EFFECT!" The 90th FA "Lobsters" fired one volley and that's all the enemy needed to keep face and POST!. The attack dwindled to a few feeble burp gun bursts and sayonara NKs!! During this ticklish fire mission, wounded soldiers were huddled in a depression next to the RR tracks running thru our btry position. After having Cpl Meares' gun crew fire his rounds point blank at the NKs, I went to this group of wounded, being tended to by Father Schaag, our Div Arty Catholic Chaplain. (What a night he picked to sermonize with "A"Btry)! It was from here that I conducted the fire mission with the 90th. The men groaned when they heard my initial command to DROP 100, so I changed to DROP 50 since I felt they had not my kamikaze spirit. I probably shouldn't bring this up BUT I'm sure the statute of limitations has long since expired,—I had squirrelled away a fifth of Old Granddad in my musette bag I brought from Japan, for medical purposes, of course! What else!! I felt now was a good time to put those spirits to better use than what I had intended,—-sore throat, etc. The WIAs were thus nursed back to that level of health that eased the bumpy ride back to the the Bn Aid station for proper routing to insure recovery from their wounds. As exec of the firing battery, my hands were full with insuring we could carry out our vital DS mission with our cannoneers. Others were tending to btry hq personnel. Such action I will discuss later. But all during the attack, I was concerned about the AA Cal.50 half-track emplaced atop the hill just in front of the guns on the south side of the RR. When the attack began, its crew deserted the .50, and enemy in this engagement saying its automatic traverse was not working. I quickly sent 3 of my men to man the track and prevent any NKs from firing it against us. (I later found out from an AA crew in another battery that such disabled halftrack could yet be tracked manually.) The BC, Captain Anderson, helped the commo platoon wrestle with its problems. Altho I never, understandingly, saw him as we carried out duties in different areas in pitch dark, he was an experienced Redleg and helped these men do battle with the invaders. I did run across C/FB Germanus Kotzur who maintained good control of the two hows just N of the RR tracks. The btry 1st Sgt, M/Sgt William Parker, standing near the battery switch-board(SWB) dugout close to the MSR, noticed several men coming down the MSR. When they ignored his challenge, he ordered them to halt. Instead, they being 3 NKs pulling a mounted MG, they dropped down in a roadside ditch and opened fire on the battery's right flank. The NKs had also emplaced other MGs on the ridge line in front of the guns. So the action this night was divided between our howitzer sections and the admin components of the battery. I fought with the guns and Capt Anderson with his commo and other sections. The wire team chief, Sgt Herbert L Rawls, Jr, of Edgecomb County in NC, saw the NKs moving out and he ran to the huts occupied by his wire section and to the SWB to alert his men. This was to little avail, unfortunately, as all three men were killed as they ran out the door, viz. Pfc's Harold W Barker, Thomas A Castello and Sanford B. Moore. They were all gunned down by a group of NK soldiers gathered about the hut. Two Campbell brothers, twins, survived these fusillades. In other action, Sgt Joseph R Purseley of Wilson County in Tennessee was kneeling on the ground splicing wire to insure constant commo between battery and battalion, when he was killed by a burp gun blast. Sgt Rawls was also killed soon afterward. A grenade tossed into the SWB dugout killed 2 of the 3 operators in and around near there. The third, Cpl John Pitcher, a 16-year old from New Orleans, survived, remaining at his post during the the attack, maintaining contact with bn, most important during an attack. Another commo man, Cpl Bobbie H McQuitty, dashed to a 2 1/2T truck with a ring-mounted cal.50 MG and tried to fire but the MG jammed. He leaped off the truck and headed down the MSR to where he had seen a tank earlier in the day. Two battery medics, Cpls Beaton and Attikouzel, raced about the battery area tending to the wounded, placing them in a central location within the battery area, as described earlier, all the while exposed to the heavy enemy fire. They were both awarded Bronze Stars for their heroic action. So it can be seen, nobody was spared the attention of the enemy in this engagement. (KIAs/WIAs in App "B") As stated, the attack was over at about 0430, but as soon as the attack ended, 4 or 5 enemy artillery rounds landed in a rice paddy about 200 yards off our right flank. Immediately, several Koreans dressed in civilian clothing, rose from the rice paddies and clambered back onto the the road(MSR). How could they know the firing was over? Their timing was too coincidental to satisfy "A" Btry's MG Sergeant Saxon. So he asked my permission to gun them down. Worn out, like everybody else, losing 20 men during the night, I could not take the chance of this being another "sortie"; I told Sgt Saxon to "go ahead." Many instances like this occurred during the fighting in Korea, such as "civilians" concealing weapons on their person and being waved on thru our lines, only to gun down unsuspecting troops. What to do? In combat it's kill or be killed, nothing in between. Tough decisions have to be made on the spot. Yet stateside news media and pious folk in the rear and the ZI decry such action. But as Scipio Africanus, in launching his invasion of Carthage, stated when he was criticized for his actions in Carthage: "Let those who will, criticize me for my actions in war, BUT let them come with me to Carthage." Replace "Carthage" with "Korea" and you have my sentiments exactly. When dawn broke, it was found, as reported earlier in Major Smith's bn log, that the NKs had scrawled gobbledegook on the shields of 3 of our howitzers——they never got to Cpl Meares and me! No Asian linguists present in the battery,(strange); we did not know but what the chalk writings were boobytrap alerts to NKs so as not to dampen their intended victory celebration. So, in the early dawn, I had the cannoneers dig me a pit in rear of each of the three marked hows. Turning each how around to point at the unoccupied (by US troops at least) hill to our rear and jumping into each pit just dug, I pulled the improvised long lanyard from each gun, firing a projectile with low charge. Shakily covering one ear, I listened for a dreaded explosion at each pit that would send me to Kingdom Come ——or elsewhere. But no, the good Lord spared me once again and we could resume normal fire missions in due course. Later in the day, our Div Arty

Commander, Brig Gen Barth, and some of his staff paid us a visit. An interpreter on the staff stated the scrawls were naming certain squads and platoons, announcing which were those who could brag during their victory ceremonies. But now such scrawls served as obituaries. So solly! Being wrapped up completely with moving my howitzers across the RR tracks to form a more compact body and still maintain a reasonably wide btry firing front, I was not queried on the events transpiring during the attack. Others did the talking. "A" Btry was saved this day but suffered 7 KIA and 11 WIAs. One of Cpl Meares' crew, Pfc Chauncey E Schick from Hawthorne, Pa, was hit in the shoulder He was flown to Japan but quickly returned to combat, soon to earn a battlefield commission,————a truly outstanding, always cheerful soldier amongst the top cannoneers of Fighting Able. We will read more about this hero as he fell in battle one last, sorrowful time. Sgt Jack L Cuthrell of the 35th Infantry "Cacti" Regiment has this to say about the Battle of the Pusan Perimeter: "Everyone has heard of the Punch Bowl, the Bowling Alley, Pork Chop Hill, Old Baldy, and Chosin Reservoir. Hardly anyone has heard of BATTLE MOUNTAIN The 35th and 27th Infantry Regiments of the 25th Division were assigned the area around SUBUK-SAN and PIL=BONG which became known as BATTLE MOUNTAIN. The NKs were massing for an attack thru this section which was their best route to Pusan. We had orders to 'HOLD AT ALL COSTS.' The battle raged for two weeks and changed hands thirteen times. General Kean said of the battle: "Never before to my knowledge has a unit closed the gaps in its front line and held it intact while a full scale battle was raging in the rear area.' By the time the battle was over, the NK forces were no longer an effective fighting force. 'We had whipped their A---!' In the book 'FIGHTING ON THE BRINK: DEFENSE OF THE PUSAN PERIMETER'by Brig Gen Uzal W Ent, he refers to the 35th as the 'ROCK OF PUSAN'. This is in no way meant to suggest that we were the only ones to save Pusan. Every outfit and every soldier that was at the Perimeter fought under tremendous hardship and with great courage. I for one am proud to say that I was associated with the troops that held the Perimeter. We took Gen Walker's order to 'Stay or die' to heart. We said:'Yes, General, we can do that, and we did it. I hope this piece which I am compelled to write will someday get into the hands of some troops that were there and to some that were not. History should not glaze over this part of the war. It was the first victory over communism and set the stage for what was to follow." In late morning, LtColHogan called me aside and, as we sat on some empty ammo cases, he asked me if I wanted to take over "B" Btry. Its BC had hurt his back during an attack in his area; he was being evacuated Stateside. This was, for me, a tough decision. After what I had just gone thru with our cannoneers, it would be hard for me to leave them at this time. We had trained hard together and had done well. Career-wise, I probably should have leaped at this opportunity,— a great chance to make captain before most of my USMA classmates. However, with much mixed feelings, I declined the offer but thanked my Bn commander very much. For the rest of the day, I worked at regrouping my howitzers. For protection from mortar or artillery attack, they should be dispersed as much as possible. The ideal front for a battery of six 105s is, per TAS, 150 yards, to maximize the 25 yd bursting radius of the 105 when firing a parallel sheaf to the direct front. But with the infiltration of enemy into firing batteries as just occurred, guns must be placed closer together. Finally, with the seasoned suggestions of our new Chief of Firing Battery, M/Sgt Rufus Cole, newly appointed First Sergeant Germanus P Kotzur, and experienced chiefs of section, we decided to move one howitzer across the RR track, leaving four on one side of the tracks and two on the other. By noon 3Sep, Fighting Able was back to firing DS missions for our Cacti doughboys. The finale to the 2-3Sep affair occurred on or about 5 Sep when 12 F4U Corsairs roared down the battery position, spitting bullets and dropping napalm on the small mountain to our rear. We could see the eyeballs of the pilots; the pilots were really "on the deck". Those persistent NKs had infiltrated our rear and were evidently seen by elements of higher headquarters and they laid on a heavy close air support mission. Able Btry was saved again! Made us think more highly of higher Hq lolling safely far to our rear but keeping surveillance of the battle area where we were. We estimated a company of enemy had been wiped out. We could smell their rotten carcasses spoiling in the hot sun for days as we feasted on C-rations and Australian bully beef. Pfc Howard H Sexton, one of our cooks, did a great job of creating feasts out of these entrees. Until finally debouching the perimeter, we maintained a tight perimeter about our battery, keeping all troops busy. This included our officers, e.g. I cleaned and oiled my M-1 every day. We conducted frequent registrations with concurrent metro messages sent by Div Arty. This maintained our accuracy of fire. I would try my best to adjust with bn aircraft because the pilots had much better coverage of the target area than did ground observers. They could more easily select base points more identifiable both on the ground and on the map, insuring we were all firing on the same coordinates. With my GFT in one hand and mike in the other, I would frequently complete a BP registration with but seven or eight rounds. This took good initial data, frequently enabling FFE after but one or two rounds in the adjustment phase. We got tickled with Lt Julius Duncan of Texas whose virtues have already been extolled in the Bn log. Not atypical of many Texans, he, at times, waxed eloquent during his conduct of fire. On one mission with "A" Btry, his transmissions proceeded as follows:

ROGER, ABLE, THAT LAST ROUND LOOKED GOOD. IT LANDED NEAR THE BP BUT I LOST IT UNDER SOME TREES. BETTER COME RIGHT A BIT AND ADD A FEW AND TRY AGAIN. OVER.

Our Bn CO gets on the horn:

THIS IS ROBIN SIX. CONFINE YOUR REMARKS TO FIRE COMMANDS! OUT! Immediate response from Lt Julius O Duncn: RIGHT FIVE ZERO! REPEAT RANGE! OVER. We shall read later how the state of Texas likewise extolled its own. On the subject of registration. this technique is the sina qua non of the FA. All guns cannot hit the same point even using identical firing data. For cogent reasons, this is true. For those desiring more information on the techniques and reasons for registrations, see APPENDIX "C". A radar van of the 1st FA Obsn Bn had been stationed in our area. It was well protected within the perimeter of Fighting Able. Lt Walter B Thompson of Warrenton, NC, was in charge of this van, operating with Corps Artillery. Tommy, my old roommate from bachelor days at Fort Sill, had won a battlefield commission while fighting with the 1st Ob in North Africa in WWII. He was a crackerjack officer. Tommy and his jeep driver were the last men to get back to our lines thru the Kasserine Pass in North Africa before German general

Rommel closed it off. I was best man at his wedding in Fort Sill on 7Nov48. His lovely bride, Anita, a native Okie, was a nurse in Lawton. Then, on 18Dec48, ole Bert followed suit, marrying his sweetheart from West Point days, Tommye Lou Williams from San Antonio, Tx. We were married at the Old Post Chapel at Fort Sam Houston. So here in Korea, Tommy and I were reunited but not until summer 1951. It may be appropos to describe these FA Obsn Bns, not known to many besides their TOE troops. Most of these outfits produced enviable records in WWII as target getting agencies. By successful location of hostile artillery, adjustment of fire, vast survey operations, and other such accomplishments, they have become an indispensable part of Corps Artillery. Not many Redlegs know about what exactly these "Ob" battalions are up to and how much they contribute to success in combat. The only reason I know much about them is due to my old BOQ buddy. He and I held "show and tell" presentations for our batteries at Fort Sill, my firing battery and his Obsn Bn battery that acquainted our troops with how the "other half lives." Many times, when the 1st Obsn Bn got a new commander, he and Tommy would spend hours in the living room of our BOQ, old hand Tommy explaining the intricacies of Obsn work to the new Bn commander. More on the history of the First FA Obsn Bn can be gleaned from the pages of the Nov/Dec01 issue of the GRAYBEARD magazine. The mission and operation of this battalion was the location of enemy mortars and artillery by sound, flash and radar ranging, providing survey control for friendly artillery, surveillance along the front for the purpose of collecting intelligence information, and providing meterological data for our artillery. The history of this unusal and little known organization dates back to 7Aug22 when the parent unit, the 1st Observation Battery was created at Fort Bragg, NC. The Bn participated in seven campaigns during WWII, i.e. North Africa, Sicily, Italy, France and Germany and ten in Korea. Battalion honors include two French Croix de Guerre awards in WWII and the Meritorious Unit Citation and ROK Presidential Onit Citation in Korea. In Aug 50, the Battalion departed from Fort Sill, OK, for Korea. Within four days after landing at Pusan on 22Aug50, the Bn was committed to action in the support of the 1st Cav Div, the 24th Ind Div, and the 25th Inf Div. Throughout the Korean War, the 1st Obsn Bn with call sign NATHAN HALE supported most UN divisions in major battles. Assigned to Eighth Army, the 1st Ob Bn was the only battalion of its kind in Korea. This resulted in spreading the Battalion's services completely across the Korean front and attaching each of its three other batteries to a Corps (I, IX and X). The support of an Army front by a battalion designed to support only one Corps was no mean accomplishment.

Lt Tommy and Anita Thompson at 7Dec48 Wedding at Ft.Sill

Lt Bert and T-Lou Bailey Atop the Empire State Bldg Jun50.

CHAPTER TWO

Pusan Perimeter and Breakout

6 SEPT 50

0001-0600 Fired harassing and interdiction fires. C/90 roving gun interdicting the pass at (31.4-59.9) with 4 rds per hour. 0600 Ln 2 reports that White CP was under attack; B and C Btrys were also involved and that C Btry was firing direct fire with their howitzers. 0630 Lt McFerron, BC B Btry was hit by small arms and evacuated. The following personnel of C Btry were outstanding in the Btry's defense: Lt Foss with a small patrol consisting of Sgts Chambers, Withers, and Markham and PFCs Majors, Kingsley and Correa killed 37 NK Communists and wounded 6. This happened on the flank of C Btry's position. Lt Gramlich, Sgts Edwards, Gazinski, Cpl Dixon and Pvt Faldenaur manned a howitzer and helped stop the attack on the Btry. 1130 Fired in support of attack by 1st Bn 27th Inf in the 2nd Bn 35th Inf sector. The attack was successful and the high ground cleared and taken. 1800 Capt Sherman, Asst S-3 released and assigned BC B Btry. Capt. Metcalfe assigned as Ln O, Capt McCoy joined and assigned as Asst S-3. 1830 8th FA Bn took over the FDC for the 2nd Bn sector. In reality they just passed the target location on to the Btrys (Btrys kept their own charts) and no chart was kept in the FDC. It is felt that this was not a good set up. 2100 Assigned harassing and interdiction missions to all Btrys and C/90 roving gun. 2230 fired on a column of vehicles with lights on at (39.9-73.6). Results unknown - lights went out. 2300 fired on enemy Arty piece at (34.0-75.6); 5 volleys neutralized the gun which was located by two intersecting azimuths., Bn expended 2373 rds. (Total to date 32,136 rds). C/90th expended 315 rds of 155mm.

7 SEPT 50

0001-0700 fired harassing and interdiction missions for our supported Inf. A small attack on E and G Co's 35th during the nite was repulsed by Arty fire. 0700 Dawn broke with a very heavy ground fog - visibility zero - plane reported in area but could not observe. 1615 CO 8th FA Bn, Col. Terry, notified us that his mission was changed and that B/8th would leave tomorrow 8 Sept and that the 64th would now take over the fire control. 1700 Destroyed a small, probably 37mm AT gun at (35.95-64.27). 1830 Lt Berassa, Bn Air Observer, identified 3 enemy medium howitzers at (38.5-79.4) and adjusted one how. of C/90 on them; destroyed 2 with direct hits, damaged the other by near misses and blew up their ammunition supply. 1900 Lt. Jensen returned as FO with 2nd Bn 27th Inf. - they are leaving this area on another mission - relief of 5th RCT. 2315 A Btry was adjusted by sound on an enemy Arty piece - it was neutralized and believed destroyed. Bn expended 718 rds. (Total to date 32854) C/90 expended 374 rds of 155mm.

8 SEP 50

0145 Bn received 150 rds of WP. We have been short on WP ammo for the past 10 days. 0750 Capt Bornhouser, Ln 1 was evacuated to MASAN; believed to have malaria. M/Sgt Pope took over his duties until we could get an officer replacement up there. 0850 Capt Stockton was recalled from a Platoon of C/35th, where he has been since the ROKs ran off and left him. He was sent to relieve Capt Rutherford at Leopard Blue. Capt Rutherford temporarily took Capt Bornhouser's place as Ln O at Leopard Red. 1000 B/8th moved out of posn. 1430 Displaced C/64 to B/8 old posn at (1150.4-1371.38). This move cuts down the size of and simplifies the perimeter for B/64, C/64 and Leopard White Hdq. 1535 Leopard 6, Col Fisher, ordered one gun of C/90 turned to fire on (36-79) area and also wants one to continue interdicting the pass. 1600 Capt Driscoll joined and assigned S-1; Lt Galloway joined and assigned to A Btry; Lt Goodman released from S-1 and assigned as Asst S-3; Capt McCoy released from Asst S-3 and assigned as Ln O. 1830 C/64 in posn and registered. 2235 D/A 3 requested that we lay one How of

C/90 in direction of Baldy Hill (38.2-58.2) to help repel a banzai attack on Lion Blue, 3rd Bn 27th Inf. Bn fired on concentrations of enemy troops, arty and mortars during the day and obtained excellent results. Fired a few harassing fires during the night. Bn expended 391 rds. (Total to date33,245 rds). C/90 expended 232 rds of 155mm.

9 SEPT 50

0605 FO B reports column of lights coming thru the pass. Fired C/90 roving gun - results unknown - lights went out. 0730 Bn received 66 more S. K. (ROK) soldiers. They were assigned 22 to each of the firing btrys. 0845 D/A cut us down to 40 rds per gun per day. 0900 D/A 3 requested any info that we might have relative to the Inf. leaving our FOs or of failing to protect them. Lt Bell was left in posn by G Co 24th Inf on 29 Aug while West of Sangju - they also stole his Jeep at the same time. 1045 Col Doerr, Exec of 35th Inf, directed that all of our recommendations for awards would be sent thru 35th RCT Hq. 1235 A Btry neutralized a Howitzer firing from (33.62-61.90). 1245 D/A 3 directed that we lay a platoon of A and a platoon of C/90 to be able to fire as far South as (38-59). 1400 A Btry destroyed a S. P. gun at (34.4-64.4), Air Obsn was used. 1530 Col Sandeen, CO 90th FA Bn, conferred with Col Hogan regarding a posn for his newly activated B Btry. 1830 Bn wire crew reported 9 N. K. soldiers cooking supper in village at (50.5-67.3). They have been cutting our wire lines there for past 2-3 days. Hq Btry sent a 19 man patrol. 1855 Ln 2 reported that the 2nd Bn would make a limited objective attack in the morning, 10 Sept, to regain some important high ground. He requested air Obsn at 1000 during the attack phase and recommended that we have one 155mm how layed on that area. 1900 Lt Ross relieved from S-2 and assigned to A Btry; Lt Reese, relieved from A Btry and assigned as Ln pilot; Lt Nyval relieved as Ln pilot and assigned to B Btry; Lt Berassa relieved as Air Obs and reverted to his asst S-2 duties. Lt Jensen, C Btry, appointed as Air Obs. 1930 Sgt Pogue, Bn Com Chief requested help for our patrol - more enemy than they could handle. Infantry notified and sent I & R Platoon. 2120 PFC Guarjardo was killed and left in the village. Enemy had one MG, several burp guns and were armed with M1 rifles. Patrol killed 3 of the enemy. 2210 Leopard 3 notified us that they would clean out all of the villages up the creek from us and also recover PFC Guarjardo's body and for us to furnish them a guide tomorrow, 10th Sept. 2211 A great deal of Arty firing was heard on our North flank. We were informed that it was the 2nd Inf Div Arty. 2400 Clocks were set back one hour now on I time instead of K. Bn expended 314 rds (total to date 33,559 rds). C/90 expended 501 rds.

10 SEPT 50

0001-0600 Fired harassing and interdiction missions. During this period wire communication was in and out many times. Our last contact with the radio relay was at 0330. Several times during the night we had to awaken them by telephone. 0730 Checked on radio relay station - by all appearances the 3 men, Cpl Greenwell, PFC Taylor and Pvt Wynn were captured while asleep. The equipment was strewn over the area and all present except for the telephone handset. 0740 A patrol of 50 men and one tank from Leopard Blue, went up the creek to clear the villages of enemy and to recover PFC Guarjardo's body. 0800 Ln plane returned to air strip - too much ground haze - ceiling less than 300 ft.. 0930 Lt Nyval was evacuated to Div Clearing Sta., NBC, battle fatigue. 1050 Advised Leopard 3 that it would be better to bulldoze down villages rather than burn them as the smoke and haze will prevent air Obsn in this area for the rest of the day. 1110 Col Sandeen, CO 90th FA Bn arrived at the CP on reconn for posn for his newly activated B Btry. 1115 Radio relay station now in operation in a new location - not completely satisfactory as we cannot reach all stations. 1140 Visibility clearing, plane back in air. 1200 Lt Stout joined and assigned to B Btry. 1215 RCT commander desires that we move a 155mm howitzer up behind 2nd Bn 35th to fire on troop and vehicle concentrations in 2nd Inf. Div sector. Advised that C/90 was already spread too far and in 3 positions, that the available officers and communication facilities were not available to handle another position. 1300 D/A 3 notified us that we were now limited to 25 rds per gun per day. 1450 Bn CO ordered each Howitzer Btry to send one squad of ROK soldiers to Hq Btry as perimeter defense for relay station. 1500 Capt Stockton and Ln party returned to Bn CP. 1500 S/Sgt James Campbell, Hq Btry, discharged and appointed 2nd Lt AUS and assigned to C Btry. 1605

Lt McGrady promoted to Capt. 1820 D/A 3 reports 300-500 rds 105 ammo at (46-72) and to check on it. Ammo was left in posn by B/64 and that said info was reported to D/A by Bn Exec Off on eve of 5 Sept. We will remove it as soon as the Engineers have repaired the road which at the moment is impassible. 2030 Ln 1 reports 6 different enemy arty pieces firing into the zone of the 1st Bn. We are using sound and our OPs in attempting to locate them. 2100 G/35 undergoing an attack. C and B Btrys firing in support of their defense. 2145 Ln 2 reported that the attack on G/35th had slowed down – force estimated to have been one company. 2146 Ln 1 informed us that Leopard 6, Col Fisher, had authorized the use of plenty of ammo for counter btry fire. 2200 D/A 3 warned us to watch our ammo expenditure. Bn Expended 308 rds (total to date 33,867 rds). C/90 expended 465 rds 155mm.

64 FA BN continued

11SEPT 50

0040 C/90 roving gun being shelled by 76mm SP gun believed in vic CHUNGAM-NI (34.5-64.7). 0345 G/35th Inf being attacked - fired B & C btrys. 0435 Enemy attack slipped off of G/35 and into E/35th. 0554 G/35 pinned down by MG fire; neutralized by B Btry. 0715 Bn Exec Off, Capt Stockton, M/Sgt Pogue, M/Sgt Myrick, Pvts Wise, Sides and Bault left for Div Rear Echelon to attend GCM of Pvt Iberra. 1145 Leopard 3 directed that we send a Ln plane to (34.5-74.8) as they suspect a SP gun in that area. Plane reported tracks but no gun. 1200 Ln 2 reported 600 enemy trps in rice paddies at (39-76) and requested an air strike. 1230 Ln 2 reported 2000 enemy retreating 6 miles N. E. of YONGSAN (48-84); out of our Arty range. 1345 CIC screened all of our S. K. civilian laborers as ordered by D/A CG. 1440 Gen Barth, D/A CG visited our CP and informed us that C/90 was now under control of 90th FA Bn and in a General support/reinforcing role. We are to get rid of our Korean kid mascots. He has talked to the Inf. about ammo expenditures; we will fire on any attack but use fewer volleys in effect. 1450 Air strike on YONSAN - retreating enemy columns were strafed with good results. 1500 Moved one howitzer section, with Lt Stout as Exec, up into F/35 perimeter - to be used as a roving gun. This was ordered by RCT CO. In posn at 1535. Ln plane, flown by Lt Reese with Lt Duncan as Obs, was forced down by engine trouble; landed on mud road 600 yds behind E/35; cause of trouble unknown. 1600 Plane trouble has been corrected and they are now airborne. 1630 Lt's Milleren, Sexton and Hart relieved as FOs. Replaced by Lt's D Campbell, Knight and Roper. 1900 Cleared Leghorn to fire on tank at (38.32-64.7) in our area. 2030 Ln 1 reported a terrific flash and explosion in CHUNGAM-NI. There was no Arty firing into there at this time cause unknown. 2215 Gen Wilson, Asst Div CG, and Leopard 6 want illuminating shell fired in front of E and G Cos 35th. B/90 has only one round. 2330 Ln 2 reported that Leopard White was planning a limited objective attack tomorrow. He has the Arty plan set up and also warned them about our ammo allowance for such an attack. 2400 Ln 1 reported that Red

6 would not let C/90 roving gun fire at night as it drew too much return Arty fire into his posn and the Red CP area. Suggest that it be pulled out and returned to the battery if they don't intend to use it. Leopard 6 says that it will stay and interdict the pass. Bn expended 659 rds (total to date 34,526 rds) C/90 expended 223 rds 155mm.

12 SEPT 50

0200 G/35 under attack again. Broken up by 21 rds from C/64. 0320 notified that A and C 159 FA Bn were under enemy attack. 0350 A Btry fired on sound location of enemy arty at (34.81-63.87). Neutralized the piece. 0445 Ln 2 reported a series of small attacks being made on G/35. One platoon lost 150 yards. Fired C/64 in support. 0550 Ln 2 needs plane to observe behind hills across river NW of G/35. Plane sent immediately – located and neutralized two mortars. 0815 Gen Barth, D/A CG, called about moving one of our batteries from the Northern sector of 35th RCT to the W to a posn at (66.0-43.6); old posn of C/159, to be layed on CA 6000 to support the attack of 2nd Bn 35th and to move today. Advised against the move. Btry will move today. 0914 Gen Barth arrived FDC and conferred with Bn Co and directed that we move one Battery. 1005 D/A 3 advised us that B/65th Engineers and Div Recon Co are being attacked at (44-72) and to have our planes check this area as they come and go. 1040 Leopard Red 5 wanted to know just what is status of 90th FA Bn and what is meant by Gen Support Reinforcing; what communications his Arty Ln O has to the 90th and whether he could get a medium concentration in front of each of his companies? Bn Exec Off advised him of Gen Support reinforcing; we have a direct line from FDC to FDC and that he may get a concentration in front of each Company, but it's not probable. Will register on enough check points so that satisfactory transfers can be made. 1048 D/A 3 advised us that Gen Kean was concerned about the local defense of all Arty. They must be wired in with barbed wire out beyond hand grenade range, all entrances to the posn to have removable barricades. All Btrys and S-4 were notified. A Btry is already wired in. 1105 Authorized by D/A 3 an additional 300 rds for attack of 2nd Bn. 1107 CO 90th requested info as to whether or not A Btry had drawn any arty or mortar fire and if there was room for his roving gun within A

Btry's perimeter as the roving gun draws fire on itself and Red CP. 1200 Lt's Guill (B/64) and Beverly (C/90) relieved as FOs by Lts Ross and Galloway (A/64). 1238 D/A 5 called said CG wants Bn CO to know what he's doing before he decides to move his Battery and for him to check with Leopard 6 prior to movement, (we were ordered by D/A CG to move one Btry) that there is an enemy piece behind our lines at (43-71). 1320 Gave C Btry march order to move to posn in creek at (43,6-66.2). 1500 B Btry retrieved 632 rds 105mm ammo that had been left in their old posn area at (45,7-73.0). They left approx 200 incomplete and unserviceable rds and will in all probability have to destroy them. 1720 C Btry in posn, laid on CA 5500. 1830 D/A allocated 100 rds for support of attack by White Bn. 1900 D/A alerted all units in CHUNG-NI area to be on alert tonight - another Arty hunting unit reported to be in that vicinity. 2210 D/A authorized 300 addnl rds for attack of White tomorrow. 2315 D/A 3, stated ASP critically short of 105mm ammo we must keep within our allowance. 2320 Ln 2, arty piece at (35.45-78.45). Located by 3 intersecting azimuths. Out of our arty range. Bn expended 722 rds (total to date 35,248 rds)

C/S M/Sgt Hammer/FO Lt Galloway

l/Sgt Germanus P Kotzur and I

64th FA BN Continued

13 SEPT 50

0110 Ln 2 reported G/35th receiving 4-5 rds of mortar fire every few minutes. The mortars are behind hill 63 (39.0-74.7); arty piece located by intersection at (35.45-78.4) but out of our range. 0150-0500 All quiet on entire RCT front. 0505 G/35 under attack - enemy continues to harass this Company. Fired B/64 in support. 0630 Ln plane fired on group of enemy dug in at (43.2-71.3). Casualties were noted however the enemy was stubborn and would not move. We could not use VT as our troops were too close. 0930 Air strike on tank and Inf at (37.0-69.6) – tank destroyed. 1300 Air strike on Arty btry at (31.8-61.2) with good results. 1345 90th FA Bn requested clearance to fire on enemy troops in (42-70). Mission cleared by Leopard 5. 1404 90th FA Air Obs says troops in (42-70) are friendly and did not fire. 1405 Div Air Off ordered all planes back to strip; ground winds of 50 to 60 MPH expected in next 20 minutes. 1415 Ln 2 says 2nd Bn attack progressing slowly but steadily - they have reached phase line "L". 1421 Requested permission of Leopard to withdraw B/64 and C/90 roving guns as Red 6 does not desire C/90 roving gun to fire at night. 1433 Leopard 5 directed that we leave the roving guns in position and that Red 6 denies saying not to fire the "Little Professor", C/90 roving gun, at night. C/90 roving gun has not fired for past 2 nights - interdiction concentrations have been assigned to them and Ln 2 confirms that Red 6 says no night firing. 1535 FO G reported 75-100 NK crossing the river NW of G Co at approx (38-75). 1610 RCT Commander complained of unsatisfactory Arty support for todays attack of 2nd Bn directed that CO 64th report to him at White Bn CP. 1630 CO 64th reported to RCT Commander and was referred by Col Fisher to Capt Hammerquist, White 3, for details of unsatisfactory Arty support. Capt Hammerquist stated that the Arty support was excellent all day, that his only complaint was when attempting to move up about 25 yds in range across the edge of a ridge, the rounds then went way over. The RPE at the firing range was approx 35 yds – this explanation was satisfactory to him. Rgtl Commander then complained that observers were attacking tgts by firing one rd at a time and that adjustment took too long. He wanted all howitzers to fire. Ln O2 was contacted. Adjustments referred to were precision destruction missions on individual MGs and were being destroyed at the request of the Infantry. Ln O2 was informed by CO 64th that if destruction of individual enemy MGs was holding up the attack, to change to area fire to neutralize the MGs. Ln2 informed CO 64 that Inf were going to withdraw to phase line "L" for the night and that they wanted area fire to cover their withdrawal. Above information and explanation passed on to Rgtl CO and also explained that area fire required greater ammo exp. to accomplish the mission. 1640 A Btry adjusted on 2 Arty pieces and destroyed one but could not observe any visible effect on the other as it was under a bridge. 1645 RCT Commander passed on a complaint of CO 2nd Bn 35th Inf that the Arty FOs communications had been "spotty", that is, had not worked consistently. No specific instance was stated but Col Wilkins, CO 2nd Bn, gave as an example that each FO started a mission direct with a Btry and that Inf personnel knew that all missions didn't get fired. Ln O2 was questioned and he stated that one of his 4 FOs had a defective receiver but could transmit, that the other 3 FOs and his equipment was working. The FO fired direct with the Btrys or through him (Ln O) whenever necessary to relay. That to the best of his knowledge the FO radios failed only when their line of sight characteristics were exceeded. In his opinion, any failure of the FOs to fire was due to lack of observation. 1650 Major Wolfolk, CO 3rd Bn 35th Inf, entered 2nd Bn CP and stated that the Arty FO fired two rds too close and caused 4 casualties among our own troops. 1655 Col Wilkins, CO 2nd Bn 35th interrupted a fone conversation between CO 64th and Ln O2 to call "Cease firing", rds were falling on our position. FO said "no". 1650 D/A notified us that MASAN police had reported 40 enemy in foxholes near temple on MT MUNUNG (53-73) and that they have rifles. Notified B/64 and B/90 as this area is approx 1000 yds behind their positions. 1830 A Btry fired on and destroyed a SP gun at (32.54-62.36). 1900 D/A 3 stated that 8th Army has notified us that we will have to live within our ammo allowance; no emergency allocations to be considered; for us to hold down on our firing so that we may get a little ahead. 1915 Informed Leopard 6 of ammo situation and requested permission to displace B/64 roving gun to posn with remainder of Btry. Permission was granted to displace it in the morning. 1925 Leopard 6 informed the Bn CO that (1) Maj Wolfolk, CO 3rd Bn reported FOs inefficient, their communications didn't work and that they didn't fire frequently enough; (2) he desires a heavy volume of fire from B/90 tomorrow morning with the entire btry firing on the hill being attacked; (3) he desires harassing fire on the "pocket" tonight. CO 64 informed him that he would inform CO 2nd Bn of his wishes and prepare to deliver fires desired. 1955 Notified B/90th to relay on CA 5000 to cover tomorrow's attack. 2005 Notified all Ln Os that there would be no harassing from the 105s tonite - fire only to repel an actual attack. 2045 Comm O started to change to new frequencies that are effective tonite at midnight. He is unable to change the FO radios and will leave the old K channel on all Ln O radios and one of the S-3 sets. 2050 Received notification that a tropical storm would hit this area at 0300 14 Sept, expect rain and winds of 40-50 MPH - expected to be clear by noon. 2245 Ln O1 reported C/90 roving gun under arty fire from Az 4100 and vicinity of (35.8-64.8). Approx 10 rds have landed in their posn; no one hurt and no damage so far. They have not fired tonight. 2305 Ln O2 located, by 3 intersections, two arty pieces at (35.45-78.40). Neutralized by C/90; out of range of 64th FA Bn. Expended 609 rds (total to date 35,857 rds).

14 SEPT 50

0030 Ln 1 reported C/90 roving gun undergoing another shelling by a SP gun. Roving gun has not fired tonight. 0100-0600 All quiet however F/35, which had changed posns with G/35, underwent a small attack. The enemy was repelled. 0600 Displaced B/64 roving gun back to Btry posn. 0610 Ln plane sent to sector of 2nd Bn for surveillance in their sector. 0730 Sent 5 men of each Btry to Sv Btry to make barbed wire concertina rolls. Bn needs approx 120 rolls. Cpl Anderson, an ex Engineer, in Sv Btry is supervising the making of the concertina rolls. 0950 Leopard 6 called, said, "another of those deals of one rd at a time on a tgt, have Hogan meet me at White CP". 1000 D/A CG visited FDC and informed us that we would fire no prepatory fires unless cleared by Div., that there would be no emergency allocations of ammo, a max of 3 volleys in fire for effect, to save ammo at every opportunity, that the 155s are now limited to 50 rds per gun per day, that we would probably get 25 SK ROK soldiers for Hq and Sv Btrys. CO and Exec Off of 90th FA Bn arrived at FDC requesting info as to the 35th RCT plan of attack and our plan of support. At present we have not received the RCT plan of attack we expect the opns order tonight. 1050 Lt Lee, ROK Ln O with Div Arty, visited all firing Btrys to see how the ROK troops were progressing. 1350 Ln plane reports 25 or more enemy dug in on a steep bank near F Co at (39.2-73.8). 1335 Ln 2 reported that the 2nd Bn attack is not going very well, very slow. Inf has had two air strikes on their objective. 1635 D/A directs that we are limited to 30 rds per day per Arty Bn for harassing and interdiction fires. 1730 Bn received five 1/1000000 maps from D/A Asst 3 as TIP material. 1800 Received Div Opn order, Adm order and intelligence annex covering our future operation. 1910 Requested of Leopard 6 permission to displace C/90 roving gun to posn with remainder of Btry. This gun has not fired a rd after dark for the past 3 nights. Permission was granted. 1922 C/90 roving gun displaced to remainder of Btry. 2020-2135 Vehicles with lights coming through the pass, also entering CHUNGAM-NI. 2150 Defensive fires were fired in by Ln 2 to cover new posn of Leopard White. Leopard White 6 stated that Arty support was slow and not enough of it. 2250 Ln 2 reported column of trucks with lights at approx (36.0-74.3) - out of our range. 2255 Ln O1 reported trucks in CHUNGAM-NI. Fired C/90 into there. Bn expended 332 rds (total to date 36,189 rds)

ON THE NEXT PAGE, SEE SGT CUMMINS AT HIS 105mm HOW POINTING NORTH AND STREAM OF TERRIFIED SOUTH KOREANS HEADING SOUTH

64 FA BN continued.

15 SEPT 50

All quiet during the night. 0530 F/35 under attack, B/64 firing in support. 0630 Plane reports that visibility is too low to observe. 0800 Have 6 flights of high performance aircraft in the vicinity waiting for visibility to clear up. 0845 D/A 5 reported that PW states that a Company sized unit is between HAMAN road and MASAN road with the mission of knocking out the Arty. Div Recon Co is going to clean them out but probably won't get started prior to tomorrow. Notified A and C Btrys, who are in that area. 099 Lt Griffin released from FO by Lt J. Campbell. 1140 Ln plane back in area – reported unable to observe – ceiling too low. 1415 Ln 1 reports activity at tunnel entrance (38-59), suspects there might be an arty piece there; has seen flashes from that area at night. 1425 Ln 2 reported a SP arty piece firing form (40.78.5). 1600 Leopard 6 visited CP and requested a Ln Plane land at the strip near Leopard CP. 1702 D/A 2; at 0507 this AM the 1st Marines and ROK Marines made a two beach landing off

INCHON. Objective KIMPO airdrome. There is additional information but not for publication at this time. 1705 Bn Co and Exec Off 159 FA Bn conferred with Bn CO about future plans. 1840 Bn CO left for Leopard White to see about their plans for tomorrow's attack. 1850 Lt Chapman, Bn Ammo Off. recovered 190 projectiles and 23 propelling charges in B Btry's old posn. 1925 Ln 1 reports Arty piece of approx 37 to 50mm firing from az of 3850 and located at approx (32.3-62.3). 1932 FO "E" reports an estimated Co. of enemy crossing the river at (37.3-76.7) coming our way. Fired B/64, observer reported 98% effect on the tgt. 1933 FO "F" reports large caliber arty piece firing from az 6280 at approx 6-7000 yds range. Out of range of our arty and requested an air strike on it in the morning. 1945 Ln 2 reported that all of the "pocket" was cleaned out except about 40 enemy. The total in the pocket so far, 167 new dead, 26 old dead, 35 POWs, 15 HMG, 11 LMG, 23 auto rifles, three 90mm mortars with 16 boxes of ammo, 19 burp guns, 91 rifles, 29 carbines, 5 AT rifles and 32 cases of ammo. 2012 Ln 2 will send us an overlay tonight for transmission to the air strip and briefing of observers prior to tomorrow's attack. Want plane tomorrow as much as possible. Put civil Sv "K" channel on the planes – they can work direct with B/90. 2044 Ln 1 Arty piece firing from (34.1-62.1). Located by two intersecting az. Fired on by C/90 using sound adj. Neutralized or destroyed, caused a large explosion and fire. 2200 Lt Berassa left for air strip in MASAN to brief the observers on tomorrow's plan of attack. Bn expended 120 rds (total to date 36,309 rds).

FOLLOWING COMMENTS ADDED BY AUTHOR:

When the brilliant General MacArthur again demonstrated his uncanny ability to turn failure around and launched his Inchon Landing on 15 September, the pressure on our troops within the Perimeter slacked off as the NKs retreated to protect their bases of supplies to the north. This was the same strategy MacArthur used in the War in the Pacific, bypassing those islands heavily infested with Japanese to hit much lesser protected areas or islands, more nearly assuring victories with unbelievably low losses of his own troops.

Inchon was a most tough nut to crack. Its tides ranged from over 31 feet at high tide to less than one at low. Troops would have to land against 16-foot high seawalls within a two-hour time frame. The generals of all services objected to this choice of landing. One suggested Osan. But MacArthur at 70 years of age was adamant and confident of his planning. It was approved by the Pentagon and the General, once again, displayed his genius with masterminding brilliant amphibious landings. As in his Pacific campaigns in WWII, MacArthur forced the enemy to retreat while his troops advanced with very few losses. The Pusan Perimeter was saved. Now the path is clear for Seoul. With supply lines cut, the NKs, like the Nips in WWII, must beat a hasty retreat

NOW BACK TO THE 64th FA Bn LOG:

16 SEPT 50

No harassing and interdiction. We are saving ammo for attack of 2nd Bn 35 in the morning. All quiet during the night. D/A reported that it was quiet on the entire front of the 25th Div. 0615 Laid C/64 on CA 6000 to support the attack of the 2nd Bn. 0620 Ln 02 notified that he could have 250 rds to support the attack of the Inf but was to fire no preparation for them. 0700 Lt Ceravsky sent out as FO with I Co 35th. 0710 Ln plane was directed to area of Ln 02. 0925 Received the 35th RCT Opn Order, Adm Order, Intelligence annex and overlay for 15 Sept. 0930 D/A CG visited the FDC. He reported that the marines were in YONDOK and that we would receive 25 SK ROK soldiers for Hq Btry to be used as security for wire crews and linemen. 1055 Forward elements of 2nd Bn attacking force at (39.8-73.9). 1227 FO K reported arty piece at (36.5-72.5) and that it was shelling F Co.. Adjusted 90th FA on it – piece was destroyed. 1310 Ln plane reported up again and was sent to 2nd Bn area. Visibility was poor and the ceiling very low. 1450 Lightning 5, Gen Wilson, requested an air strike on (37.7-79.9). We reported this to TAC air and D/A. 1500 D/A advised us that when VT was fired by us or our reinforcing unit, it was our responsibility to notify TAC air.

1500 B Btry Exec notified FDC that he has fired 140 rds with good effect, wants to continue. Told to shoot up to 250. 1522 Twenty five SK ROK soldiers assigned to the Bn. 1610 Have fired 200 + rds so far in 2nd Bn attack. Authorized 90th FA to fire VT on troops crossing the river at (37-75). 1618 RCT CO, Col Fisher, directs that a Ln plane be over 2nd Bn area at all times when this attack is going on. One of ours is deadlined for maintenance, other is in the air. Requested Lobster (90th FA) help us on the planes – they said that they would. 1650 FO K destroyed or neutralized 2 arty pieces – adjusted C/64 – one piece hit with 2 rds WP. 1730 Ln plane reports 3 arty pieces on edge of school yard and that 800 yds North by the bridge there are 3 more (37.9-79.4). Notified TAC air to get on these tgts. 1733 B Btry has expended 289 rds – told Btry to expend 50 more and report when expended. 1850 Notified by D/A that Wolfolk was going on a mission to the South and would take the Recon Co, B/65 Eng, I/35th, a Co from the 27th Inf and his own staff. 1900 FO "K" reported 2 tanks firing and has seen as many as 300 NKs gathering. Tanks are shooting at L Co. Relayed this to Ln 02 and D/A 2. Capt Loftin gave authority to shoot 150 more rds. 2010 Leopard 6 wants plane up at dawn to observe to North and NW of hill 127k, look along all rds and to the sides of roads. 2015 D/A 3, your FO with I/35 will accompany TF Mongrel and 64 will furnish the Ln O. Your Comm O will set up 159 FDC and C/159 channels on your radios with this TF. 2100 From Ln 02, the 64th can take credit for at least 250 enemy killed today and probably lots more. 2230 D/A 4 called and asked how many 608 radio equipped vehicles would we want to send by rail if we had to move 100 miles or more? He was told none, as we need them for column control. 2305 Lobster notified us that Lighthouse (24th Inf) had had a small attack and that it had been repulsed. Bn expended 135 rds (total to date 36,444 rds).

17 SEPT 50

No harassing or interdiction missions were fired. We are trying to stock up a little emergency Ammo. 0545 Capt Stockton and his Ln party left the area for Ln with the composite Bn task force Mongrel. 0645 Ln plane checked in and was directed to hill 127. Saw no enemy activity; ceiling less than 1000 ft and visibility less than one mile; returned to strip at 0710. 0840 Comm O had A and B firing channels placed on plane's radios as their alternate frequency. 0900 25 Sk ROK soldiers attached to Hq Btry. They will be used as wiremen and security for our radio relay set. 0920 Leopard 2 requested that we get a Ln plane in the air. Called the strip, pilots said no visibility from the air but would come up. 0932 Plane reported in area. Confirmed no visibility. 0935 Ln 01 reported little if any activity in his sector and that ground visibility was extremely limited. 0945 Plane reported that it was returning to strip. 1020 D/A 2 reported the EEI for today: prompt reporting of all enemy, whether large or small groups, organized or disorganized, which way moving, and what type of arms? 1055 Bn Ammo O reported that he will have to stay approx 300 rds below our basic load as he cannot haul it since we received no extra section of trucks on the activation of C Btry 64th FA Bn. 1105 FO C reported arty pieces firing at 938.5-75.2). Mission was given to the 90th FA Bn. 1205 Ln 02 reported 12 NK enemy at (38.4-76.8) and that 100 disorganized NKs without weapons withdrew across the river at (39.8-76.7). For past week enemy has been digging in and sandbagging the village at (40.5-82.5); however only 4-5 were seen there today.

1200 Lt Sexton, B Btry, relieved Lt D Campbell as FO with E/35. 1255 Sgt Stampley returned from FO with task force Mongrel – had enough Fos already from other Arty Bns. 1305 Air strike on enemy arty not on tgt – 1000 yds off the tgt at (35.88-75.44) and (36.16-74,88). 1330 D/A 2 requested plane look at (38.5-75.2). Plane reported negative. 1600 Ln 01 a patrol from K Co located an OP at (36.8-72.3), there are 7 NK there. 1825 Leopard 6 directed Bn CO report to Leopard CP. Bn CO was located at B Btry. 2015 Ln 01 The 24th Inf intercepted a NK radio transmission in the clear on the 300 radio: instructions to 3 Cos, one to attack between A and B, one between K and L and one direct into C. It is unknown whether instructions for attacking into the 24th or 35th RCT. 2135 Ln 01 arty piece located at (34.25-64.45) by intersecting azimuths from A and B Fos. 2145 Bn Co returned from RCT with attack plans for the 18th. 2150 Requested of Lumber (65th Eng) that they furnish us a bull dozer in SAGA at 0700 18 Sept to dig in FDC and howitzer emplacements for B/64th and B/90th. 2210 Notified B Btry to be ready to move at daylight 18 Sept and for BC and his party to report to FDC at 0645. 2230 Notified 90th FA Bn to have their B Btry prepared to follow B/64. 2245 Leopard 3 stated OK to use RTO in

SAGA as FDC and CP area, however Col Fisher wants your FDC and CP close to Leopard CP. Don't know yet where Leopard CP will move. Informed that we had to have our CP and FDC forward now that our Btrys in the North were moving to posns behind the 1st Bn on the MSR. Communication problems with the FDC too great from the present posn of the FDC. 2400 Enemy counter attacked in the Index area tonight with two Bns. Bn expended 422 rds (total to date 36,866 rds).

18 SEPT 50

0230 Directed 90th FA to lay C/90 in two platoons on CA 5000 and one platoon on CA 5400 prior to daylight and to have an FO ready to join the 25th Recon Co when they pass. 0255 F/35 is being attacked by an undetermined number of NK. B/64 firing in their support. 0255 Directed C/64 to lay on CA 5900 by daylight and to have an FO with complete party stand by to go with A/65th Eng when called for. 0615 Hq Btry CO, Capt Rutherford and a detail went forward to SAGA to prepare posn for FDC and CP in the vicinity of the RTO. 0700 BC B Btry and party arrive at CP for instructions. Was given location of new Btry posn, CA4500 and directed to pick up the SCR 625 Mine Detector from Hq Btry. They failed to pick up the mine detector. 0830 B Btry in posn at (42.3-67.9), laid on CA4500 and ready to fire. 0830 One half of FDC personnel, Comm Sect, Comm O and S-3 left for SAGA to set up the forward FDC and Swb. 0840 Bn CO left for RCT Hq and then to our forward CP and posn area. 0950 Forward FDC and swb in new posn ready to take over fire missions. Displaced 9.6 miles to (41.3-66.9). 1000 Closed out rear FDC and CP. 1015 B Btry registered by Air OP. 1030 Leopard 5, Col Doer, complained our Ln plane was flying over friendly territory in attempting to observe. An immediate check was made on the spot – the plane was West of CHUNGAM-NI – 2 miles beyond our most advanced friendly elements. This complaint positively unjustified; they think that every Ln plane in area belongs to the 64th. 1030-1300 fired observed missions, both air and ground, on several enemy arty pieces. No missions were fired on enemy personnel. 1303 B Btry given march order and to displace to posn at (41.1-67.25). 1310 Ln 01 Our most advanced elements are at (36.2-65.5) and we have the ridge

South from there. 1410 D/A CG was in the area and questioned the reasoning behind our 2nd displacement of B Btry. It was explained that this was done to give C/90 a posn if and when they moved today. 1440 B Btry in posn laid and ready to fire. 1520 Ln 01 A Co at (36.2-64.2), C Co at (36.0-65.7) 1520 Leopard 6 complained about Ln planes for not flying far enough forward to observe – at that very moment observer was directly above the enemy battery on which he was adjusting. 1700-2000 fired in defensive fires for A and C Cos. 2020 B Btry received one rd of HV fire in their posn area from az 4600. 2050 Fired TOT, our first with another Bn on an enemy btry at (34.24-64.0). Results unknown, however the btry was neutralized. 2200 B and C Fos getting arty fire in their posns. 2230 D/A will arrange for continuous air coverage by Pickle Barrel and Mosquito. 2250 Lightning 6, Gen Kean, directs that we place harassing and interdiction fires in CHUNGAM-NI all during the night. Bn expended 74 rds (total to date 36,940 rds)

AT TOP OF NEXT PAGE IS SHOWN AN AT-6 TEXAN ADVANCED TRAINER USED BY THE USAF FOR "MOSQUITO" MISSIONS, THOSE FLOWN ACROSS THE FRONT UNDER THE COORDINATION OF USAF HEADQUARTERS AND HIGHER LEVELS OF THE ARMY WITH AN ARMY OBSVR IN THE BACK SEAT

64FA BN Continued

19 SEPT 50

0800 B Btry outpost fired on a 3 man enemy patrol, killing one of them. He was dressed in peasant clothing, carried a burp gun, 300 rds of ammo and 5 hand grenades. 0300 A Btry fired on and stopped a banzai attack on C/35. 0430 D/A 2 reported an ambush and road block at (47.5-65.3), number of enemy unknown. 0725 Directed C/64 to lay on CSA 5600. The 2nd Inf Div has moved forward on our North. 0740 D/A 3 notified us that beginning tomorrow nite our ammo allotment will be increased; how much they couldn't answer. 0835 Have located 8 different arty posns. Firing all btrys and the 90th FA Bn; notified TAC air. 0843 D/A 3 We can use 300 rds above our daily ammo allowance if we have the tgts and can observe the fire. Mortar ammo is critical. 0925 Ln O2 reported his location at (38.2-70.4). 1000 An AT-6 plane, the mosquito that controls the high performance aircraft in our area, was shot down by ground AA fire at (33.4-63.4) and exploded. No one was seen to escape. It was witnessed by our Ln plane. 1020 Capt Stockton and Ln party returned from TF Mongrel which has been disolved. 1030 Col Sandeen, CO 90th FA Bn, arrived at CP and conferred with Bn CO about plans of 35th RCT and 64th FA. 1035 D/A 1 notified us that Sv Btry would receive 25 ROK soldiers. 1140 B/35 jumped off on attack, ran into trouble on hill to their front; B Btry fired 2 rds in effect and neutralized the area. 1200 Lt Hart sent out as FO with D Co/35th. 1320 Bn CO left for B Btry and forward posn area reconn. 1345 B Btry received one rd of arty fire from Az 3743, believed to be a howitzer. 1400 Ln plane located arty pieces at (33.2-62.1), adjusted A Btry with good effect, however results unknown. 1415 Ln O1 reported B/35 at (35.2-67.3) and C/35 at (351.5-66.2). 1440 Capt Stockton and party reported as Ln O with 3/35th. 1510 Col Preston, CO 159 FA Bn arrived at our CP and conferred with Col Hogan about our future plans; also gave us the situation as regards the 24th Inf sector. 1550 B Btry received 2 rds Arty fire from Az 3743. 1605 B Btry received another rd from same Az. No casualties or damage have been caused by the fire that has landed in their area. 1745 FO "L" reports lots of enemy activity at (37.5-74.1) and (37.7-76.4). Enemy laying wire and carrying supplies. Lt Nicols and TAC party arrived. They are the relief for Lt Petkov and his TAC. 1810 D/A 5 notified us that we are allocated 150 rds for harassing and interdiction fires tonight. 1815 Ln plane sent to area of (32-62), suspected arty in posn. 1950 Ln O1 arrived with 1/35 plan of attack for tomorrow. 2015 Leopard Red 5 arrived at FDC with plan of attack for TAC air officer. Bn CO showed him air photos of attack area, avenues of approach, etc and arrived at a new attack plan to take the high ground in certain sequences; we can now support it better. 2128 S-2 159 FA Bn brought plan of attack of 24th Inf. Informed us that max resistance had been at (35.5-61.8). We informed 1/35 of this. 2400 Leopard 6 wanted to know if we had been firing any missions? Have had no firing except harassing and interdiction missions, otherwise all quiet. Bn expended 443 rds (total to date 37,383 rds)

64 FA BN IN KOREA (continued)

20 SEPT 50

0001-0060 Fired harassing and interdiction fires throughout the nite. All quiet in all sectors of 25th Inf. Div. 0835 D/A notified us to pick up approx 1200 rds of 105 mm Ammo at the Div. ASP. Gen. Kean is desirous of cleaning out the ASP today. 0900 Lt. Milleren relieved Lt Roper as FO with A/35. Lt Roper was sick. 0900 Leopard 3, discontinue your arty support to the North, mass your support to the West. 0907 C/90 displaced forward to B/64 old posn. 0910 Capt Daprato returned to duty and assigned as S-2. 0915 Col Sandeen, CO 90th FA Bn arrived at FDC and conferred with Col Hogan about our future plans. 1100 Ln 3 reports 8 Arty pieces in area (34-77), requests Ln plane take them under observation and adjust on them. 1100 D/A CG visited FDC, stated that 90th FA will have to leave a platoon covering the North until we know the location of the forward elements of Ivanhoe (2nd Inf Div). 1150 F FO reports his Company now on the objective at (31.9-66.3). 1235 Bn Exec Off notified C Btry to cancel their plans for displacement today and to be prepared in the morning - their BC party to pick up the mine detector from Hq Btry. 1315 RCT CO, Col Fisher, arrived at the FDC and requested that we look for and find the Arty piece that was holding up the attack of his 2nd Bn. Plane was dispatched to the suspected area. The Air OP located the piece at (34.5-63.3). It was destroyed by A Btry and proved to be a 47mm AT gun. 1320 CO 90th FA Bn arrived at CP, requested current situation and future plans. Was told that we would sit tight remainder of the day, tonight and displace tomorrow 21 Sept. 1320 Ln O1 reported C Co 200 yds short of CHUNGAM-NI (34.4-64.8). 1600 D/A notified us that the Div. Ord. team would be out to star gauge C Btry's How. 1650 Ln 2 now located at (32-66.4). 1700 Air OP located 3 light Arty pieces being towed by NK soldiers and oxen. Fired A/64 and B/90 using VT. Killed oxen, personnel, and disabled the guns. 1730 Lt Foss, C Btry, was injured by a trip flare and evacuated. 1920 Gave no fire lines to Leghorn and Lobster. 1930 Lumber 3 (65th Eng) notified us that he would have a D-7 dozer here for us at 0700 21 Sept and that the 89th Tank Bn needed it first to pull a disabled tank out of the ditch. 1942 D/A 3 notified us to have one or two howitzers in B Btry ready for star gauging by the Ord at 0800 21 Sept. There is no extra ammo allocation tonight for harassing and interdiction fires; 30 rds maximum on such fires and we must stay within our 25 rds per gun per day allocation. 2050 LnO 1 reported A Co in posn at (34.5-63.4) in the pass. They are not occupying the high ground. 2055 No fire line at (29.7-67.0) to (32.0-64.5) to (34.0-62.0) to (35.0-62.0). Sent to D/A. 2250 Notified C Btry to have recon party report to FDC at 0730 21 Sept. Bn Expended 504 rds (total to date 37,887 rds).

21 SEPT 50

0315 FO K reported vehicles with lights at an az of 335, possibly located at (28.0-72.8). 0710 Ln Plane reported that the NKs had cratered the road last nite in the vicinity of the pass at (31.8-60.8) and (31.2-59.8). 0755 TAC AIR reported seeing many enemy troops on the high ground North of the pass. D/A and Leopard notified. 0745 LnO 1 sent in today's attack plans for Leopard Red, complete with intermediate objectives and phase lines. This is the first complete plan that this unit has ever received from any element of the 35th Inf Rgt or the RCT. 0750 LnO 2 sent in attack plan for Leopard White, complete with phase lines. 0800 C Btry advance party moved out for CHUNGAM-NI. 0850 Lt Galloway, A Btry, notified to relieve Sgt Stampley as FO C today. To be complied with as soon as LnO 1 is in posn. 0910 Air OP reports that the enemy has blown the bridges at (31.8-60.8) and (31.2-59.8); D/A and Leopard notified. 0910 Bn Co left on recon for posns West of CHUNGAM-NI. 0940 Air OP reports an estimated enemy Bn of troops at (33-56) now being taken under fire by TAC AIR using bombs, napalm and MG fire. 1000 LnO 3, FO I reports a large caliber Arty piece firing from az 6150; estimated location in (32-79) or (34-77) areas (CHUNGYON-RI). 1020 LnO 1 reported A Co on first objective. 1057 C/64 given march order, to move forward until met by their Btry guide. 1120 6 rds of medium caliber arty landed in Hq Btry area; coming from az 2600. 1128 Air OP reports a camouflaged object with shell cases about it at (37.3-76.4), will adjust on it. 1140 Bn CO returned to FDC. LnO 1 reported that Leopard Red was on their final objective. Relayed this to Leopard

6. 1240 CO 90th FA Bn called and asked the present situation. He has one platoon ready to displace forward. 1250 CG D/A at FDC. 1315 Bn CO and D/A CG left on fwd recon. 1400 A Btry given march order. 1405 Lobster 3 reported a gun at (37.3-76.4) and desired that our plane observe in that area. 1420 D/A 3 reported that the guns firing on Ivanhoe are well dug in at (40-181) out of arty range. 1500 From Bn CO; have B BC and party move fwd at once, Btry follow in 20 minutes, Lay C Btry to cover Northern sector. 1550 Leopard 6, get an air strike on (33.5-58.0) enemy troops moving SW. 1600 A Btry closed in posn at (32.66-62.77) layed and ready to fire. 1620 Hq Btry moved out. 1800 Hq Btry in posn at (32.70-62.95), marched 9 miles. 2100 Leghorn 3 (159 FA Bn) states that Lion's (27RCT) fwd elements now at (26.9-56.0). 2100 B Btry located at (26.9-56.0), however they have not reached the posn area; held up on the road by jammed 35th RCT vehicles. 2105 LnO 2 reported that Leopard White is now on their objective. 2240 Leopard 5 reported that the 24th RCT west of the TUNDOCK rd, didn't know how far. That Index has reached the river; on the rt of Index the other 2 RCTs are across the river. 2250 D/A 2 gave us the same info as Leopard 5 did at 2240. Fired no harassing or interdiction fires. 2400 B Btry still halted along the road approx 3 miles short of their new posn area. Bn expended 172 rds (total to date 38,059 rds).

22 SEPT 50

0230 B Btry closed in posn at (26.9-55.9). 0645 C Btry's advance party moved forward; the Btry will move out after bkfast. Hq Btry will follow C Btry by 30 min. 0658 Ln plane reports bridge at (29.2-53.0) blown during the night. 0715 Directed BC party of B/90 to move fwd to meet Col Hogan in vicinity of B/64 posn. 0826 C Btry moved out. 0850 Hq Btry moved out. 0915 C Btry closed in posn at (27.62-57.54). 1020 Hq Btry closed in posn at (26.9-56.3). 1030 Col Sandeen, CO 90th FA arrived at FDC and requested the gen situation and our plans for his B/90. 1100 120mm shellfire falling in the vicinity of B/64. This is observed fire and was directed at 35th Sv Co and the Med Collecting Co who were jammed bumper to bumper on the rd. Rgtl Hq Co was jammed up in the same fashion farther ahead. 1135 Air OP reports that the enemy is digging in and cutting trees at

(21.7-53.2). 1150 FO A adjusted C Btry and destroyed a MG at (20.5-57.5). 1225 Air OP adjusted C Btry and neutralized a 122mm how at (17.0-53.3). 1230 Lt Berrassa, Asst S-2, left for MASAN to relieve Lt Jensen, C Btry, as Air Observer. Lt Jensen was unable to orient himself quickly and is too slow in bringing effective fire to bear on his tgts. 1300 Bn CO left on recon. 1325 B/64 receiving med arty and mortar fire; 12-16 rds, minor material damage. PFC Thompson, Hq Btry lineman for LnO 1, was hit by fragments and evacuated. 1330 Air OP adjusted B Btry, destroyed a med arty piece at (16.0-53.9). 1340 Lt Galloway relieved Sgt Stampley as FO C. 1330 Bn Exec O left on recon for posn for A Btry. Btry still behind the pass and out of range of our front lines. Roads are too jammed with RCT vehicles to get them into posns already reconnoitered. 1400 B/90 in posn at (29.05-56.28). They were placed here due to the roads being blocked. 1540 Bn Exec O reported A Btry posn at (27.1-56.9), a burned out village. He has two D-7 dozers and will have the posn prepared. 1730 A Btry given march order and told to move fwd. 1800 TAC AIR knocked out 2 arty pieces. 1805 A Btry in posn at (27.1-56.9). 2005 FO G receiving shell fire from az 4400. 2022 LnO 1, FO's are at (23.4-55.0) A Co in reserve; (26.0-55.0) B Co; (23.0-55.0) C Co. 2045 PW reports two 122mm how in posn at SAMUN-NI; on N side of ridge at (17.1-53.6). Given to Lobster. 2120 LnO 3. 3rd Bn to attack tomorrow morning 23 Sept. K Co in the lead, attack in column of Co's to first objective. Request 5 min preparation on call at (21.4-55.2). Preparation denied. Div CG has ordered that no preparations will be fired as long as we are under ammo restr. We are limited to 25 rds per gun per day. 2325 LnO 1. 1st Bn to attack tomorrow 23 Sept, request preparation on hill 152, then walk the fire up in front of the Inf. Preparation denied. Bn expended 285 rds (total to date 38,344 rds)

64 FA BN IN KOREA (continued)

23 SEPT 50

0010 Bn S-4 delivered 180 pieces of Eng Pierced Steel planking to the Btrys. Basis of 2 strips for each 2 1/2 ton truck and 4 for each howitzer. It will facilitate rapid shifts in direction of fire for the howitzers. 0001-0600 All quiet. Bn fired no harassing or interdictory fires. 0625 LnO 3 reported that L Co will make a right hook to take the high ground to their North. 0700 Air OP observed enemy OP on hill at (21.4-55.7). Adjusted B Btry. Had 2 direct hits on OP and killed the personnel on the reverse slope. 0730 registered all 3 Btrys on a common base point. This is the first time that we have been in position and able to utilize a common base point. 0915 Ln plane reports no activity on hill 152. 0925 LnO 1 Leopard Red wants a preparation fired on hill 152. Advised no enemy there and that we would not fire. Red 6 became very indignant as to whether we would take his word or the word of a Lt in an airplane regarding presence or non presence on enemy on hill 152. 1025 LnO 1 reported Leopard Red on their objective. Met no opposition. 1045 Air OP reported enemy Inf and mortar at (22.5-54.0). 1050 FO B reported 2 rds of arty fire in his Co. area. 1130 D/A 2 reported heavy fighting in SEOUL; 1st Cav Div broke thru 20 miles, 2nd Inf Div in Army reserve. One Div has moved South across the 38th parallel; however is it not a Chinese Div. 1150 LnO 1 reported that a SP gun is firing into A Co's posn from (22.0-154.0) and requests that our air OP take a look in that area. Air OP reported no visible activity in that vicinity. 1232 Air OP located 2 SP guns firing from (13.6-52.4) and (11.2-52.1). Info given to TAC AIR. 1520 D/A CG and D/A commo arrived at FDC and informed us that the 2nd and 25th Divs make up the IX Corps and that a task force had been made of the 25th Recon Co with additional tanks and armored personnel carriers and was to pass thru the 27th RCT. The 27th RCT is in Div Reserve with one Bn of the 27th to protect the exposed rt flank of the 25th Div. 1520 FO G reported enemy troops at (21.2-56.9). Adjusted B Btry with excellent results; area neutralized and many casualties noted. 1650 Bn CO and CO 90th FA returned to FDC. Said Gen Kean, Div CG, had issued orders to

35th RCT CO to attack all nite and to keep on going - he was extremely dissatisfied with the progress of the 35th RCT. 1705 90th FA Bn moved their FDC and Comm O up to our CP area and adjacent to our FDC. This area now very crowded and congested; there is no other place for them to get off the road. 1800-2130 Fired in defensive concentrations for 35th RCT and 2nd Bn 24th Inf. 2135 LnO 2 reported that Leopard White will jump off and attack at 0600 24 Sept. 2220 Lightning 6, Gen Kean, directed that we interdict tonight the road junction at (10.8-52.0). This is beyond our maximum capabilities. The mission was given to the 90th FA Bn. The target is on the maximum range for their most forward platoon of B/90. 2330 LnO 3 reported that Leopard Blue would move West of K Co position tomorrow 24 Sept, time of attack unknown. Bn expended 500 rds (total to date 38,844 rds).

24 SEPT 50

0001-0600 All quiet. All troops remained in place. 0620 Ln plane reported visibility very poor - too much ground mist, however we did get each Btry checked in on the base point. The weather closed in at 0715 with visibility less than 50 yds. 0730 received overlay and plan of attack for Red from LnO 1. 0745 LnO 3 reported that K Co was moving to the SW with the mission of taking hill 261 if they can. 0830 Bn CO left for D/A CP. 0855 LnO 2 arrived at FDC with plan of arrived at FDC requesting fire on (16.9-54.2) and (17.17-54.1). The enemy is moving to these areas, request med arty fire on them. 1030 D/A CG arrived at FDC, "wants us to hit Col Fisher's tgts intermittently whether we can see any activity there or not. They are worth expending ammo on. Do not displace any of the 90th FA Bn fwd until they can occupy posns that will enable them to hit CHINJU. Use the 90th for harassing fire on the objectives as they have plenty of ammo available. The 64th to fire on all tgts that the Inf request; give the Inf all the fire they want as the 159th hasn't used their allowance. D/A has 2000 rds in reserve". 1105 D/A 3 notified us that if we need extra ammo today or tomorrow to let him know. 1120 Leopard 2 requested that we send our Ln plane far to the South to report on the progress of TF Thurman. The RJ at (11-50) is his objective. We complied. By doing so we lost 70% of our effectiveness due to the lack of sufficient ground observation. The Infantry do not appear to realize how valuable the Ln plane is to the D/S Arty Bn. Div has organic Ln planes for such recon missions as the Inf have requested of us. 1225 BC A Btry and party went fwd on posn area recon. 1300 FO G reported 16 enemy dead and many small arms, auto weapons and equipment on our Conc 419. 1328 C Btry closed in posn at (22.44-55.80), laid on CA 4400 and ready to register. 1415 A Btry displaced fwd to new posn area. 1432 D/A CG arrived at FDC, stated, "he wanted all arty well fwd". B Btry was alerted to move when called. 1437 Bn CO and D/A CG left on recon. 1439 B/90 displaced to (22.08-54.88). 1540 A Btry in posn at (22.28-54.8) laid on CA 4950 and ready to register. 1542 Ln plane reported TF Thurman at (10-52). 1605 B Btry displaced fwd. 1630 FO L reported many enemy swimming and wading the river at (12.8-54.1). 1700 D/A 3, "have Ln plane, less observer, meet Col Dolvin, CO 89th Tank Bn or Maj Moran at the strip N of CHUNGAM-NI at 0700 25 Sept, to be used on a special TF mission".1730 Leopard 5 "requested the Bn CO report to Leopard CP immediately to receive a warning order for tomorrow's operation and to name one Btry to go fwd, attached to 1st Bn. Maj Danley will pick up the BC and take him to the 1st Bn CP. Btry will move out early in the morning. 1735 Bn CO not present in the area. Bn Exec O left for Leopard CP to receive the warning order. 1800 Lt Nichol, TAC AIR controller and party left to join TF Dolvin. 1835 Leopard 5 requested info as to whether or not the MSR was open to SOMUN-NI? 1852 Bn Exec O returned from Leopard CP. Plan calls for 35th RCT to cross river at CHINJU, N to HAMYANG, SW to NAMWON, N thru CHONJU to the Div obj KUNSAN. A Btry 64th, attached to 1st Bn, 64th minus on the rear of 3rd Bn followed by the 2nd Bn 35th. TF Thurman to pass thru CHINJU tonight and TF Dolvin to clear CHINJU by 0800 tomorrow 25 Sept followed by 1st Bn 35th, 3rd Bn 35th, 2nd Bn 35th. 1900 B Btry in posn (18.25-53.42) laid on CA 5050. 1940 D/A 3 requested the most advanced location of Leopard. We are out of communication with our LnOs and FOs and do not know at the present time. 2035 LnO 1 reported that he was at the same location as early this afternoon, (14.4-52.0) and did not have communication with his FOs. 2315 Bn CO returned to CP. Previously made plans are cancelled; our troops havn't crossed the river yet. TF Thurman is halted at the RJ at (11-50). Bn expended 301 rds (total to date 39,145 rds). 64 FA BN IN KOREA (continued)

AUTHOR'S INSERTION. 35 Inf Battle Plan shown on map on next page followed by another map showing areas around MASAN and SANGJU, followed by two pages describing the FA's FDC and means used to measure firing elevations.

35th RCT Battle Plan
Late September
to break out of
The Perimeter

A most important team of a firing battery is its Fire Direction Center or FDC. Shown below is a typical battery FDC truck and a battery FDC set up in the open. The battery Executive Officer is in full charge of the FDC. He has help from his team of EM which includes a Fire Team Chief or computer (not a machine!), chart operator and radio-telephone opr or RTO. At battalion FDC chart operators are provided for vertical and horizontal control. This is the basic TOE for a 105mm howitzer battery. Guns and howitzers of larger calibers will require more personnel because their targets are often larger and more sophisticated, requiring, for instance, more exotic, heavier projectiles.

FA guns are usually pointed in the correct vertical dimension of elevation by the sight placed at the gun. In the 105, a change in elevation must be accompanied by a change in site if there is a difference in altitude between the shifts in deflection or horizontal direction at or to the target. Again the 105, for simplicity assumes a 300 mil value for a 0 degree difference in altitude between that of the gun and of the target. However, when extreme accuracy is mandatory, gunners use the Gunner's Quadrant. This instrument uses quadrant elevation which includes both the angle to the target itself and the angle caused by any difference in height between gun position and the target. Any US FA gun is fired using the mil. In the US a mil is that angle subtended at the target by a measurement of one yard e.g. one yard at 1000 yards subtends one mil. One day I ran across a Russian gunner's quadrant captured off a Chinese 37mm AT gun. I was amazed at its apparent inaccuracy. As I delved into the problem, I found out the Russian artillery uses a 6000 mil circle. (We use 6400) Assuming the chord equals its intercepted arc at these small measurements, the true value of the mil with the 6400 mil circle is 0.98 yards and 1.07 meters with the 6000 mil circle. Another plug for our FA's accuracy. As the Fort Sill motto states.

CEDAT FORTUNA PERITAS
(Skill Rather Than Luck)

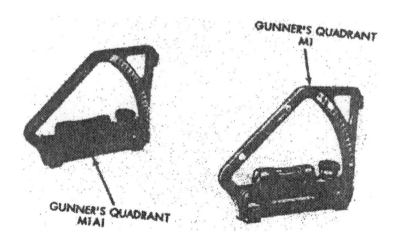

64 FA BN IN KOREA (continued)

25 SEPT 50

0030 All Btrys notified to feed bkfast by 0420. Capt Rutherford,

Hq Btry BC notified to report to 89th Tank Bn by 0500 and report to FDC when they have started to move. Bn minus moved out after the 89th Tank Bn in the order Hq, C, and A Btry. B Btry to support the Inf. in vicinity of RJ at (10-52); ammo sections to move with the Btrys and Sv Btry to remain in place. 0100 Leopard 3 reported that the 1st Bn, located in the vicinity of RJ (10-52) and moving; 2nd Bn 400-500 yds from the river; TF Thurman in the vicinity of RJ (10-52) and in a fire fight. Everything is in hand. They have killed a lot of enemy and also captured some. 0400 LnO 1 reported that the 1st Bn was receiving Arty fire and requested the 90th FA Bn fire on CHINJU (09-56). 0600 A Btry displaced fwd. 0640 Bn CO, S-3, S-2, Comm O, wire sect and ½ of the FDC displaced fwd to SOMUN-NI. 0715 Remainder of Hq Btry displaced fwd. 0715 C Btry displaced fwd. 0725 A Btry in posn at (12.2-51.1). 0755 C Btry in posn at (16.2-53.7). 0815 Hq Btry in posn; CP located in SOMUN-NI (16.7-53.5). Marched 10.5 miles. 0825 BC A/90 and party moved fwd on recon. 0915 POW reported enemy Arty at (07.8-57.3), neutralized by C Btry, observed by Air OP. 0948 Leopard 2 reported that TF Thurman was in CHINJU. 0950 Leopard 6 reported a SP gun firing from vicinity of (07.8-57.3) into the MSR, neutralized at 0955. 1000 A/90 in posn at (16.2-53.53). 1015 D/A CG stopped by CP on his way fwd. Bn CO was at Rgtl CP and returned at 1035. 1045 FO E reported enemy troops along ridge at (09.4-55.8). Fired B and C Btrys with good results observed. 1250 Ln plane reported having engine trouble and that they will try and make it to the strip at SACHON (08.5-41.3). Made it OK. Lt Reese reported water in the fuel as the cause of motor failure. 1305 LnO 3 reported his leading elements at (10.5-53.9) moving slowly westward. 1420 LnO 2 reported his unit at (09.0-55.8) to (10.0-55.7). 1410 D/A CG visited the CP, spoke to all Off present about road discipline; column doubling; only higher commanders and staff officers in single vehicles could double the column (BC parties under no circumstances) and about criticizing Divisional units. 1648 FO E reported his location at (07.3-55.4). 1800 fired in defensive fires for FO I and FO L. 1810 A Btry moved out with the 1st Bn 35th. 1900 Leopard 3 called for Bn CO to report to Leopard CP. Bn CO not present. Bn Exec O left immediately for Leopard CP. 1905 A/90 displaced fwd. 2000 Bn CO returned to CP. 2010 Bn Exec O returned with the RCT opn plan. One btry 64th to be attached to each Inf Bn; Hq Btry, Sv Btry and A/90 follow RCT command group which will march as a part of the 2nd Bn. The 1st Bn will be completely motorized; 2nd and 3rd Bns will have to be shuttled. 2110 A/90 in posn at (12.2-51.1). 2115 Notified B Btry to be ready to move by 0800 - probably will move between 1000 - 1200. Notified to have vehicles prepared, in so far as possible, to ford up to 3 feet of water. 2220 LnO 1 reported that they are not moving tonight and will probably cross the river sometime after daylight; time unknown. Bn expended 106 rds (total to date 39,251 rds)

26 SEPT 50

0645 BC B Btry and party arrived at FDC and were given instructions pertaining to displacement into CHINJU. 0725 Ln plane reported TF Dolvin 5 miles beyond CHINJU. 0800 Sv Btry displaced fwd. 0810 Bn CO, S-2 and Commo O left for Regt CP left instructions to have Bn Cmd Gp ready to move by 1000 and to carry 5-1 type rations. 0920 Received msg from TF Dolvin, "how about a plane from D/A?" We had Lt Duncan in the air and observing his column at that time; told him same. 0945 Capt Daprato, Bn S-2, returned from Rgt and reported that the column was still waiting for the bridge at CHINJU. Dolvin forded the river there with his tanks. 1000 B Btry displaced fwd to vicinity of river crossing.1030 Commo O reported that the bridge would be usable within 2 hrs. 1030 C Btry displaced fwd to vicinity of river crossing. 1145 Sv Btry in posn at (16.3-53.7). 1245 B Btry in posn ¼ mile S of bridge at (08.1-54.7). 1300 C Btry closed in posn 1/3 mile SE of bridge at (08.5-55.5) 1310 Bn S-2 returned with opn order #6, 35th RCT. 1330 Col Doerr, Rgt Exec O, called and "wondered if we had noticed that the 64th minus and the Medium arty btry were in the 4th serial and that serials 1 and 2 would get out today." 1330 Ln plane reported that an enemy arty btry was moving out of posn at (94.2-67.1). Fired C Btry and neutralized them. 1340 D/A CG, Gen Barth, arrived at CP area, ordered us to get the brass picked up in C Btry's old posn area at (27.62-57.54), on the road to the N by Leopard CP (approx 14 miles to our rear). 1400 Ln plane reported enemy arty at (1094.4-1367.2). We cannot reach it; notified D/A. 1530 Bn CO called and notified CP that A, B and C Btrys would be attached to the 1st, 2nd and 3rd Bns of the 35th as they cross the NAM-GANG river into CHINJU. 1545 A Btry crossed the NAM-GANG into CHINJU with the 1st Bn 35th. 1630 Ln plane reported enemy arty at (1095-1372) along the road. 1700 B Btry moved over the bridge into CHINJU. 1920 Bn CO and Bn Cmd Gp displaced fwd to Rgt CP area in CHINJU. 2005 Bn minus with A/90 attached displaced fwd under Exec O in order A/90, Hq and Sv. 2300 A Btry halted on road for the nite at (97.0-69.0). 2345 Bn minus closed into CHINJU, marched 12 miles. Bn expended 30 rds (total to date 39,281 rds).

27 SEPT 50

0510 B Btry moved out with the 2nd Bn 35th column. 0815 C Btry displaced across the NAM-GANG into CHINJU and went into rendevoux area at (06.9-56.3) on the NW side of CHINJU. 1000 A Btry placed one platoon into posn at (96.0-69.2); fired one mission on Inf in the open. 1218 Bn Cmd Gp displaced fwd; located in the column between 2nd Bn and 3rd Bn 35th Inf. 1300 A Btry reported that the column had captured 100 motorcycles, 23 armored cars and 3 arty pieces. They were located by Lt Campbell, FO with B/35th. 1445 LnO 4 reported that the 3rd Bn had been ordered to proceed on foot; approximate time of departure 1600. 1530 Ln plane reported head of column at (91.0-76.0) and that a mile from the head of the column there were 2 companies of enemy on foot heading for the 38th parallel. 1530 LnO 4 reported that L Co would remain in CHINJU as protection for Div Hq. Lt Ceravsky, C Btry FO with L Co, relieved Lt Ross, A Btry as FO with K Co. 1543 3rd Bn 35th moved out on foot. 1645 C Btry moved out in column behind the foot elements of the 3rd Bn 35th. 1745 Bn with A/90 attached moved out under Exec O in order A/90, Hq, and Sv Btrys; followed the Sv elements of the 3rd Bn. 1630 Lightning 6 ordered us to relay message to 90th FA Bn, "get out of CHINJU, stay along the road and follow the column". 2030 A Btry was attacked by enemy with auto weapons and small arms. Fired 3 how direct fire; had 2 casualties. 2115 TF Dolvin located near check point 14; relayed this to Lightning 6. 2135 Lightning 6 requested information from LnO 1 as to whether or not lst Bn had contacted the 2nd Inf Div at ANUI (80.0-09.0)? No! 2200 A Btry halted along road for the nite at (86-85). 2230 C Btry halted along the road for the nite at (99.1-64.5). 2300 Bn minus halted on road for the nite at (99.2-67.1). Marched 8.3 miles. 2310 A/90 sent forward, doubling the halted column to occupy A/64 old posn area at (94.0-75.8). 2330 D/A 3 requested total ammo expended during periods 1200 25 Sept to 1200 26 Sept and 1200 26 Sept to 1200 27 Sept. Bn expended 35 rds (total to date 39,316 rds).

28 SEPT 50

0010 BC A/90 requested fuel pump for an M-5 tractor. Stated necessary in order not to abandon the equipment. notified D/A. 0110 LnO 3 reported that the column would move forward in one hour. 0130 Leopard 3, Division has ordered all elements of 35th RCT to be N or RJ at (1098-1367) by 28 Sept before the 27th Inf closes at that point. 27th Inf due there on morning of 28 Sept. 0230 C Btry displaced fwd. 0645 Bn minus moved fwd. 0730 Bn Cmd Gp moved fwd with RCT Hq. 0840 Bn minus halted at (1089.61381.6) marched 15 miles. All light vehicles were off the road and dispersed in dry rice paddies. 0845 Ln plane reported a bridge blown at (1078-1340), that contact had been made at the bridge with recon elements of the 23rd Inf on our right. No enemy resistance; that there would be a delay of 1-2 hrs at the crossing while a ford was being prepared. 1110 C Btry BC party encountered an enemy patrol near UNBONG (1053-1386); small arms fire was exchanged - no casualties. 2305 Bn minus and A/90 halted at (1060.0-1388.13); Hq and Sv Btrys bivuoacing in a school yard and A/90 remained on the road. 2345 C Btry in posn at (53.1-85.6). Bn expended 29 rds (total to date 39,345 rds)

29 SEPT 50

0025 Bn Cmd Gp arrived at UNBONG (1053-1386). 0700 Bn Cmd Gp displaced fwd with RCT CP. 0730 Bn Exec O notified CO 3rd Bn 35th that the 64th minus could carry one Co of his Inf. 0900 A Btry reported that they had abandoned a 105mm how along the side of the road and down the mountain bank at (1037.7-1385.1). Capt Cole, Bn Motor Officer notified to salvage and recover the how. 0900 Bn Exec O received msg from CO 3rd Bn 35th that Div H column was receiving small arms and mortar fire at HAMYANG and that he was ordered to march his Bn back to HAMYANG. 0905 Bn Exec O moved parts of Hq and Sv Btrys out of the school yard and placed a platoon of A/90 into firing posn laid on CA 1100. Ln plane was directed to HAMYANG (1072.0-1396.1) to observe and report on enemy activity. No enemy activity observed. 1215 Bn minus displaced forward under Exec O in order Hq, Sv and A/90. 217 D/A 3 ordered A/90 detached effective on arrival at NAMWON (1038-1382). Btry is to go into an assy area there and prepare to furnish all 2 1/2 ton trucks to shuttle supplies on Div order. 1242 Bn minus halted on road behind 3rd Bn 35 who was waiting for infor- mation as to the location of the nearest POL supply point. Bn Exec O donated 13 drums of gasoline to refuel their shuttle trucks. 1245 A Btry in posn at YONGAN (CQ15.9-98.1). 1300 Bn Cmd Gp arrived at CHONJU (1015-1432) with Rgt CP. Lt J Campbell, C Btry, went out as FO with L Co 35th. 1550 Bn minus with A/90 attached dis- placed fwd under Exec in order, Hq, Sv and A/90. 1635 A/90 com- plied with D/A orders and halted in NAMWON. 1610 B Btry in posn at (1022.6-1423.2) 2200 C Btry halted along road South of CHON- JU for the nite. 2230 Bn minus closed in bivouac at CHONJU (1015- 1432). Marched 55.9 miles. No ammo expended (total to date 39,345 rds).

30 SEPT 50

0845 C Btry displaced fwd to IRI. 0915 Bn CO and party left on recon for posns vicinity of IRI (315.0-97.8). 1500 C Btry in posn in school yard NE edge of IRI. 1545 Bn CO returned. 1600 Bn CO left for IRI with Hq and Sv Btry's kitchen trucks. 1615 Bn minus displaced fwd under Exec in order Hq, Sv. 1830 Bn minus closed in IRI and occupied a school yard; marched 21 miles. Hq and Sv Btrys spent most of the day doing much needed motor maintenance and the care and cleaning of radios and small arms. No ammo expended. (Total to date 39,345 rds).

64 FA BN IN KOREA (continued)

1 OCT 50

0845 D/A 3 requested our training schedule and that the Fort Sill questionnaire be filled in as soon as possible. 1225 D/A 3, "Gen Barth will inspect our howitzers tomorrow 2nd Oct." 1400 Two Cos of the 89th Tank Bn moved into our area; one Co to furnish the perimeter guard for us. 1600 D/A 3, 1st platoon A Btry 25th AAAW is relieved from your command effective 020800I. Have platoon report to BC A Btry 25th AAAW Bn at Div Arty Hq. 1700 Capt Bornhouser relieved as Ln O and assigned as BC A Btry; Capt Anderson relieved as BC A and assigned as Ln O. 1835 All FOs returned to their Btrys. The 35th Inf has the mission of patrolling and searching their assigned area of responsibility for any enemy personnel and equipment. Arty FOs are not needed to accomplish this mission. 1930 Capt Baird, D/A Special Svs officer brought out a movie which was shown to all personnel of Hq and Sv Btrys. This was our first movie. The day was spent in the maintenance of motor vehicles, small arms, radios and reloading vehicles. Howitzer Btrys inspected and inventoried all Arty ammo.

2 OCT 50

0800 Received overlay of patrol plan of 3rd Bn 35th and a request that we send our Ln plane up to observe hourly progress of each patrol. The air strip was notified and we will observe the patrols. 0930 The AAAW platoon left the Bn area for KUMSAN. 1000 Col Fisher, CO 35th Inf, arrived at CP and conferred with Col Hogan about a close support Arty demo for replacement Infantry Offs and NCOs. 1100 Gen Barth, D/A CG, visited the CP and informed us that he would not inspect the howitzers today but that he would hold a command inspection of the Bn on 4 Oct 50. 1145 Notified all btrys of coming command inspection and ordered all btrys to move to this area. 1215 WO Mullahey, Pers. Off arrived with the Sept pay for the Bn. 1600 Sv Btry moved out of the school yard and into bivouac area across the road to our N. 1710 C Btry closed into the compound. 1820 A Btry closed into the compound. 1900 B Btry closed into the compound. 2030 Leopard 6 alerted us for movement to TAEJON (CR60-24) with the RCT at 0800 3 Oct 50; the 64th FA Bn to furnish 23 2½ ton trucks to carry the Infantry. 2240 Leopard 3, the 3rd Bn will cross the IP at 0930. Trucks report to the 3rd Bn at 0730. 2330 Capt Daprato notified to accompany the RCT recon party and to be at the RCT CP at 0500 3 Oct. The day was spent in the maintenance and care of equipment.

3 OCT 50

0910 Bn moved out under the Bn CO in the order Hq, A, B, C, Sv. 1300 D/A 1 notified us that the Div Finance office opens at Div Fwd CP (KUMSAN) at 1300 today and for us to send our agent officers there to pick up the Bn pay. WO Mullahey paid the Bn yesterday. 1500 Bn CO left for RCT CP to obtain information as to their dispositions. 1615 Bn closed in assy area at (CR59-21) in a large creek bed. One of the Sv Btry 6 ton ammo trucks broke thru a bridge on the way up but was undamaged. Sixty feet of the bridge was dismantled by the motor Off, Capt Cole, in extricating this vehicle. Bn marched 50.6 miles. 1700 Lt Barrow returned from the Inf with our 23 2½ ton trucks and took 11 of them back to IRI to pick up the personnel, equipment and ammo that we had to off load in order to haul the Infantry. 1700 Bn CO returned to assy area. The 1st Bn 35th with A/64 attached is to occupy posns in the vicinity of YONGDONG (CR90-04); the 2nd and 3rd Bns 35th to remain in the vicinity of TAEJON (CR60-24). A Btry was alerted for movement tomorrow to YONGDONG with the 1st Bn 35th. Bn will remain in assy area tonight. 1815 Mail truck was dispatched to KUMSAN to pick up the Bn mail. 1945 Capt Dexter, 13th FA Bn, 24th Inf Div, visited the CP. He was cadre from this Bn to the 24th Div Arty on 2 July 50.

4 OCT 50

0630 LnO 3 notified us that the 3rd Bn 35th was going to YONGDONG and requested maps of the area. C Btry was alerted to accompany them. This is not in accordance with the Inf plan that the Bn CO received from Rgt last night. 0700 Requested confirmation of movement of 3rd Bn from Rgt. Leopard 3 said that the 3rd Bn 35 would remain here (TAEJON). 0945 Lt Dunda, 11th FA Bn 24th Div visited CP. He was cadre from 90th FA Bn to 24th Div Arty on 2 July 50. 0945 Notified BC Sv Btry to look for posn area in TAEJON but not to move until cleared by Bn CO or Exec Off. 1045 Notified BCs Hq, B, C Btrys to reconnoiter for posn in the vicinity of TAEJON. The CP to be near RCT CP and howitzer Btrys to be outside of town to the E or SE. 1050 a Btry displaced to YONGDONG (CR90-04). 1305 Sv Btry displaced to position in the vicinity of the TAEJON RTO. Have concrete standing for their vehicles and covered sheds for Btry and Bn maintenance sections. 1315 B Btry displaced to (CR65-23). 1400 C Btry displaced to (CR65.2-23.3). 1445 Hq Btry displaced to posn on SW edge of TAEJON air strip (CR56-19), ½ mile from the RCT CP. 1640 Received Opn Order #8, 35th RCT. It does not pertain to the 64th; outlined areas of responsibility for the Inf. Bns and gave the mission of clearing area of enemy, enemy material, and equipment. The remainder of the day was spent in getting settled and establishing communications with the Btrys.

5 OCT 50

0955 Leopard 1 requested that an Officer and a clerk typist with typewriter report at 1300 to Leopard CP. They will be writing up individual citations for heroism and meritorious service. 1030 Received overlays showing dispositions of 1st and 2nd Bns 35th. 1230 Lts Chastain and Duncan arrived, with our L-4 from KUMSAN. They informed us that Lt Bourassa was bringing the air sec and vehicles by road and that Lt Reece was in TAEGU getting a new engine in the L-5; the present engine had 750 hrs on it and that Lt Reece wouldn't be in until tomorrow afternoon. 1245 A Btry reported that they closed into posn at (CR89.8-02.8) at 1630 4 Oct and that Lt Galloway had been sent out as FO with B/35. 1510 Lt Bourassa arrived with the air section and took them immediately to the air strip. 1530 Capt Anderson went on air recon for an Arty impact area suitable for a demonstration to be shown to Infantry replacement Officers and NCOs. 1420 Received a disposition overlay of 3/35th. 1625 Bn CO left to visit Sv, B and C Btrys. 1745 Leopard 6 desires 10 2½ ton trucks from us tomorrow 6 Oct., time and place of reporting later. Notified Sv Btry to unload 10 trucks and have ready to haul personnel by 0700 6 OCT. Hq Btry and the CP installations are all located in Quonset huts. All personnel have steel cots. Bn has located two Japanese style natural hotsprings baths in the area. They were utilized to their maximum by Hq Btry personnel. Bn performed normal garrison duties during the day.

6 OCT 50

0850 Bn received notification from Div G-1 that Cpl Robert A Miller, A Btry was to be returned by air to the ZI by reason of the serious illness of his mother. 0915 Bn CO was flown to YONGDONG to inspect A Btry. Lt Chastain piloted the L-4; as they neared the strip the engine failed. A satisfactory landing was accomplished without incident. 1215 Bn CO returned to CP. 1240 Lt Reece arrived from TAEGU with the L-5. A new engine has been installed in the plane. 1315 BCs of B and C Btrys each took an orientation flight over the area around TAEJON. 1440 Div Arty CG visited the CP. He made inquiry as to the number of awards and decorations that had been submitted and the number that had been approved. He also expressed a desire to visit our Btrys. Gen Barth was informed that our recommendations for awards and decorations were all to go through the RCT Hq as per verbal instr. of Col Fisher, RCT CO. Gen Barth stated that he would talk with Col Fisher about the awards and decorations for the FOs and LnOs that worked with the Inf and also about the Arty channels for administration. 1640 Lt Nichols and his TAC party left for 1st Bn 35th. They have a suspected enemy location and may call for an air strike. 1700 LnO 1 requested that we contact Leopard about suspected enemy troops near YONGDONG and send up an air observer today if possible. Notified LnO 1 that both planes were in use; one taking the BCs on orientation flights and the L-5 has been taken by Division, without notifying us, to IRI. 1720 Leopard 3 reported that they have captured the Asst G-3 of the 7th NK Div; present location (1089-1480); strength approx 4000 and that their plans call for assembling the 6th NI and 7th NK Div at (1089-1510) to start hostilities again and that the 6th NK Div should be there now. 1730 LnO 1 requested air observation on suspected enemy at (1084-1380). 1820 LnO 3, there are 800 POWs in the vicinity of KUMGU-RI; we need 17 trucks to get them into TAEJON. Message was relayed to Rgt. 1830 Notified LnO 1 to maintain 24 hr radio communication with us on SCR694 radio. 2310 Leopard 6 requested Ln plane at YONGDONG air strip at 0830 7 OCT. Bn performed normal garrison duties during the day.

7 OCT 50

0115 LnO 1 reported that the 1st Bn 35th will contact the enemy at (CR845-805), that Leopard 6 desires that one of our Ln planes be at YONGDONG air strip at 0830 and that the other plane be in the air over that area at 0845, both planes to contact LnO 1 on our K channel. Notified Maj Dobbs, D/A air Off at the strip. He said that we would have to use our own planes so that we could operate on our own K channel. (He has already taken our L-5 and sent it with a D/A pilot, to IRI). Lts Bourassa and Chastain flew to YONGDONG. 0815 Lt Reece borrowed a plane from the 159th and left for YONGDONG area. 0815 Bn CO left for D/A and B and C Btrys. 0850 D/A 3 notified us that we are under the 35th RCT for tactical control only and that our administration goes through D/A. 0920 Bn CO radioed that he and Gen Barth were on the way to B and C Btrys. 1050 Dispatched the air sec to YONGDONG with fuel for the Ln planes operating from that airstrip. 1100 Div G-1 notified us that PFC Walter Anderson B Btry was to be flown to the ZI due to serious illness in his family. 1305 Leopard 5 reported B and C Cos 35th had advanced to (81-86) and (81-87); had located and killed 15 enemy. An estimated enemy Bn located at (86.6-and the river) were now being fired upon by A/64. Notified D/A 3. 1307 Bn CO radioed msg to A Btry to fire Btry 10-12 rds in effect. 1335 Notified Sv Btry to send 300 rds ammo to A Btry at YONGDONG. A Btry occupied position at (CR96-05) for this mission. 1515 Chaplain Schagg visited CP, gave information regarding time and place of tomorrow's church services. 1530 LnO 1 reported that A Btry's firing had killed an estimated 400 NKs. 1725 Bn CO returned CP. 1730 Lt Nichols and his TAC AIR party returned to CP. 1741 Ln planes returned to TAEJON strip. Reported that one plane sat at YONGDONG strip most of the day. Only service performed was to bring RCT CO back to TAEJON. 1835 Bn CO left for RCT CP and 90th FA Bn CP. 2040 Bn CO returned to CP. All Btrys except A Btry were in a normal garrison status performing necessary maintenance on vehicles, weapons and equipment. Capt Anderson completed the plans for an arty demonstration that is to be fired for the Inf replacement. Bn expended 415 rds (total to date 39,760 rds).

IN KOREA, IT WAS ONE D————————D HILL AFTER
ANOTHER AND THESE SHOWN
HERE WERE THE SMALLER ONES

64 FA BN IN KOREA (continued)

8 Oct 50

1045 Capt Moran, Asst D/A 3, brought Lt Sterling and 3 EM, British Arty, to the CP. They desired to watch American Arty methods and were sent to A Btry to observe them today and tomorrow. A Btry notified to meet them in YONGDONG. 1053 Notified D/A 5 that our practice demonstration was being held this after noon. 1300 Bn CO, S-2, S-3, COMMO O, LNO 2 and all EM that could be spared from Hq Btry left for service practice demonstration. Fire problems were fired; Lt Guill 2, Capt Metcalfe 1, Capt Sherman 1, M/Sgt Parker 1. Methods used were those that would enable the Inf to adjust fire on a tgt in the easiest possible manner. While on the OP a SK native reported 30 NK soldiers in the vicinity. B Btry posn at (CQ52.6-89.9), OP at (CQ51.5-82.2). 1800 Leopard 3 requested an officer from the 64th report to Leopard CP at once. One of the 35th Bns will move tonight and it involves moving one of our

Btrys. Capt DaPrato was sent to RCT to obtain the information. 1845 Sv practice called due to darkness, personnel returned to base camp. expended 33 rds. 2100 Major Wolfolk, CO 3rd Bn 35th requested that we have no more Sv practice in that area because 1500 NK soldiers were reported to be in the vicinity of where our OP was this afternoon 2130 Capt DaPrato returned from Rgt. The 2nd Bn is moving now to TAEAM-NI (CR62.5-02.5) and KUMSAN (CQ64.5-96.0) where 10K NK enemy have been reported. LnO 2 and B Btry alerted to move at 0730 tomorrow. 2200 Air section returned from YONGDONG. They brought 4 VT fuzes that were picked up in a position that had been occupied by the 1st Cav D/A. 2210 Sv Btry notified to contact B Btry and make necessary arrangements for ammo, fuel and rations. 2210 Notified A Btry to report, by coordinates, the location of all abandoned ordnance materiel and ammo in their vicinity. 2220 Notified Air section that one plane will have to fly surveillance over all 3 of the Inf Bns tomorrow. A Btry fired on some concentrations of NK soldiers. Bn expended 216 rds (total to date 39,976 rds).

9 OCT 50

0730 LnO 2 and B Btry displaced to vicinity of KUMSAN (CQ-62.5-95.5). 0900 Bn CO left for Rgt and B Btry. 0910 Bn CO reported large numbers of enemy troops in CHILLANSAN (46-62) and NAMI-NYON 1000 Received overlay of 3rd Bn dispositions from LnO 3. He stated that a patrol had reached our OP of yesterday's service practice and no contact had been made with the enemy. 1035 Negative report from Air OP. 1145 Leopard 6 requested that we drop leaflets today. Leopard will notify us when they are available as we have been unable to procure any. 1247 LnO 3 reported approx 3000 enemy in area (CR72-07), (CR69-08) and (CR71-09) and requested Ln plane observe these areas. The 3rd Bn has had a motorized patrol through them but no enemy contact has been made. LnO 3 told that a plane would be in that area at about 1400. 1255 LnO 3 desired information as to whether we had anything that could shoot into that area. No! but we could contact C Btry and have them move a platoon or the Btry into the position occupied by B Btry for yesterday's service practice. (CQ52.6-89.9) 1530 Capt Frazier, 35th Inf, visited the CP and wanted to know if we had selected a position for the demonstration by the 35th Inf? No! 1615 D/A 5, Col Dick, notified us that we have to furnish a complete air section; 2 planes, pilots, observers, ground crew and a security platoon of 30 men, 1Officer and a suitable number of NCOs. Ground crew and security platoon to leave tonite. Vehicles to consist of two 1/4 tons, one 3/4 ton and two 2 1/2 ton trucks. One of the 1/4 tons to have a 608 radio complete. Their mission is to adjust Naval Gun Fire. Take necessary rations, POL and wire. To report to the KMAG LnO at 3rd ROK Div at TONKCHON. There is an air strip at KOSONG (1125-1780) 30 miles N of TONKCHON. Planes can gas at POHANG-DONG will call later and give coord locations of other strips where planes can gas. Planes should patrol over the column from POHANG and on up the coast. 1835 Lt Worth, Ln pilot for 17th FA Bn 24th Div arrived at CP. He oriented the pilots and observers on the problems involved and the type missions flown for the 3rd ROK Div. He stated, that the road N from POHANG-DONG was more or less unsafe as the mountains and hills had not been cleared of enemy. An Air section had been ambushed along the road and all personnel killed, that he was unable to locate or contact his own Air section that was supposed to be coming S to POHANG-DONG. 1900 Bn CO called D/A about the possibility of an LST movement from POHANG-DONG to KOSONG? The set up doesn't look good. Request that D/A contact Corps or Army and give them the details as given to us by Lt Worth. 1900 B Btry reported their posn at (CQ48.4-66.1) with 2nd Bn 35th. 1935 LnO 1 requested Ln plane at 1000 10 Oct and the observer bring maps 6722III, 6722II and 6721I He was informed that our planes would not be available. 2020 Called D/A 3 about leaving some planes behind when they left tomorrow. After tonite, the only Arty planes will be those of the 8th FA. If they are not too busy, the 64th may call on them for missions. 2145 From D/A 3, "the 64th Air Section is to arrive in POHANG-DONG between 0900 and 1000 10th Oct and to contact a Navy supply ship, FSO 803, in the harbor there. This ship will water lift and transport trucks and personnel to KOJO (1085-1815). There is an Air strip at KOJO. Gasoline and rations are already enroute for the Air section and will be landed at KOJO. The ship has been ordered to wait for the Air section." 2345 Capt Anderson, Lt Duncan, Lt Bourassa, air ground crew and the security platoon departed for POHANG-DONG.

Above shows gunner Cpl Dodson standing next to
the M12A1 panoramic sight which is used to lay
the gun in deflection. When the exec lays the
battery with his aiming circle, he is actually
lining up the sights in parallel with each other.
When the guns are boresighted, the tubes are placed
in parallel with their sights.
Boresighting is done in the field, using a distant
aiming point at least 2000 yards away. In garrison,
calibrated boresighting charts can be used.

Bn received notification that Cpl Walter Greenwell, one of the 3 men who were captured early on 10 Sept while asleep at the Bn relay radio, had been rescued and transferred to 8069 Replacement Bn. Lt McFerron, absent in hosp, was promoted to Capt; Lts Chapmen, Duncan and Milleren were promoted to 1st Lts. Bn expended no ammo.

10 OCT 50

0330 Capt Anderson notified us that one of the 2 1/2 ton trucks had broken down in YONGDONG and requested permission to trade trucks with A Btry. Permission granted. 0900 Bn CO left for Rgt. 0945 Lts Chastain and Reece left for POHANG-DONG with the Bn Ln planes. 1630 Leopard 3 requested air surveillance and an Air Strike in the vicinity of the 1st Bn 35th. They were told to contact Div for the plane and G-3 Air for the Air Strike. 1610 Bn CO up on recon in Div L-17. 1710 LnO 1 reported that the CG, his staff, and 400 men of the 7th NK Div were in TOPSON-NI (CR94- 08) 4 1/2 miles NE of YONGDONG, requested an Air Strike. Bn was unable to arrange for the TAC Air. 1910 Bn CO returned to the CP. 1930 D/A Sp. Sv. Off, Capt Baird, showed a movie in the CP area for Hdq and Sv Btrys. 1930 Called Div Air Strip, requested a Ln plane and pilot for tomorrow at 0800. Request granted, would use L-5 #625 and to install our own radio. No ammo expended.

11 OCT 50

0715 Bn CO left for C Btry to observe their Sv practice. 0800 Bn Exec O flew to YONGDONG on an observation mission - low ceiling, poor visibility, rain, - unable to observe. 0840 Leopard 3 notified us that the Inf demonstration for the 64th had been called off for today. They will notify us when it can be put on again. Hq and Sv notified of the cancellation. 0850 Div G-3 notified us that Capt Anderson, 159th FA Bn, who is working on a USAK special project, will be here tomorrow to look at our S-3 reports for period 6-13 Aug. 1145 A Btry reported their present posn at (CR91.7-05.4), have two FOs out and they are now firing at a group attempting to escape N. 1200 LnO 3 reports approx 2000 enemy troops at (CQ58-81) and that the 3rd Bn is sending a patrol to that area. Blue 6 wants LnO to remain with him. LnO will remain with Inf even tho they are not in contact. 1200 LnO 2, Capt Metcalfe, and his section arrived at CP area and reported that the 2nd Bn had no further need of B Btry. The Btry has been told to return with the Inf.

1630 Lts Chastain and Reece returned to the CP area from POHANG- DONG. They reported that the Navy ship, there in the harbor, was unable to load the trucks, rations and personnel; that the Navy was unaware that they were to carry our ground crew and security section to KOJO; that the 17th FA Bn ground crew has been missing along the coast road for 5 days and that 8th Army has cancelled the detail for the 64th FA Bn. Capt Anderson, with the personnel and vehicles will leave POHANG-DONG for the CP early tomorrow morning 12 Oct. 1715 LnO 1 reported that of 40 enemy located at TAPSON-NI (CR91-08) 12 were killed by Arty, 21 taken prisoner and the remainder dispersed. The village was burned by Arty fire. The civilian reports about this village were unreliable. 2310 Lightning 7 notified us that PFC William P McCombs, B Btry, is a sole surviving son and is eligible for reassignment to a non- combat area. Get him out of hazardous duty until the Div Rear Echelon arrives here, at which time he will be transferred from the 64th. Bn expended 231 rds (total to date 40,207 rds).

12 OCT 50

0740 Capt Sherman, BC B Btry, arrived at the CP and was instructed to reoccupy his old posn at (CR65-23). 0815 Bn CO left for Rgt CP and from there to the Btrys. 0920 Lightning 3 notified us that 3 Off. and 5 EM from the 10th BCT, Philippine Army, will arrive today and be attached to the 64th. 1000 LnO 3 reported that the 3rd Bn 35th would send a patrol from each Company into SODAE-SAN (CR69-09) area today and will notify us when they go out. 1625 Lightning 3 reported that Capt Robbis, 2 officers and 7 EM will arrive at the 64th at approx 1730 today. 1630 Major Lawrence and Capt Anderson arrived at the CP to recheck the S-3 records for the period 6-15 Aug. 1710 Capt Robbis and party of the 10th BCT, Philippine Army, arrived at the CP. They are to study our Arty methods, techniques, and the manner in which our Arty has been employed during the Korean Campaign. 1830 LnO 3 reported negative reports from all of the 3rd Bn patrols today. 2300 Lt Chapman, Bn Ammo Off, reported 225 M-67 Mechanical Time Fuzes on hand. No ammo expended.

13 OCT 50

0800 Bn CO, Asst S-3, FDC, Surv Crew and the 10th BCT personnel left for C Btry's service practice. We will use two charts; the Philippine Army personnel will operate one of them. 0815 Inquired of Rgt whether or not they needed any Air surveillance today? They will notify us if needed. 0820 LnO 3 requested Air surveillance on the E side of SODAE-SAN (CR69-09). The Inf also want us to fire some arty into that area. Notified them that the arty would not fire unless they made contact with the enemy and could not handle the situation themselves. 0955 Bn CO notified SV Btry that the M-67 fuzes would not fit into the cavitized shell. Ammo Off to investigate and report to Ordnance. 1000 Leopard 6 directed that we have a plane available at the Air strip at 1300 today for use by the CO 2nd Bn 35th, and another plane to pick up Leopard 6 at YONGDONG strip at 1500. 1410 Div G-3 notified us that our ammo allocation for the period 1800 10th Oct to 1800 15th Oct is 1833 rds of 105mm How ammo. 1700 Leopard 3, 1st Bn is moving from YONGDONG to TAEJON. They are being relieved by 65th RCT. 1745 Notified Lightning 3 that Lt Sterling and 3 EM, British Army, were with our A Btry. 2000 Div G-3 authorized Sv practice tomorrow, 14th and 15th Oct. C and B Btrys notified. Bn expended 216 rds (total to date 40,423 rds)

CHAPTER THREE

On to the Yalu

14 OCT 50

0755 Capt Sherman, BC B Btry, arrived at CP. He is on recon for Btry posn W of TAEJON. 0800 C Btry displaced to (CQ52.6-89.0) for Service Practice. 0810 Bn CO, S-2, Capt Robbis and his Philippine personnel left for C Btry's service practice. Hq and B Btrys survey sections will check C Btrys survey. 0940 B Btry displaced and closed in posn at (CR52.2-24.1). The BC did not like the area as it was "too filthy". It had previously been occupied by Hq 11th FA Bn and 2nd Bn 38th Inf. 1100 An M-10 trailer of A Btry, loaded with small arms ammunition, burned and exploded during their march from YONGDONG to TAEJON. Cause of the fire unknown. It is believed that it was caused by a faulty WP hand grenade as the first smoke from the trailer was white. AUTHOR'S NOTE: Btry "A"s Ammo Chief Sgt Gunn heroically unhooked the burning M10 trailer and pulled it off the MSR, surely saving lives among those in the column. Put in for a Bronze Medal for valor, it was knocked down to a Soldier's Medal because the action, however brave, did not involve actual contact with the enemy. (Sgt Gunn earned his first Soldier's Medal back in Japan.)

APPENDIX "A"

Lt Kelly, an able FO ABLE. Later flew with me and became an outstanding observer in the air, also.

BACK TO HERODOTUS:

1235 A btry displaced from YONGDONG and closed into B Btrys old position at (CR65-23). 1430 BC A Btry reported to the CP. He was given the latest situation and information that was known by this Hq. 1440 Capt Robbis and his party left the Bn area for WAEGWAN. 1440 LnO 3 reported CP of 3rd Bn 35th at (CR75.5-11.5). 1815 Notified B Btry that they would have service practice on 25 Oct. Hq, A, C and Sv btrys will continue with their normal training, guard and maintenance of individual equipment, weapons, radios and vehicles. 2030 LnO 1 reported that a Co. sized patrol from 1st Bn 35th was going out 15 Oct to NONSON (CR28-07). LnO 1 will accompany the patrol with a SCR 694 radio to maintain contact with us. On 16 Oct a Co. will go to HONGON on the coast, N up the coast and back to HONGON. The patrol will be gone two days. They have requested an FO so that they can have radio contact with the Ln plane and all of the air surveillance that they can get during the two days. 2245 Leopard 5, Major Wolfolk, notified us to be ready to move to HAMCHANG (DR27-456) at 0800 15 Oct. One Btry to be attached to and remain here with the 2nd Bn 35th. 2300 Leopard 4, Major Andrews, wanted to know how many trucks we could furnish the Infantry for a 3 or 4 day operation? He was told 20 trucks. 2330 Bn CO and Capt Metcalfe, LnO 2 left for Leopard CP for more complete details of tomorrow's movement. Bn expended 119 rds (total to date 40,542 rds).

15 OCT 50

0100 Btrys notified of coming movement. B Btry, Sv minus, S1 Sect and personnel section will remain behind. The supply sections of A and C Btrys are to remain with Sv Btry. Sv Btry to send two ammo sections, ration truck, POL truck, Bn wrecker and one maint. crew. 0700 Hq Btry and Sv Btry elements departed from the CP area enroute to A and C Btry posns. 0730 B minus moved out under the Exec O in order C, A, Hq. 0900 Bn CO left by plane for SANGJU and will meet the Bn there. 1510 Bn minus halted at S edge of SANGJU. 1742 Bn minus closed in posn 4.5 miles W of HAMCHANG. Marched 103.7 miles. Bn CP with Rgt CP in school house at (DR23.9-47.8), C Btry in posn at (DR20.5-45.8), A Btry posn at (DR24.1-47.3). 1800 Bn CO directed that no single vehicles were to move after dark as the NKs were very active in the area, mining roads, ambushing single vehicles and raiding small installations. 1930 Estab comm, by CW with Div and D/A. Notified Rgt. 2230 LnO 1 sent in overlay of lst Bn dispositions. 2335 notified A Btry by radio to have FOs report to LnO 1 at 0730 16 Oct.

16 OCT 50

0015 Raining very hard. 0115 LnO 1 notified us that we would receive 1st Bn overlays and operation order by 0530. 0620 A Btry notified to make an immediate recon for a new posn area that will be tenable if it continues to rain. 0710 BC A Btry arrived at CP for maps and lst Bn operations overlay. 0900 RCT CO notified us that H hour has been postponed indefinitely due to rain. Recon and preparation for attack will be continued. All Btrys notified. 1030 CWO Greer, asst S-4, and Capt Cole, Motor Off, left CP area for TAEJON. They will report on the condition of all stream crossings. 1105 Sent maps and overlays to the Air Sect and 9th ROK RGT in SANGJU. 1255 LnO 3 reported that the 3rd Bn was moving out by truck. C Btry to follow and go into posn #3 as shown on the overlay (DR13-48). 1350 LnO 3 requested Ln plane look for a reported enemy Rgt at (95-29) and a Bn at (96-29). At present the weather is unsuitable for Air opns and observation. Will get the plane up as soon as weather clears. 1520 Ln Plane in the air but cannot observe due to the ground fog and rain. 1540 LnO 1 reported 1st Bn still in posn. 1600 Plane sent to area N of hill 830. Reported no activity there. 1745 C Btry fired on enemy in woods - good effect was observed. 1835 Radio message from CWO Greer, Asst S-4, that he will supply us with Clas I and III supplies; for us to return the empty ration and POL trucks to TAEJON and that all stream crossings were still OK. 2045 LnO 3 reported his location as (DR12.2-48.7), I Co at (DR10.2-50.1), L Co at (DR15.9-47.1) and C Btry in posn at (DR12.29-48.88). A patrol will go up hill 830 prior to 0700 tomorrow. Bn expended 40 rds (total to date 40,582 rds). Still raining at close of period.

17 OCT 50

0600 Still raining. 0710 Rgtl Exec O reported that the 3rd Bn moved out in attack at 0700 and that the 1st Bn will attack at 0800. 0720 Bn CO left CP for A and C Btrys. 0835 Bn CO notified Exec O to have FDC, Comm sect and part of the mess sect prepared to displace fwd at approx 1400. Bn CO will recon posn A-3 (DR10-51) as soon as the Inf pass thru it. 0847 Ln plane reported that they could not observe the N and W side of hill 830 because of rain and fog. 1015 LnO 1 reported that he has reached Phase Line A and that the road beyond is impassable for vehicles. No enemy have been encountered. 1100 LnO 1 reported his location as (DR20.7-51.7). 1200 Ln plane returning to strip due to heavy rain. No enemy activity was noted. The road net starting at (DR1655) goes NW approx 2000 yds, W to (DR0659) and appears passable for 2 1/2 traffic. 1330 LnO 1 reported all 1st Bn patrols converging on objective 1. 1355 One platoon of A Btry displaced fwd to (DR13.8-52.2) 1400 Bn CO requested whether or not we had contacted the 8th FA Bn on their command channel? Answered no! We are continuously monitoring their channel. 1430 Bn CO ordered the FDC group displaced fwd to the vicinity of C Btry (DR09.8-51.2) 1445 LnO 1reported leading elements of the 1st Bn on their objective. 1550 FDC closed in the vicinity of C Btry. 1710 RCT CO desires that we fire on the village of CHONG-NI (DR16.25-59.80) Informed him that it would have to be unobserved fire - "fire at it anyhow after checking with CO 1st Bn". 1800 LnO 3 requested harassing fire on hill 830 (DR95.3-26.2), 3rd Bn CP at (DR96.9-28.0). Request for fire denied. 1825 CO 1st Bn does not desire fire on CHONG-NI. 2330 Leopard 2 notified us of Div "No Fire Line". No fire W of (CR96) grid, nor N of (CR63) grid. 8th FA Bn Ln plane tried to contact 64th FA today; monitor their channel! We have been doing this continuously. 3 FOs from 10th BLT (Philippine Army) will report in the morning and accompany 64th FOs. They are to observe our methods and techniques. Bn expended 17 rds (total to date 40,599 rds) Raining at end of period.

18 OCT 50

0600 Raining and foggy, visibility extremely limited. 0615 LnO 3 called in the plans of the 3rd Bn for today. 0745 LnO 3 reported K Co moving out by truck, N up the river and turning W at (DR11-58). 1017 CO 8th FA Bn reported that he can support Leopard Blue (3rd Bn 35th Inf). 1030 LnO 1 called in 1st Bn plans for today.1230 LnO 3 reported L Co at (DR96.3-33.5) and that road W of (DR11-58) is not passable for vehicles larger than 1/4 ton. 1245 LnO 3 requested that 2 ambulances be sent to 3rd Bn 35th. They have had a serious truck accident. Capt Began, Bn Med Off, and our ambulance was sent. Leopard notified. 1500 Stopped raining. Heavy overcast clouds with 1000 ft ceiling. Ordered Ln plane into the air. 1700 Plane returned to strip. no enemy activity noted. Bn expended 73 rds (total to date 40,672 rds). Raining at close of period.

19 OCT 50

0600 Weather clear and cold. 0650 Leopard 3 reported that the 1st Bn was moving back to the vicinity of the Rgtl CP at 0800 today; K Co is attacking W at 0700 and that the remainder of the 3rd Bn would sit tight. 0700 notified A Btry to relay one platoon on CA 5600 and leave the other platoon as is, to cover the withdrawal of the 1st Bn. 0900 LnO 3 reported 3rd Bn dispositions. 0900 Bn CO left for 3rd Bn CP. 0910 Contacted 8th FA Bn on SCR 193 radio. 1030 BC C Btry notified us that a civilian had reported 2000 NK soldiers on a hill approx 3000 yds W of his Btry posn, that he was establishing a Btry OP on the high ground in front of him. 1035 Leopard 6 desired a position report on K Co and for us to contact the 8th FA Bn on their command channel. Lightning 6, Gen Kean, desires the same information on K Co. 1050 BC A Btry reported one platoon now located in the vicinity of the 3rd Bn CP at (DR12.0-57.5) and laid on CA 5000. 1300 Notified Ln plane to look for and report the location of K Co patrols moving W from Objective #1, also find out if they have contacted the 27th Inf. 1330 Ln plane reported returning to strip as weather had closed in. Will try to get back to SANGJU by flying N S road. Have not seen K Co nor any enemy; have contacted the 8th FA Bn and they know of no contact having been made between the

27th and 35th Inf. 1550 Requested permission of Leopard 6 to displace C Btry and the FDC back to the vicinity of the Rgtl CP. We cannot get C Btry far enough fwd to support the 3rd Bn 35th. They can receive any needed support from the 8th FA Bn. Permission was granted. 1700 C Btry and FDC displaced to vicinity of Rgtl CP. 1825 C Btry closed in posn in dry creek bed in vic of Rgt; FDC returned to Hq Btry. 2055 Notified air sect to pick up Capt Dahlman, Leopard S-1 at HAMCHANG strip in the morning and take him to TAEJON. Plane to return to SANGJU. 2150 Received a march order from Rgt. Rgt will march back to TAEJON tomorrow; 64th is the second serial and will cross the IP in HAMCHANG at 0830. Btrys notified; air section notified of movement and to cancel flight for Capt Dahlman. Btrys to have one Off and vehicle at Bn CP at 0645 tomorrow to leave with the advance party. 2230 Radio msg sent to BC B Btry to locate positions for A and C Btrys in the vicinity of the Bn CP in TAEJON. Try to get buildings. Raining at end of period.

20 OCT 50

0600 Raining very hard. 0700 Bn Exec O left with advance party. 0800 Bn minus, under the S-3, Major Braatz, moved out for TAEJON in the order of march C, A, Hq Btry. 1850 Bn minus closed in posn in TAEJON. One accident during the march; hq Btry 3/4 ton survey truck struck a tree and was damaged. Marched 104 miles. A and C Btrys at (CR55.88-22.36) on the S edge of TAEJON air strip. All personnel of the Bn are now billeted in bldgs. 2015 Bn CO arrived at the CP. Bn had a little trouble fording the KUM river. The fan belts had to be removed from all the jeeps as the water was quite deep. B Btry had a Special Service Movie.

Typical "spoony" Able cannoneer

FDC Chief, Sgt Francis, and I

64 FA BN IN KOREA (continued)

21 OCT 50

0800 Notified LnO 1, Capt McCoy, and LnO 2, Capt Stockton, to return to Hq Btry with their sections. 1000 Ln sections 1 and 3 arrived at CP area. Their vehicles, field glasses and communications equipment were in poor shape and badly in need of 1st echelon maintenance. 1400 Bn CO left for Rgt CP. 1400 BC B Btry arrived at CP and informed the Exec Off of his bathing facilities. B Btry has 4 natural hot springs baths in their CP bldg and sufficient room to bathe a Btry at a time. Btrys notified. 1445 Gen Wilson, asst Div CG, visited CP. Inquired as to what the Bn was doing today. He was informed that the Btrys that returned from HAMCHANG yesterday (A, C, and Hq Btry) were performing maintenance on their vehicles, weapons and Comm eqpt while B Btry was following a regular training schedule. 1510 Bn CO returned. 1515 Requested of G-3 for range clearance for week of 23-28 Oct. 1900 Bn had a movie in A Btry area for all Bn personnel. Weather clear and cold at end of period.

Kincheon H (Bert) Bailey

22 OCT 5

0910 Lt Seeley, C Btry, returned to duty from hosp. 1000 Bn CO left by Ln plane to reconnoiter for Arty posns and the road net in the vicinity of HWANG-GAN (DR02-08). 1515 Lt Reece took S-3, 2nd Bn 35th on an air recon to the vicinity of HODONG (CR40-10). Approx 30 enemy were observed - ran as the plane approached. 1516 Capt Sherman, BC B Btry, flew on recon to KUMSAN (CQ64-95) to check the road net, possible gun posns and the disposition of the 3rd Bn 35th Inf. 1615 Bn CO returned from RGT. 1620 Lt Hoffman, assigned and joined the Bn. he was assigned to A Btry; Lt Roper, A Btry, transferred to B Btry. 1845 Leopard 6 directed that we move a Btry to KUMSAN to support the 3rd Bn 35. 1900 B Btry alerted for movement on 23 Oct to KUMSAN to support the 3rd Bn 35th. B Btry was sent on this mission as they had previously occupied posns in that vicinity and also were idle when the remainder of the Bn went to HAMCHANG (DR27-46). 1910 Received an overlay of the 35th RCT zone of responsibility. 1910 Alerted Capt Stockton, LnO 3, for movement on 23 Oct to 3rd Bn 35th. 1930 Capt Knight, Bn Special Sv. Officer showed a movie in A Btrys area for the Bn. Weather clear and cold.

23 OCT 50

0730 B Btry moved out for KUMSAN. 0730 A Btry left for Service practice; GP at (CR67-18). 0815 Bn CO left for A Btry's Sv Pr. 0830 Hq Btry holding familiarization firing of all small arms and crew served weapons. Range at (CR22.5-54.8). 1300 Leopard 3 notified us that they would have a representative to observe our command inspections. 1615 Ln plane dropped surrender leaflets on the road between KUMSAN (CR64-95) and UNSON (CQ43-94)l. 1630 D/A 1, Col Moore, arrived in the area, requested that we furnish four 2 1/2 trucks to the 90th FA Bn to haul their winter clothing to SUWON (CS22-28), approximately a 4 day round trip. 1805 Sv Btry dispatched 4 trucks to haul 90th FA Bn winter clothing to the vicinity of (YO42-32). 1900 Capt Knight, Bn Sp. Sv O had a movie for the Bn. C and Sv Btry's performing maintenance and following a training schedule. Bn expended 241 rds (total to date 40,913 rds).

24 OCT 50

0930 All personnel, who desired to see Bob Hope's show troupe, departed for the 66th Ord Bn area. Performance started at 1000. 1245 Maj Danley, S-2 35th Inf and 2 other Officers arrived at the CP to observe the Bn Cmd inspection of C Btry. 1300 Sv Btry conducted familiarization firing of all small arms and crew served weapons. 1300 Bn CO and staff inspected C Btry. This was a command inspection as required by recent Division directive.

AUTHOR'S INSERTION:

Elements of the 25th Div, which included the 35th RCT, as mentioned on the previous page, had the pleasure of a most welcome visit by Bob Hope and his typically arousing entourage in an outdoor stadium in UIJONGBU. His usual bevy of beauties included Marilyn Maxwell, with whom I conversed for a few pleasurable moments. She was the fill-in for Marilyn Monroe and just about as alluring. Bob offered his well-known type of genuine, unrehearsed humor: "When I was a young man, I always dreamed of someday visiting those three best known, most beautiful cities in the whole, wide world,—- LONDON, in Jolly Olde England, with its famous Buckingham Palace and the London Bridge,——GAYE PAREE, with its exciting Can Can dancers, the Champs-Elysee and the Eiffel Tower,—-and, that city in the exotic, fragrant wonderful Paradise of the alluring, magical Orient—-UIJONGBU! Birds fell out of the sky, the surrounding mountains rumbled as thousands of combat clad GIs let loose with low-pitched raucous laughter there in that stadium in UNCLE TOWN. Ole comedian Bob had once again captured the hearts and minds of American fighting troops sitting out in the open not that far from the front lines. AFTER LOOKING AT PHOTOS on NEXT PAGE, BACK TO HERODOTUS.

Bob Hope and Marilyn Maxwell in Uijongbu

Gun Crew Basking in Subfreezing Weather

1320 Div CG, Gen Kean, arrrived at CP and visited the inspection of C Btry. 1640 Ln plane returned from surveillance mission for 3rd Bn 35th. Lt Bourassa, the observer, reported that he saw a 3rd Bn patrol ambushed by NK troops. There were US casualties. 1650 LnO 3 radioed in that the 3rd Bn will remain in vicinity of present posn until all enemy are cleared out. 1900 Capt Knight, Bn Sp Sv Off had a movie for the Bn in A Btry's area. 1940 LnO 3 reported that I and L Cos 35th will clean out the ambush area tomorrow 25th Oct. He was notified that no preparation was to be fired, however the Btry may register. 2050 LnO 3 requested that we register on 3 reported enemy concentrations at (CQ51-97), (CQ47-01) and (CQ45-02), all temples are reported by priests to contain 200 NKs. A and Hq Btrys followed regular training schedules. Weather clear and cold. Bn expended 193 rds (total to date 41,106 rds).

25 OCT 50

0700 A Btry departed for Sv Practice. 0830 Major Danley, S-2 35th and two other officers arrived at the CP to observe the command insp of Hq Btry. 0900 Sv Btry firing clean up on their familiarization firing of small arms and crew served weapons. 0900 Bn CO conducted cmd insp of Hq Btry. 1000 Air OP registered on 3 temples as requested by LnO 3. An estimated 30 enemy were observed. Casualties were noted and 6 dead counted. 1145 A B Btry 2 1/2 truck carrying a patrol from the 3rd Bn 35th hit a mine; the truck was damaged, no casualties. 1405 Col Fisher, CO 35th RCT, directed that all trenches in the 35th zone of responsibility be filled in. Native labor is to be used and no payment will be made for the work done. 1530 LnO 3 reported that the 3rd Bn 35th was cleaning out all villages in their Z/R, screening all personnel and burning all known and suspected enemy hiding places. 1620 Bn CO authorized 200 rds of 105mm to B Btry for use on night harassing missions. 1900 Bn had a Sp Sv movie. 1932 LnO 3 reported that the mission of the 3rd Bn 35 for tomorrow is the same as today. C Btry followed normal Tng Sched. Bn expended 83 rds (total to date 41,189 rds). Weather clear and cold at end of period.

26 OCT 50

0800 Bn CO left for B Btry. 0845 Major Danley, S-2 35th and two other officers arrived at CP to observe the Cmd Insp of A Btry, 0930 Bn Exec Off conducted the cmd insp of A Btry. 1015 Div CG, Gen Kean, visited A Btry and inspected their howitzers and motor vehicles. 1145 Col Fisher, CO 35th, directed that B Btry harass road junctions and ridge lines only. 1650 Major Danley, S-2 35th requested air obsn of a 38 man ROK patrol that was reported as being surrounded at UN-DAE-RI (CQ65-87). We will fly the mission tomorrow morning. 1830 Capt Knight, Bn Sp Sv O had a movie for the Bn. Weather clear and cold at end of the period. Bn expended 120 rds (total to date 41,309 rds).

27 OCT 50

0830 Bn CO and inspection staff left for Sv Btry Cmd Insp. 0840 Major Danley and two other officers arrived at the CP to observe the Cmd Insp of Sv Btry. They were sent to Sv Btry posn in the vicinity of the RTO in TAEJON. 0900 Cmd insp of Sv Btry conducted by Bn CO. 1000 Gen Barth, D/A CG, visited Sv Btry, inspected their motor vehicles and 3 trailers that had been built by Capt Cole, the Bn motor Off. 1300 Bn CO returned to the CP. 1800, Capt Metcalfe, LnO 2, attended a briefing at 35th RCT CP. A, C, and Hq Btrys conducted scheduled maint. and training during the day. Weather cold and clear. Bn expended 124 rds (total to date 41,433 rds).

28 OCT 50

0001-0430 B Btry fired harassing fire on ridge lines and trails in the 3rd Bn 35th Z/R. 0815 Bn CO left for B Btry. 1715 Bn CO returned to CP. 1800 Capt Metcalfe, LnO 2, attended a briefing at Rgt. 2045 Lts Chastaine and Bourassa left on night aerial recon over 35th RCT Z/R. This is our first attempt at flying nite missions. We hope to be able to locate enemy groups by their fires. 2230 Ln plane returned - no activity noted. Bn minus B Btry spent the day performing scheduled maintenance and tng. Weather cold and clear at end of the period. Bn expended 90 rds (total to date 41,523 rds).

29 OCT 50

0001-0530 B Btry fired harassing fire on ridges and trails in the 3rd Bn 35 Z/R. 1515 BC B Btry, Capt Sherman, requested authority to fire 150 rds for harassing fires nite of 29-30 Oct. 1530 Bn CO authorized B Btry 150 rds for harassing fires but no firing on towns unless the Inf has received fire from the town. 1800 Capt Metcalfe, LnO 2, attended briefing at Rgt. 1830 Capt Stockton, LnO 3, requested Ln plane to fly nite recon in the vicinity of (CR46-05). Reported that two platoons of L Co 35th were in trouble. 1845 LnO 3 reported that Lt Sexton, B Btry, an FO with L Co had been wounded by small arms fire. 1915 Exec Off, 35th Inf, cancelled the request of the 3rd Bn for a nite recon flight. Bn minus B Btry conducted scheduled maintenance and training. Weather cold and clear at end of period. Bn expended 174 rds (total to date 41,699 rds).

30 OCT 50

0800 Bn conducted clean up small arms and crew served weapons firing. Capt McCoy was in charge. 1205 C Btry alerted for movement at 0930 31 Oct to TOKEI-RI (CR46-20). 1300 Bn CO left on recon for Btry posns in the vicinity of TOKEI-RI. 1430 Gen Kean, Div CG, visited Sv Btry and desired the time of their next Cmd Insp. 1730 Bn CO returned to CP. 1800 Capt Metcalfe, LnO 2, attended a briefing at Rgt. 1800 Capt Knight, Bn Sp Sv O, had a movie for the Bn. Bn minus B Btry conducted scheduled maintenance and training. Weather raining and cold at end of period. Bn expended 170 rds (total to date 41,869 rds).

31 OCT 50

0001-0400 B Btry fired harassing fire on ridges and trails in 3rd Bn Z/R. 0400 B Btry was attacked by 30-40 NK enemy; one ROK soldier attached to B Btry was killed and Pvt Volack, 25th D/A Med Det (B Btry Aid man) was seriously wounded. Enemy withdrew at 0500 leaving 3 dead behind. 0730 Bn CO and Comm O left for B Btry. 0820 B Btry fired preparation for attack of 3rd Bn 35th. 0830

Bn CO notified C Btry by radio to execute plan A (move to their preselected posn vic TOKEI-RI.) 0845 Capt Waddell, BC C Btry and party departed. 0900 C Btry moved out for TOKEI-RI. 1010 Gen Barth, D/A CG visited the CP, talked about recommendations for awards and inspected A Btry's howitzers. 1100 Gen Barth departed from CP. 1430 C Btry in posn at (CR46-15), layed and ready to fire. 1610 Lt Col Gassett, Div G-4, and Lt Col Baker, Div Ord Off visited the CP; wanted to know if we had any problems regarding supply, Ord, etc. Inspected Hq and A Btry's motor parks. Complimented Capt Cole, Bn Motor Off and CWO Greer, Bn Asst S-4. Informed us of the new method of marking motor vehicles and that anti-freeze was on the way. 1800 Capt Metcalfe, LnO 2 attended briefing at Rgt. 1910 Bn Exec Off departed for Div JA sect to attend pre-trial investigation of PFC Gregg, Hq Btry. 1920 Bn CO returned to CP. 1948 B Btry closed into their old posn at (CR52.5-24.1). 2210 C Btry notified to send out their FOs at 0700 1st Nov to replace B Btrys FOs. Bn minus B & C Btrys performed scheduled maintenance and training. Weather clear and cold at end of period. Bn expended 45 rds (total to date 41,914 rds)

1 NOV 50

0720 LnO 3 reported 3rd Bn 35th advancing in zone. C Btry is in support. 1006 Alerted B Btry to be prepared for cmd insp at 0900 3 Nov. 1130 LnO 3 reported that he has no further need of Ln plane. 1425 Received notification that the Ordnance would make a tech insp of Hq, A & Sv Btrys on 2 Nov and B & C Btrys on 3 Nov. 1500 D/A 1 notified Bn that we would lose excess ROK personnel over 100; to be at Div Repl Co at 1000 2 Nov. 1515 LnO 3 reported that C Btry was released from attached to 3rd Bn 35th but will remain in posn until 0700 2 Nov. 1800 Capt Knight, Bn Sp Sv O, held a movie for the Bn. 1930 Leopard 6 informed us that the 64th is alerted to move on order anytime after 2400 4 Nov. Bn less C Btry conducted scheduled training and prepared for coming Ord Tech Insp. Bn expended 183 rds (total to date 42,097 rds) Weather clear and cold at end of period.

64 FA BN IN KOREA (continued)

2 NOV 50

0845 C Btry displaced to TAEJON. 0845 Bn CO spoke to the ROK soldiers who were to depart this morning. 0930 Excess ROK soldiers departed by motor convoy to 25th Repl Co. None of them were very anxious to leave the Bn. This has been their home for most of the Korean campaign. A large portion of Hq and A Btrys turned out to watch their departure - they left the Bn area singing and waving. 0915 Col Dick, D/A 5 visited CP area and conferred with Col Hogan. 1025 C Btry closed in their old posn area on S edge of TAEJON airport (CR55.88-2236). 1035 D/A 3 informed the Bn that RR flat cars are available for our 6 ton trucks, M-4 tractor/wrecker, and M-2 trailers. Time of loading and departure are unknown. Bn will take a basic load of ammo. 1500 LnO 3, Capt Stockton, and section returned to the CP area from 3rd Bn 35th Inf. 1830 Bn CO left for briefing at Div CP. 1830 Capt Knight, Bn Sp Sv O, held a movie for the Bn. 2220 Bn CO returned from Div CP. Bn spent the day on scheduled training, maintenance and preparation for Ordnance Technical Inspection. Bn expended 19 rds (total to date 42,116 rds). Weather clear and cool at end of period.

KAESONG: Where CG, 25th Infantry
Division, General Kean,
presented me the Silver Star

3 NOV 50

0015 D/A 3 notified us that we could start our RR loading of the 6 ton trucks, M-4 tractor/wrecker, M-2 trailers and 2 M-10 ammo trailers at 0700 today. 0730 Sv Btry started their RR loading. 0830 Bn CO and staff left for B Btry. 0900 Command Insp of B Btry conducted by Bn CO. 1000 Capt Knight assigned as BC Sv Btry. Capt Block relieved as BC Sv but remains as Bn S-4. 1130 Received annex A (rail movement) to march order #3 and Incl 2 to annex B from 35th RCT. 1200 Sv Btry completed their rail loading for movement to MUNSON-NI (CS0593). 1300 Ordnance Tech Insp team in Hq, A & Sv Btry's areas. 1330 LnO 2 with Lt Chastain as pilot left on aerial recon for noon meal halting position in the vicinity of SEOUL Municipal City Airport. 1600 Lt Barrow, Sv Btry, and trucks returned from 35th Inf ammo hauling detail. Bn less B Btry performed scheduled training and maintenance. Weather clear and cool at end of period.

4 NOV 50

0545 Bn advance party consisting of S-3, Comm O and one officer per Btry departed for KAESONG (BT8605). 1100 Bn CO departed by motor vehicle for KAESONG. He had planned to fly up, however the heavy rain and low ceiling has kept our planes grounded today. 1600 LnO 1, Capt McCoy, was evacuated to the clearing station with a bad ear infection (NBC). 1800 Advance party arrived at KAESONG. 2315 Capt Metcalfe, LnO 2, departed for SEOUL with A & C Btry's kitchens and a representative from each Btry. He is to pick a halting place for the Bn and be prepared to feed a hot noon meal for the Bn. Bn spent the day in loading and preparation for motor movement to KAESONG. Weather rainy, overcast and cool at end of the period.

5 NOV 50

0035 Bn moved out under the Exec Off in order Hq, C, B, A and Sv Btrys; destination the Div Assy area in the vicinity of KAESONG. 0310 C Btry's 4th Sect prime mover was hit by an unlighted train at a grade crossing between CHOCHIWON and CHONAN. There were no injuries, the vehicle was evacuated to 1725th Ord Det # 2. 0935 Bn halted on the S Side of the SEOUL Municipal City Airport and fed a hot noon meal. There were many tires to be changed and repaired. 1245 Bn departed for KAESONG. 1710 An M-10 ammo trailer in C Btry exploded and burned on the road. Cause of the fire was thought to have been WP hand grenades - that the constant bouncing and jarring of the unsprung M-10 caused the safety pins or the triggers to work loose. The column was halted here for 30 minutes. 1745 Bn closed in an assy area in a dry stream bed E of KAESONG at (BT905039). Bn marched 159 miles, had two accidents and no injuries. Weather clear and cool at end of the period.

6 NOV 50

0645 Major Andrews, S-4, 35th requested that all of our available 2 1/2 ton trucks be dispatched to MUNSON-NI (CS0592) to haul the 35th Inf to their assy area. 0730 Lt Chapmen, Sv Btry, departed for MUNSON-NI with 50 2 1/2 trucks. 0845 Major Braatz, Bn S-3, departed for conference at D/A CP. 0900 Gen Barth, D/A CG arrived in the CP area and conferred with Col Hogan, the Bn CO. 1030 Capt Metcalfe, LnO 2, departed for MUNSON-NI to coordinate the movement and use of our trucks. 1300 Bn CO departed for MUNSON-NI. 1815 Maj McMann, D/A 4, notified us that we were to furnish 15 2 1/2 ton trucks on 8 Nov to move the 159 FA Bn from the RTO to their assy area. 2135 Lt Chapman and the last shuttle of trucks returned from their mission with the 35th Inf. 2310 Div G-3 directs close security of all Btry posns on 7 Nov as it is a Communist holiday. All Btrys were notified; also to keep all Koreans out of the Bn area. Bn engaged during the day in transporting Infantry and performing necessary maintenance. Bn rcvd notification that Lt Hoffman, A Btry had been promoted to Capt on DA orders. Weather clear and cool at end of period.

7 NOV 50

0823 Maj Andrews, S-4 35th Inf notified us that we would furnish30 2 1/2 ton trucks this afternoon at 1300. Trucks are to be used to shuttle the 27th Inf to the NE. Do not know how long they will be gone. 1045 Capt Hoffman and convoy of 30 trucks departed for 27th Rgt area on N side of KAESONG. 1100 D/A 4 notified us that the 15 trucks for the 159 FA Bn may be called for at any time after 2400 today. He will try to hold it off until around 0700 tomorrow. 1101 S-3 departed for D/A CP. 1150 Bn S-3 called from D/A stating that KMAG had reported an enemy force moving from (CT1445) in this direction and that the 8th FA Bn has been firing today in the vicinity of (BT9640) at enemy Inf. They are reported moving from (CT1445) to a point between (BT8420) and (BT9118). There will be a Co of the 35th on each posn. The enemy force had previously retreated from the S and reorganized at (CT1445) and are attempting to cut the MSR. Request a Ln plane fly surveillance in that area. 1320 D/A 4, our 15 trucks are to report to Capt Tanniscoli at MUNSON-NI RTO at 0700 8 Nov. 1330 Capt DaPrato with Lts Milleren, Galloway and Ross as FOs left for 1st Bn 35th. 1330 Bn CO left for RCT CP. 1345 Div Asst Ord Off requested 15 drivers this afternoon to be flown to PUSAN and drive 25th Ord Repl vehicles from PUSAN to KAESONG. 1445 Fifteen 1/4 ton truck drivers departed for 725th Ord CP. 1445 Leopard 3 notified us that the Div QM cold weather demonstration would be available to us tomorrow 8 Nov. 1445 Lt Bourassa, air observer, reported no enemy activity in area of his surveillance today. There appears to be a road block at (CT0341) and a small bridge that has been blown at (CT0741). 1600 Bn CO returned from RCT CP. 1650 Lt Duncan, Air observer, reported that in the village of POCHON (CT153-455) there were approx 30 enemy troops in the school yard. They waved at the plane but did not fire. 1830 D/A Comm O notified us to shut down our SCR 193 radio until 0800 tomorrow 8 Nov. Bn performed maintenance during the day. Capt Hoffman and 30 trucks remained out with the 27th Inf. 1830 Received overlay and operations plan of 1st Bn 35th for 8th and 9th Nov. Weather clear and cool at end of period.

8 NOV 50

0500 Lt Chapman and 15 trucks from Sv Btry departed for MUNSON-NI RTO. They will haul the 159th FA BN from the RTO to their assy area. 0800 Capt Metcalfe, LnO 2, left for 2nd Bn 35th; he is to get their plan of operation. 0845 Bn CO left on aerial recon of 1st Bn 35th area. 0900 Leopard 3 informed us that the cold weather demonstration team would be in the area at 1330 and that a training film on cold weather clothing would be shown at 2000 tonite. 0945 LnO 2 returned to CP with opn plan of 2nd Bn. 1000 LnO 2 and FO Lts Griffin, Guill and Stout departed for 2nd Bn CP. 1020 Lt Duncan, air observer, reported a short barreled howitzer located at YUGA-DONG (CT0741). 1110 Air observer reports a 57mm AT gun in school yard at (CT1731), village of SANGUYONG. 1330 Cold weather demonstration for the Bn in C Btry area. 1730 Bn CO arranged for the 17th FA Bn 8" how to support the 1st and 2nd Bns 35th Inf. 1800 Capt Baird, D/A Sp Sv Off held a movie for the Bn. 2000 A tng film on cold weather clothing and Trench Foot was shown to the Bn. Capt Bornhouser, BC A Btry, had received notification from the War Dept that he had been appointed 2nd Lt RA. All btrys performed maintenance during the day. Weather clear and cool at end of the period.

9 NOV 50

0840 Air observer reported that he had searched the area assigned and no enemy activity was noted. There is a friendly patrol just S of the 1st Bn objective. 0910 Bn CO left for D/A CP. 0915 LnO 2 reported that F Co will remain in present posn, E Co will move N along road to (9215) and then to (000155). 2nd Bn will return to base camp tonite. 1100 Capt Block, Bn S-4, was evacuated to Clearing Co because of pleurisy attk (NBC) 1235 Bn CO returned to the CP. 1320 LnO 2 reported that he could register the 8" how on the road fork at (97.5-17.8). 1350 LnO 2 stated CO 2nd Bn does not desire arty fire in his sector until he has an enemy tgt. 1410 S-3 requested LnO 1 to pick a base point and register the 8"how. 1420 LnO 1 stated CO 1st Bn doesn't desire any arty fire in his sector because he has two companies scattered throughout his area. 1430 Directed LnO 1 to relieve Lt Ross as FO and send him to the Bn CP. Lt Ross will assume command of A Btry tomorrow when Capt Bornhouser leaves to take his RA physical. 1545 Col Preston, CO 159th FA Bn, arrived in area and conferred with the Bn CO. 1600 Leopard 3 reported enemy observed digging in the vicinity of SINDAE (BT733-008). Ln plane was sent to check over the area. 1720 Air observer reported that there are a lot of mines in that area and that the people appear to be mining coal or something. 1730 Bn convoy, under Capt Stockton, left for 17th FA Bn area to see a movie. 1800 Col Preston departed for his CP. Btrys performed maintenance and care of equipment during the day. Weather clear and cool at end of the period.

10 NOV 50

0700 Capt Bornhouser, BC A Btry, left for Div Air strip. He is to be flown to PUSAN and get a final type physical exam in connection with his appointment as a 2nd Lt RA. 0855 Lt Milleren, A Btry, FO with A Co 35th, reported an enemy ammo dump in an old Korean Army Camp at (CS83.3-13.8). There are three truck loads of 76mm and 120mm. 0900 Div Ord Det # 2 maintenance team arrived in Bn area. They are making on the spot inspections and repairs. 0920 Notified Div Ord Off of the ammo dump located at (CS8313)l. 0930 Bn CO left for RCT CP. 1130 Bn CO returned. 1630 Bn CO left for 159 FA Bn CP. 1920 Bn CO returned. 1930 Capt Stockton took a convoy of Bn personnel to 17th FA Bn to attend a movie. Capt Driscoll was relieved as Bn Adj and assigned as Bn S-4. Btrys performed maintenance during the day. Weather clear and cool at the end of the period.

11 NOV 50

0800 Bn CO left the CP to inspect the Btrys. 0830 D/A 3 desired our S-3 attend a meeting at D/A at 1500 this afternoon, to discuss plans for movement to the N. We may send up to 6 vehicles as advance party; to leave with D/A tomorrow morning. 0840 Maj Andrews, S-4 35th requested 55 trucks for movement of 24th RCT, to be at 24th CP (CT0603) at 1800 today. Each truck to have two drivers and carry 5 days rations. All maint, mess and supply trucks will have to be unloaded. We cannot comply with this request unless Capt Hoffman and the 26 trucks that are out with the 27th RCT return. 55 two and a half ton trucks of a 62 total completely immobilizes this Bn and puts 150 tons of ammo on the ground. 0910 Bn CO returned to the CP. 0945 S-4 35th notified us to send our trucks to the 24th Sv area (BT9901). 1045 Div SJA called and requested that Pvt Gregg, Hq Btry, and all witnesses to report to the Div Rear Echelon for GCM of Pvt Gregg. It is 62 miles over rough narrow roads to YONGDUNG-PO. 1101 Pvt Gregg and enlisted witnesses left by 3/4 ton truck for YONGDUNG-PO. 1235 Maj Smith and Capt Rutherford left by Ln plane for Div Rear Ech. 1300 D/A notified Bn that the movement to the N had been temporarily cancelled. The 25th Div is to remain in this vicinity, protect the MSR and clean out all enemy pockets in this area. Request Bn CO attend unit commanders meeting at D/A Hq at 1500. 1430 Bn CO departed for D/A CP. 1700 Bn CO returned with information that Rgt has received a mission and an area to sweep. Rgt will operate as three separate BCTs. The 2nd Bn attacks tomorrow morning with B/64 attached. 1708 Leopard 3 informed us that the 3rd Bn will move out complete. 1710 Leopard Blue 6 desired 3 FOs report to his CP at 0630 tomorrow; his Bn is moving out at first light. 2110 Capt Hoffman and 26 trucks returned from the detail with the 27th Inf. 2245 Received Div Opns Ord #14 with overlay. Weather clear and cool at end of period.

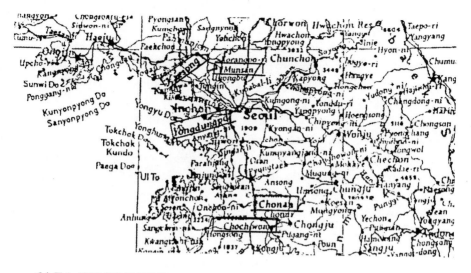

64 FA BN IN KOREA (continued)

12 NOV 50

0500 Capt DaPrato, LnO and FO Lts Bynum, Galloway & Milleren left for 1st Bn 35th. 0500 B Btry displaced to 2nd Bn 35th area. 0730 Received 1st Bn Opns O. 0912 LnO 1 reported his location as Hill 475 and that he will be there all day. 0915 LnO 3 reported his location as (CT125005). 0930 LnO 1 requested Air observation N of (BT911101), enemy has been seen there. 0930 Bn CO departed for Rgt. 1000 Capt McGrady, Bn Comm O, established a radio relay station on the high Mt at (BT8408). 1132 Leopard 6 requested the location of the leading elements of the 2nd Bn. 1135 LnO 2 reported leading elements at (CT280102). Info fwd to Rgt. 1205 LnO 3 reported leading elements of K Co at (BT993031). Given to Rgt. 1305 Ln plane reported B/64 located at (CT295099). 1315 Leopard 3 reported that there was a British Brigade in the vicinity of (CS2878) blocking to the S and patrolling to the N. 1315 D/A 1 notified us that it was permissible to keep our Bn personnel section with us for 2 more days at which time they are to report to the Div Rear Ech in YONGDUNG-PO (CS1444). 1400 LnO 1 reported A Co at (BT860190), C Co at (BT931501) and requested that A Btry displace to (BT918116) and register in front of both Inf Cos. Informed Rgt.

1420 C Btry displaced from Bn base camp to vic of 3rd Bn 35th. 1445 A Btry displaced from Bn base camp to (BT918116). 1445 LnO 2 reported leading elements at (CT291912) Notified Rgt. 1448 LnO 3 reported K Co at (CT032095) and L Co at (CT680900). Notified Rgt. 1450 LnO 2 reported that the 2nd Bn had contacted the British troops at (CT297899). Notified D/A and Rgt. 1530 Leopard White 6 requested that we relay to CO 35th, "We have reached our 1st objective; have contacted a British unit who has same mission, request instructions". Relayed to CO 35th. 1540 Leopard 6, "Tell White 6 to coordinate with the British and continue on your mission. 1550 Col Dick, D/A 5, visited CP. 1550 Air Obs notified us that B/64 was in posn at UIJONG-BU (CS280790) and requested delivery of fuel and rations there. They need 300 gal gas. 1600 Capt Block returned to duty from hosp. Assigned as LnO. 1620 A/64 in posn at (BT923127), Btry laid, one platoon on CA400 and other on CA6000. 1635 LnO 1reported A Co at (BT860190) and C Co at (BT930150). Notified D/A and Rgt. 1645 C/64 in posn at (CT;068094) and B/64 in posn at (CS294794). 1725 notified LnO 2 that the supply truck can return unescorted if it will go S of town to the MSR and then on to the base camp. 1800 Bn received word that Capts Metcalfe and Waddell were promoted to Maj on WD order. 1800 Bn CO returned to CP area. 1800 LnO 3 rptd his Co dispositions and that 1 platoon of I Co was with C Btry for their perimeter defense. 1820 LnO 2 reported his Co dispositions and the 2nd Bn plan for tomorrow. Rgt and D/A notified. 1930 Notified BC Sv Btry to recon for posn in town of KAESONG tomorrow morning. Bn communications during the day were superior. Each LnO, Btry, Bn S-3 and Bn radio relay station were equipped with the tall antenna. The Div and Rgt were completely dependent on this unit for communications with and reports of the Bns. Weather clear and cold at end of the period. Bn expended 8 rds (total to date (42,124 rds).

13 NOV 50

0730 Maj Waddell assigned as Comm O, Capt McGrady asssigned as BC C Btry. 0850 Lt Bell, Exec B Btry, reported that Sv Btry trucks were returning via the MSR. 0900 Bn CO departed for 1st Bn 35th. 0925 LnO 1 reported the 1st Bn CP moving to (CT932155).

Rpted to Rgt. 0940 LnO 2 reported his leading elements at (CS335812). 0950 Air OP observed a 57mm AT gun at (CS374882) prepared for action, no personnel present. Reported to 2nd Bn and Rgt. 1005 LnO 1 rpted the locations of his Cos, fwd to Rgt. 1104 Rcvd Rgt Opns O #15 and overlay. 1137 LnO 2 reported his advance elements at phase Line B. D/A and Rgt notified. 1225 Bn CO reported that he was enroute from 2nd Bn to A Btry. Plans call for A to displace at 1400. 1230 Sv Btry started to displace into KAESONG (BT784904). Located in a schoolyard, room enough for CP and Hq Btry. 1310 LnO 3 reported that I Co has reached (CT080170). Notified Rgt. 1400 B Btry radioed a request for automotive parts. Message given to Bn Motor Off who will send the parts out with the ration truck. 1415 LnO 1 reported that A Co is on final objective, C Co located at (BT950183), S-3 informed D/A and Rgt. 1500 Hq Btry displaced to school house in KAESONG; now located with Sv Btry. 1515 LnO 2 reported 2nd Bn operations completed for today and returning to base camp. CO 64th at C Btry and will stay there tonite. Notified Rgt. 1740 LnO 2 reported locations of his Cos and the plans for the 2nd Bn tomorrow. Notified D/A and Rgt. 1840 LnO 3 reported his troop dispositions and plans for tomorrow, that C/64 was in posn at (BT996215). They need 400 gal gas and 2 front springs for GMC. Communications worked fine all day. D/A 3 insisted that we report all dispositions and movement of our troops even though he was monitoring our radio channels and posting the information. Bn expended 11 rds (total to date 42,135 rds). Weather clear and cool at end of period.

14 NOV 50

0935 LnO 3 reported leading elements now at Phase Line C-3. D/A and Rgt notified. 1010 LnO 3 reported his dispositions. Notified D/A and Rgt. 1155 Bn CO returned to CP reported that Sv Btry truck had brought in a load of 60 and 81mm mortar ammo from the village of KUKWA-RI. Ammo was turned over to the Div Ord Coll Pt. 1222 LnO 2 reported his leading elements on Phase Line E. D/A and Rgt notified. 1230 LnO 1 reported the road cratered at (BT989279) Notified D/A and Rgt. 1340 Lt Ross, BC A Btry, reported that Lt Milleren was returning to the Bn area and bringing an ammo truck with a broken front spring. 1430 The 15 1/4 ton drivers that were sent to the Ord returned from PUSAN with a convoy of new vehicles for the Div. 1445 Air OP reported the locations of the 1st and 3rd Bns of the 35th, reported to D/A and Rgt. 1630 Notified B Btry to return their two disabled vehicles to UIJONG-BU tonite. The Bn Motor Off will meet them there in the morning and make repairs. 1700 LnO 3 reported C Btry in posn at (CT124255). 1705 LnO 1 reported the location of his Cos and that A Btry was in posn at (BT950328), D/A and Rgt notified. 1715 Air OP reported location of 2nd Bn 35th and that B Btry was in posn at (CS418954) within the Inf Bn perimeter. D/A and Rgt notified. 1855 BC B Btry reported that there was an air strip at (CS428963), that it was in good condition. He needed 5 sets of maps to extend the coverage of his area. 1930 BC B Btry reported that 50 SK police at (BT458068) had been attacked by the enemy at 1800. Attack came from the NE and SE; enemy used auto wpns and mortars. Casualties unknown. 150 SK police have heen sent to reinforce. Notified D/A and Rgt. 1955 LnO 3 radioed in the 3rd Bn plan of attack for tomorrow. D/A and Rgt notified. 2200 LnO 2 radioed the 2nd Bn plan for tomorrow. Informed D/A and Rgt. Weather clear and cold at end of period. Bn radio comm functioned perfectly despite the rugged terrain and the distances to the Bns and Btrys. Bn expended 11 rds (total to date 42,146 rds)

15 NOV 50

0908 LnO 2 reported that the LD for today was Phase Line H+2. 0911 LnO 3 requested the location of the Turkish Brigade that is attached to the 25th Div It is located 5 miles SW of KAESONG. 0910 Lt Chastain reported that the Air strip was fogged in and that they would take off as soon as the fog cleared. 1000 Bn CO left for Rgt. 1010 LnO 2 reported his leading elements at H+4, requested Air Obsn on village at (CT480120), suspected enemy mortars there. Notified D/A and Rgt. 1010 Ln Plane in air. 1020 Maj Andrews, S-4 35th, requested 21 trucks at 1300 to pick up 3rd Bn 35th and haul them to KUMCHON (BT7926). We do not have that many trucks available. All three of the Btrys are out and attached to the Inf Bns. We can send 14 which will completely immobilize us again. 1110 Leopard 3 reported that the 3rd Bn would send in a security platoon to lead the trucks to the 3rd Bn area. 1120 LnO 2 reported that their motorized elements were at Phase Line I+4. Informed D/A and Rgt. 1220 B Btry Exec reported that B Btry was in posn at (CT459051). 1230 Lt Cook, Hq Btry Motor Off, and 14 trucks left for 35th Rgt Sv area and then to the 3rd Bn. 1230 WO Mullaney, pers Off, and pers sect departed for Div Rear Echelon at YONGDONG-PO. 1240 Notified Air OP to check the air strip at (CS428963) and advise as to its suitability for operations from there, including security, messing and quarters. 1330 LnO 1 reported the 1st Bn plan for this afternoon. D/A and Rgt informed. 1345 notified A Btry not to send any single vehicles in to Bn; that A Btry personnel now here will remain until A Btry returns to Bn Control. 1400 Contacted Col Gassett, Div G-4, for permission to occupy the area in KAESONG that was previously occupied by the 17th FA Bn. We intend to move C Btry into there temporarily. Permission was granted. 1510 Bn CO called in from Rgt CP. Informed him that the 8th FA Bn cannot contact our LnO 1. Air OP reports that the plane received small arms fire from the vicinity of (CT4813), possible mined bridge there. Observed a GI 6x6 loaded with troops at (CT4917). D/A and Rgt notified. 1525 Air OP reported that White 6 desired constant Air coverage but if action occurs in another sector we will divide the coverage. D/A and Rgt notified. 1535 Air OP reported B Btry posn for the nite at (CT435080). 1540 LnO 3 reported that the trucks for the 3rd Bn have arrived but the Bn has no orders to move. "Request clarification from Rgt". Rgt stated "that Capt Frazier was on his way to the 3rd Bn with their orders".1600 Bn CO returned to CP. 1630 LnO 3 reported that they would remain over nite and come in tomorrow morning. Trucks would remain there. C Btry in posn at (CT125255). Notified Rgt. 1655 D/A 3 reported that B/8 was in communication with A/64, that A/64 was in posn at (CT130405). 1800 LnO 3 reported that the Turks have not arrived there to relieve them. Notified D/A and Rgt. 1815 LnO 2 reported tomorrow's plan and that B Btry was in posn at (CT442081) and laid on CA1100. 1920 Bn Motor Officer and Maint crew returned from repairing B Btry trucks. 1940 LnO 3 reported that the Turks had arrived at the 3rd Bn and that the relief would be effective at daylight tomorrow. Notified D/A and Rgt. 2045 Lt Chastain reported that the Air Sect will have to work out of SEOUL tomorrow in order to cover the opns of the 2nd Bn 35th. 2255 Notified

Kincheon H (Bert) Bailey

LnO 3 for Leopard 6 "that upon the relief the 3rd Bn was to move to (BT791261) via my location. Have advance party and recon elements depart at first lite and rpt to Rgt CP for details". Bn radio communications worked well, however the 1st Bn is completely out of range. Weather clear and cold at end of period, trying hard to snow. Bn expended 36 rds (total to date 42,182 rds).

16 NOV 50

0735 LnO 2 requested two additional trucks. He was informed that the 14 that went with Lt Cook took every 2 and a half ton and two 6 tons that were in the area. 0810 LnO 3 reported that the Inf were moving out now and that when C Btry arrives in KAESONG, the Inf will need 4 more trucks to go on to destination. 0820 Maj Metcalfe reported from the Air strip that it was sleeting and that the plane would take off as soon as the sleeting stopped. 0915 Exec Off B Btry reported the motorized elements of the 2nd Bn at Phase Line I+8. Notified D/A and Rgt. 0915 D/A 1 notified Maj Braatz, Bn S-3 that he had been promoted to Lt Col. 0944 LnO 2 reported 2nd Bn motorized elements now at Phase Line J+5. D/a and Rgt notified. 1000 Bn CO conferred with S-3 8th FA Bn about moving into their area in KUMCHON (BT7926) when they moved out. 1015 Lt Col Wilcox, Exec Off, 8th FA Bn, reported that the 2nd Bn 27th Inf had been attacked by approx 150 NK enemy and that the results were unknown at this time. 1020 Leopard 3 reported that the Turkish relief of the 1st Bn was not yet firm. It is expected today or tomorrow and Rgt will move the 1st Bn laterally to SIBYON-NI (BT9941). 1020 Requested permission of Rgt for C Btry to remain in KAESONG over night and move to KUMCHON tomorrow. Permission was granted by Leopard 6. 1130 B Btry Exec reported leading elements of 2nd Bn at Phase line J+6. Notified D/A and Rgt. Leopard 2 reported an estimated 300 enemy vicinity of (BT9835). Requested our Ln plane take a look, also contact LnO 1. A Btry in posn at TOSON (CT1240). 1250 Ln plane in air to look at (BT9835). 1255 BC B Btry reported motorized elements of 2nd Bn at (CT483120), that the foot elements had a fire fight at (CT480110). He is sending a truck, with security, to the Bn area for rations; need one C and one A, further that they have consumed 2/3 of their C rations. Notified D/A and Rgt about the 2nd Bn. 1308 B Btry Exec reported that it has been definitely established that the enemy is in the town of KIMGOK (CT 4992115). Inf desires the town to be covered with Arty and requested Air obsn. Notified D/A and Reg. 1310 C Btry closed in KAESONG. 1312 Air OP reports weather very cloudy and visibility very poor over 1st Bn area, he will go to 2nd Bn ara and check KIMGOK. 1316 Air OP reports

1st Bn expects to move Westward to relieve the 27th Inf. 1st Bn is at (BT943370). 1321 B Btry exec reported that it wasn't too cloudy in the 2nd Bn zone and that it had stopped snowing. 1330 B Btry BC reported the 2nd Bn in a fire fight, killed 8 and captured 2; interrogation shows 50 NK enemy at (CT499115) and 150 NK enemy at (CT495153), no USA casualties. Informed D/A and Rgt. 1400 Air OP reported that the plane was icing up from the sleet and that they are returning to the strip. 1400 Bn CO departed for D/A and Rgt CPs. 1440 B Btry fired on 35 NK enemy troops in village at (CT499115) and set the village afire. 1550 LnO 2 reported that all elements of 2nd Bn will be in (CT4915) grid square by 1630. Notified D/A and Rgt. 1600 Requested that B/8 try contacting A/64. They are unable to do so. 1625 Leopard 1 requested one Off to leave on an advance party at 0730 tomorrow. 1630 Bn CO returned to CP area. 1750 D/A 3 reported that 1st Bn 24th Inf received a civilian report that 2000-6000 NK enemy troops were massing in the vicinity of (CT505365) and at (CT565369); they are going to attack CHORWON. A/159 will be firing in that vicinity. Notified Rgt and LnO 2. 2035 Capt DaPrato, Bn S-2, returned from 8th FA Bn CP in KUMCHON. 2035 Bn Med Det jeep was fired on as it passed near the CIC bldg in downtown KAESONG. Informed D/A and Rgt. 2235 Capt Fletcher, S-2 8th FA Bn, reported that the 8th FA CP and C/8 were moving out of KUMCHON at 0900 tomorrow. 2240 C Btry was alerted and directed to move to KUMCHON at 0830 tomorrow and to occupy C/8 posn there. 2255 Notified D/A 3 that the Bn minus Sv Btry would displace to KUMCHON at 0830 17 Nov. Hq Btry will have to move by echelon; all trucks are out with the Inf. 2310 D/A 1 notified us to have 1st Lt Duncan report to Div Rear Echelon as soon as possible as he is to be returned to the ZI for separation. Lt Duncan was elected to the Texas State Legislature at the 7 Nov elections. Weather clear and cold at the end of the period. 1st and 2nd Bns are now too far away for satisfactory FM radio communications. Lts Fazenbaker and Epstein assigned and joined. Lt Fazenbaker was assigned as Bn Adjutant and Lt Epstein assigned to A Btry. Bn expended 13 rds (total to date 42,193 rds)

AUTHOR'S INSERTION:

Lt Abraham Epstein, FO "Able", standing to the right of another "A" Btry FO, Lt Jackson Showalter,—see next page—, came to Korea with very little experience in firing FA, being an "ack-ack" type. So he and I went to work training in all aspects of adjusting FA. We sat together on a small hill in the btry area firing "match-box" problems, taking on simulated targets of opportunity and the all-important firing of registrations. Abe and I spent two days off-and-on hammering on the importance of accuracy in firing and sticking with that doughby commander like glue. A quick learner, realizing that men's lives would depend on his proficiency, he really tried hard to absorb all that he could. He studied our battery firing; I told him to forget those 90s, go UP15 and do his best with our 105s. Abe wound up as "A" Company's FO, 35th Infantry, commanded by Sid Berry, already a combat hero and some years later the Supe of the USMA. Abe was the only FO who met the captain's challenges, which were really nothing more than doing the job expected of a competent FO and the FA. As you will or have read, ole Abe showed how an old "ack-acker" could really cut the mustard as a topnotch Redleg. 'Nuff said. NOW BACK TO HERODOTUS"

17 NOV 50

0730 Capt DePrato left for KUMCHON with the Rgt advance party. 0730 Leopard 3 requested Ln plane over 2nd Bn area this morning. 0830 C Btry moved out of KAESONG for KUMCHON. 0830 D/A 1 notified Lt Col Braatz that he is placed on TDY with Div to report to Div G-1 this morning. Maj Metcalfe assigned duty as S-3. 0830 Air OP reported as on way to KUMCHON to look over the air strip and from there would fly over the 2nd Bn Z/R. 0845 Bn CO departed for B Btry, took an SCR 694 and operator. Will attempt CW radio communication between B Btry and the Bn CP. 0845 Notified Air OP to contact A Btry and have Lt Duncan report to the Bn CP. 0910 Bn Advance party departed for KUMCHON. 0920 LnO 2 reported that at 1500 yesterday the Ranger Co contacted 20 NK enemy, killed 12; ammo dump located at (CT490155) and that the 2nd Bn was proceeding N to (CT490155). Notified D/A and Rgt. 0950 D/A 3 requested the Inf locations and report on any enemy contact. 1020 D/A 3 requested info on TF Johnson. Had nothing current. 1030 Advance party closed in KUMCHON. 1045 D/A 3 inquired if we had received a report of the ambush of a POL convoy 16 Nov in the vicinity of (CT0505). We had not, must have been the Turks; we have no troops from our RCT in that vicinity. 1100 Leopard 6 informed us that we will move N tomorrow as his Bns cease present opns here. 1117 Air OP reported TF Johnson motorized elements at CHIPORI (CT519221), an enemy atrocity discovered at (CT503187) and an abandoned GI truck at (CT521240). Notified D/A and Rgt. 1150 D/A 3 notified us that 35th RCT will move on 18 Nov as the advance element of the Div. Details later. 1200 Div. G-2 directed that all maps of this area be turned in today. 1210 Bn CO reported that he was going to the 159 FA Bn CP and could be reached there by phone. 1242 Leopard 3 informed us that B/64 was released from attached to 2nd Bn and to move the Btry to KUMCHON. 1300 C Btry closed in posn in KUMCHON (BT 792278) 1300 Hq Btry displaced by echelon to KUMCHON. 1325 Directed A Btry to move from present posn to KUMCHON and into posn vicinity of C Btry. 1435 A Btry BC reported A Btry in posn W of the road and within 200 yds of C Btry. 1605 Leopard 1 directed that we have our advance party of 5 vehicles formed on the road 1 mile N of KUMCHON at 1845. 1645 Bn CO radioed that B Btry should close in KUMCHON in 3-4 hours. 1715 Hq Btry closed complete in KUMCHON; moved 22 miles. 1830 Maj Waddell and advance party departed. 1900 Sent radio msg to 90th FA Bn requesting that they find and reserve an area for our Sv Btry. 1950 B Btry closed in KUMCHON. 2000 Hq and C Btrys 8th FA Bn moved in and will share areas with our Hq and C Btrys. 2000 Lt Duncan, A Btry left for Div Rear and then to the ZI. The Bn is sorry to see him leave. He has been an outstanding aerial observer. 2100 Bn CO and S-3 departed for SUNCHON (YD5367). 2320 Bn CO reported that the roads to the N were very bad and to take this into consideration tomorrow on our march up. 2330 Div movement Order arrive at CP by courier from Sv Btry. 2345 BC Call; Bn Exec O gave out the details for tomorrows motor march. Lt Aultman assigned and joined. He is assigned to Hq Btry. Bn was issued shoe pacs and heavy socks Weather raining and cold at end of period. Bn expended 5 rds (total to date 42,200 rds).

18 NOV 50

0840 Sv Btry closed in posn in creek bed on S edge of KUMCHON (BT793325). 0845 LnO 3 reported 3rd Bn moving out at 0900. 0937 LnO 2 reported 2nd Bn moving. The 1st Bn was supposed to follow the 3rd but since their trucks haven't arrived the 2nd will follow the 3rd Bn, 64th FA to follow the 2nd Bn. 1045 Bn moved out under the Exec O in the order Hq, A, B, C, Sv. 1100 Column halted, 2nd Bn hvy Wpns Co halted on the road. No traffic guides are posted. 1310 Bn less Sv Btry bypassed the 2nd Bn 35th as they were halted for lunch in NAMCHOJOM (BT7245). Sv Btry will follow the 2nd Bn. The noon halt for the column was supposed to have been at 1200 for 30 minutes. 1930 Bn passed through PYONGYANG (YD4020) and NK Capital. Weather clear and cold. Bn on the road at the end of the period.

19 NOV 50

0515 Bn, less the Bn Maint Sect, closed in posn near ANJU (YD3782). Marched 161 miles. 0730 Div G-4 requested 40 trucks with drivers and assistant drivers report to 27th RCT at KUMCHON. Drivers have had little or no sleep, trucks need gas, tire repairs and maintenance. They will go regardless. Gas will be furnished at Div POL dump. 0800 Bn CO left for D/A CP and 90th FA Bn CP. 0900 Capt DaPrato, Bn S-2, and 4 Off left with 40 trucks for Div POL dump and KUMCHON. 0900 Bn S-4 notified to obtain as much POL as possible, up to 5000 gal. 1215 Bn CO returned to CP. 1530 Capt Cole, Bn Motor Off, and Bn Maint Sec closed in Bn area. 1800 Capt Driscoll, Bn S-4, reported that he had 3600 gal POL on hand. 2040 Leopard 3 informed us that the RCT was sending an advance party across the river at 0900 tomorrow and requested that we have our advance party accompany them. 2100 Capt Cole, with 2 vehicles left for SEOUL for badly needed truck parts; especially front springs for 2½ tons. Weather clear and cold at end of period.

20 NOV 50

0850 D/A 3 requested that the Bn CO report to D/A CP at 1000. 0900 CO 35th RCT visited CP and conferred with Col Hogan. 0905 Bn CO left for D/A CP. 0910 Maj Metcalfe, Bn S-3, Comm O and BC parties left on recon for posns in vicinity of YONGSAN-DONG (YE3011). 0915 Exec C Btry reported 500 rds of Russian 57mm ammo in the rear of his Btry Posn. Notified Rgt. 1240 Div G-4 directed that we have 20 trucks report to the 24th Inf Rgt CP. Bn Exec Off informed Asst G-4 that we have only sufficient transport including the 4 ton Bn Wrecker and two 6 ton ammo trucks to move the 18 howitzers; that he already had 40 of our trucks hauling the 27th Inf and that we could send no trucks at this time. 1400 Maj Andrews, S-4 35th Inf, arrived at the CP and conferred with Bn Exec regarding trucks. He was given the same information that was given to the Div Asst G-4. 1710 Alerted all Btrys except Sv to be ready to move at 0630 tomorrow. Btrys will all have to make the move in two echelons due to the shortage of trucks. 1730 S-3, Comm O and BC parties returned from recon. 1850 Bn CO returned to the CP. 2210 Div G-3 and the D/A 3 were notified of the location of our fwd posns. They are just outside of the 35th RCT bdry and in the ROK sector. 2230 C Btry revd 3 rds of small arms fire into their Btry posn. Weather clear and cold at the end of the period.

AUTHOR'S INSERTION. Following are comments made by the CO, "A" Company, 35th Infantry, Captain Sid Berry (later Lt Gen Berry):

"As Able Company's commanding officer—Able Six—I must have been a cross to bear to the commander of "A" Battery, 64th Field Artillery, who provided artillery forward observers to Able Company. I was demanding and hard to please and sent several FO's back to their home battery and demanded competent replacements.

The source of conflict was my high regard for field artillery's effectiveness in putting my infantrymen on the objective with minimum loss of life and limb and my expectation that artillery lieutenants would be as physically fit, alert, determined, reliable. and effective as infantry lieutenants. I expected artillery FO's to be an integral part of Able Company in every way—professionally and personally, and I knew that Able Company depended upon effective artillery fire to hold defensive positions and seize objectives with minimum human loss. Perhaps I expected too much of artillery FO's, most of whom were junior lieutenants with relatively little artillery experience.

Then, in November 1950, 1st Lt Abraham Epstein joined Able Company as our artillery FO. His appearance was unimpressive. Epstein was short, balding, gentle, soft-spoken. He wore thick-lensed-eye-glasses and sported a little Hitler-like mustache beneath a large nose. Our new FO looked more like a meek high school teacher than a stalwart soldier. Thankfully, I was unaware that Epstein was an experienced anti-aircraft artilleryman who had never directed artillery fire in support of infantrymen.

In fact, Abe Epstein proved to be a superb artillery forward observer who became a close friend and a valuable source of canned Mexican food that his wife, Wilma, mailed from their home in El Paso, Texas. We soon accepted Lieutenant Epstein as an integral part of Able Company, called him "Ep" and referred to him as "Able Seven", an honor we granted to no one else. To his battery commander's consternation, only Ep fully satisfied me as Able Company's artillery forward observer.

What made Abe Epstein such a effective artillery forward observer?

First, he was a friendly, intelligent, poised human being who respected others, had high personal and professional standards, and was willing to work hard at accomplishing common tasks. Second, he was an effective field artillery forward observer who understood artillery's role in supporting the infantry. worked hard at learning how he could better support the infantry, advanced his ideas to improve our combat effectiveness, was tireless in seeking more and better artillery support for Able Company, and respected and coordinated the role of all weapons available to us. Third, he pitched in to help the company effort in every way possible and never complained that 'this is not an artillery FO's job.' Finally, Lieutenant Abraham Epstein felt at home in Able Company; and as time passed and platoon leaders were evacuated as casualties he became one of the company's trusted "old-timers."

When Able Company defended, Ep had a central role in coordinating mortar and artillery defensive fires. He placed his radio jeep where best he could direct supporting fires when needed and stayed in close contact with me. I always knew where Ep was located.

When Able Company attacked, I usually followed the lead rifle platoon to sense how the battle was going and to determine when and where to to commit other rifle platoons. Ep, the mortar FOs and the company executive officer normally coordinated supporting fires from a nearby observation post. But when appropriate, Ep and radio would accompany me. For example, about 0100 hours, 28 November 1950, when a close-in Chinese attack panicked one of our rifle platoons, Ep joined the company executive officer, first sergeant, and me in turning soldiers around to retake their position, which they did. Ep later humorously wondered aloud if leading a counterattack was included in his contract as field artillery FO.

I was aware that I complicated life of the commander of "A" Battery by sending FOs back as 'unsuitable to Able Company's needs' and requesting Epstein's assignment as our permanent regular FO. I understood the battery commander's desire to rotate FOs among rifle companies, but I was selfish in wanting the best for Able Company. Convinced that effective artillery support was essential to Able Company and its soldiers, I demanded the best available artillery FO, and Lieutenant Abe Epstein had proved best for Able Company.

In December 1950 when Able company manned the regimental combat outpost along the south shore of the Imjim River, one battery commander spent several days on FO duty with us to determine just what I expected of an artillery FO. When he returned to his battery. he reassigned Ep as Able Company's artillery FO and did so routinely for the remainder of his battery command.

My Korean War combat experience as a rifle company commander who enjoyed superb artillery support directed by an outstanding artillery forward observer shaped my professional attitude for the remainder of my active military service. I had learned that effective supporting fire permits maneuver units to to accomplish their mission with minimum casualties and was convinced that in fighting ground warfare. American military professionals should spend ammunition as if we were millionaires and soldiers' lives as if we were paupers and that field artillery was the infantryman's best friend on the battlefield."

Sign noted by the author on a range at The Infantry School at Fort Benning, Georgia

THE INFANTRY MAN'S BEST FRIEND IS NOT HIS MOTHER,

————IT'S THE FIELD ARTILLERY BROTHER!————

64 FA BN IN KOREA (continued)

21 NOV 50

0630 Bn moved out under the S-3 in the order A, B, Hq, C. Howitzers and communication vehicles moved in the 1st echelon. Bn Exec Off remained behind to supervise the maintenance of the truck convoy when it returns. He is to insure that trucks are not redispatched prior to servicing, repairs, maintenance and the drivers getting fed and rested. 0730 Capt Cole, Bn Motor Off returned from SEOUL with auto parts; springs, seals, batteries, and truck canvas. 0735 Bn CO returned to area and conferred with Exec Off, S-4 and Bn Motor Off. 0915 The first echelon of the Bn closed in Btry posn areas at (YE3111). Road clearance for the movement of the 2nd echelon coordinated with the 35th Inf. 1120 D/A 3 desired ammo report as of 1200 daily, to reach D/A CP by 1600; 1st report as of 21 Nov. 1135 LnO 2 reported that he had reached the 19th Inf CP and will report when he has received any info. 1145 Capt DaPrato and truck convoy returned with 38 of the 40 trucks. 1150 LnO 2 reported that the 35th will relieve the 19th Inf in place, by Bn; in order of 1st, 2nd, 3rd. 2nd Bn will relieve 2nd 19th at 0700 22 Nov. Rgt Hq will close today, no word on 1st and 3rd Bn; their arrival depends on availability of transportation. Btry C 1st FAOB has survey control to a sound base in this valley. 1230 Leopard 3 requested the trucks that have just returned. Bn Exec Off informed him that he could not have them until they were serviced and repaired where needed, that the drivers needed the noon meal and rest prior to being dispatched again, they have driven 550 miles within the past 72 hours with little or no rest or food. Six of the trucks have broken springs and four of them must go to Ord for repair; that nearly each truck has a flat spare which must be repaired or replaced prior to going out again. The Infantry continues to abuse the Arty vehicles and they cannot understand why they are not ready to roll immediately after making 550 miles over these rough roads. 1310 Col Fisher, CO 35th Inf, arrived at the CP. He was very desirous of obtaining our trucks. The Bn Exec Off explained to him that they must be serviced, maintenance pulled, and tires repaired prior to being dispatched again. 1325 Gen Wilson, Asst

Div CG, arrived at the Bn CP and desired that the trucks be sent to the 35th Inf as soon as possible. Bn Exec Officer explained the problem as it was explained to the CO and S-3 of the 35th Inf. We are working as fast as possible to get the trucks ready to go. 1420 Col Terry, 8th FA, reported that he will occupy posns in our vicinity at 0600 22 Nov. 1435 Capt DaPrato and 26 trucks left the area for the 3rd Bn 35th Inf. The drivers, asst drivers, mechanics and Bn supply men turned out a commendable performance in the rapid repair, fueling, and minor maintenance that they were able to perform in 2 1/2 hours. 1530 All Btrys registered by Air OP on a common BP. This is the 2nd time since the start of this campaign. 1600 D/A CG desired to know what road clearance we had obtained prior to displacement? Clearance was obtained from the Corps MPs at the bridge. There was no traffic on the road at the time of our displacement. 1604 CO 25th AAAW Bn notified us that a platoon of 8 half tracks will be attached to us tomorrow; two Officers and 68 EM. Lt Jaderosa is the platoon leader. Can the 64th resupply them with POL and 50 cal ammo? Yes, we can resupply them. 1605 CO, Exec Off and Hq Btry CO 8th FA Bn arrived at CP, will remain over nite. 1625 D/A 3 notified us that the 8th FA Bn had road clearance across the bridge from 0900 to 1000 22 Nov. 1635 D/A notified us to send an agent to D/A CP to pick up the new Opns Code. 2100 Capt DaPrato returned to the area with the 26 truck convoy. 2115 C Btry notified us to have 3 FOs report to LnO 3 at 0800 22 Nov. 2135 Sent coordinates of all Btrys to D/A. 2345 Bn CO returned to the CP, brought Opns Order #15 25th Div. Weather clear and cold at end of period. Bn expended 31 rds (total to date 42,231 rds).

22 NOV 50

0800 Capt Cole, Bn Motor Officer, left by vehicle for KAESONG to get our M-4 tractor from the 21st Ord. 0915 Col Terry and Maj Farley, 8th FA CO and Exec, left our CP area. 0945 Air OP dropped message giving data on road blocks and suspected mined areas in the Z/A of the 35th RCT. 0950 LnO 2 reported that the Chinese Communist Forces had turned 27 US POWs over to the 7th Cav Rgt. 1010 Lt Guill, B Btry FO with F/35 was injured by fragments of a jeep that had struck a mine. The 64th ambulance was sent to the scene; Lt Guill, Maj Johnson CO 2nd Bn and his driver were evacuated. 1100 Lt Aultman, Hq Btry organized a mine detecting and clearing detail, left the CP area to sweep the shoulders of the road thru the Bn area, bridge bypass and exits to the Btry posns. 1115 Bn CO departed for Rgt CP. 1140 Col Dick, D/A 5, visited the CP and will stay for lunch. 1150 Platoon of Btry A 25th AAAW, with Lt Jadarosa in charge, arrived at the CP; one sect was sent to each Btry of the 64th and the 4th sect was sent to the 8th FA Bn who is reinforcing our fires. 1207 LnO 3 reported the dispositions of the 3rd Bn 35th. 1252 Capt Kruk, D/A Survey O, and the survey O of the 1st FAOB arrived at the CP with survey info and the location of the survey control point in this sector. 1310 Maj Farley, Exec O 8th FA, reported that an 8th FA jeep had struck a mine while going into the Btry posn area; requested two L-5 Ln Aircraft to evacuate the injured men. Called the Air Strip and requested the planes; alerted A Btry to block traffic on the road as soon as the planes appeared. 1320 Sv Btry displaced to KUNU-RI (YD4998)l. 1425 Notified Bn Motor Off of Bn needs in supplies and motor parts. 1430 D/A 3 requested the location of all Btrys and directions of fire of each. 1500 Lt Aultman and detail returned from clearing mines. Discovered and removed 8 USA mines 2 of which were booby trapped by US fragmentation hand grenades. It is our belief that these mines were laid by 1st Cav Div personnel. 1530 Air OP making an aerial road recon of the roads between (YE3923) to (YE2729) and from (YE4028) to (YE2839) and any interconnecting roads. 1535 Notified S-4 that the basic load for the AAAW platoon was 73,000 rds of 50 cal belted 3-3-1 and 2350 rds of 37mm HE PD. 1556 Notified DA CG that these stations Muslin, Economics, Elephant, Checkerboard, Black Dragon, Gunpowder and Scarlet interfered with our FM channels and request that the FM fequencies be changed prior to 0600 23 Nov. 1600 Air OP reported the results of his road recon. There are several cuts, blocks and suspected mined areas. 1630 Lt Keecher, USAF, and his TACP personnel arrived at the CP. 1715 LnO 2 reported that TF Dolvin had an outpost at (YE390140). Establish a NO FIRE LINE at 38 grid, do not fire to the right of it. 1745 D/A granted clearance to occupy our present posns which are just outside of the 35th RCT boundary. There is no information yet on whether we can use the 1st ROK Div MSR. 1815 Reminded LnO 2 that FOs will not accompany a patrol of less than

Company strength. 1845 LnO 2 reported the dispositions and patrol plans of the 2nd Bn 35th. 1915 Lt Andrews, C Btry, was briefed and oriented on the duties of an Arty Air Obs. He is to replace Lt Duncan, A Btry, who has returned to the ZI. 2025 D/A 3 requested the dispositions of the 35th RCT. 2045 D/A 3 informed us that the FOs with TF Dolvin are being provided by the 77th FA Bn, 1st Cav Div. 2203 D/A Comm O, Maj Draves, directed that we lay a VHF line to the 35th Inf tonite. We feel that this order is unjust and not given with the authority of the D/A CG but by a Staff Off; we have one direct line to the 35th and an alternate line to them thru the 2nd Bn 35. We reluctantly complied. 2355 D/A 3 reported that Sv Btry must move from KUNU-RI tomorrow between 0900 and 1200. Area is to be used as a Corps Class V Dump. 2400 Called D/A on FM radio but could not raise them. Weather clear and cold at end of period. Bn expended 54 rds (total to date 42,285 rds) (4 photos of TF DOLVIN)

Task Force DOLVIN

64 FA BN IN KOREA (continued)

23 NOV 50

0050 D/A 3 notified us that a Ln Plane from the 8th FA Bn will observe for TF Dolvin. Will use frequency 27.7. Notify CO 8th FA of this. Complied with. 0845 LnO 3 sent in an overlay of the 3rd Bn patrols for today. 0915 Called D/A 5 regarding order of D/A Comm O to lay another direct line to 35th. D/A 5 stated that the line was to D/A via VHF, that perhaps the Commo O exceeded his authority and that the D/A line to us would be in today. 0915 Bn Exec Off left on recon for a posn for Sv Btry. 1010 Gen Barth, D/A CG, visited the CP. 1107 LnO 2 reported that F Co patrol was on hill 325. 1135 Sv Btry displaced from KUNU-RI to posn N of the river at (YE459074). 1220 Notified CO 35th that Col Hogan and Gen Barth were enroute to his CP. 1222 LnO 3 reported on the progress of his patrols. 1230 Bn CO called from 35th CP and informed us that the Inf patrols had reached their objectives and for us to give them Air coverage on their return to our lines. 1245 Div G-4 desired Bn S-4 report to Lightning Fwd at 1600 today. 1315 Rcvd Opns O #19 and overlay. 1330 Sv Btry closed in posn. 1330 LnO 3 reported that K Co reached Ck Pt D, took one Chinese Communist PW. 1400 D/A CG ordered that there would be no preparation fires for tomorrow's attack; no saturation fires on hills to be assaulted, however this does not preclude registration. We are authorized 50 rds per gun per day. 1410 Air OP reported an estimated Co of enemy well dug in and camouflaged at (YE3832) and five new cuts in the road at (YE4026). Notified D/A and Rgt. 1425 Sent Opns O #19 and overlay to the 8th FA Bn. 1435 Requested Metros at least twice daily from D/A. 1450 LnO 3 informed us of enemy activity at (YE349169) hill 316, road block at (YE338159) occupied at nite, concrete house on hillside off the road occupied at nite. 1515 Fired the 8th FA on our Ck Pt #1. 1630 Capt Thomas, 8th FA Bn, reported to the FDC as LnO. Their mission is GS Reinf the 64th. The 64th is in DS 35th Inf. 1630. Bn had Thanksiving Dinner, including turkey with all the trimmings. The Bn cooks did a splendid job; up all night cooking the turkeys, some of which weighed 25 lbs; maintaining blackout of their kitchen areas and preparing the dinner despite the late arrival of the rations.

AUTHOR'S INSERTION:

While all these mines and minefields were being policed up and cleared, ole Ale Btry continued the march toward the YALU. With a stripped down btry—no mess, motor or supply sections—we looked for a good firing position. Spotting one that looked feasible, I stopped my jeep, dismounted and proceeded on foot to recon the area alone. With the apparent omnipresence of mines in the area, I had to ensure the safety of my men and the preservation of our direct support 105mm howitzers and ancillary equipment. I dismounted and, leaving my jeep and driver on the MSR, and I explored the area by myself. There was no point in exposing more than me to possible explosions.

At such times the ranking officer assumes the greater risk. As I measured the site to the nearest hills, I saw that the ME would be prohibitive, preventing firing at the shorter ranges. I returned to my jeep and led the battery farther to the rear where the MEs would permit safe firing at both max and min ranges we were likely to be firing at. The area I selected appeared to be free of mines.(At least I wasn't blown up!) Fighting Able went into firing position, ready for direct support missions that never came. Where was the enemy? Things were mighty quiet. Shortly after the battery was layed, a jeep carrying some Division staff officers rolled down the MSR just as we had. But BAM!! Their jeep was propelled high in the air following a sharp, loud explosion. The Division Signal Officer was killed. The driver and Division G3 were WIA. We were numb at this turn of events. Why were we not blown up? We figured we simply missed the mines or, as had happened in the past, the mines had been laid to disable tanks, set to go after activation by light vehicles such as jeeps, setting up a time delay that would detonate the mines as tanks drove over them. While waiting for the promised delicious Thanksgiving Day repast, our Bn CO, Col Hogan, paid us a visit. While we sat on some ammo boxes, discussing future operations, the colonel reached down into a shell case of a round prepared for firing and pulled out SIX powder charges! Where was Charge 7? All 105mm How rounds are packed with 7 charges, charge 7 being used to fire at maximum ranges. That means if we had to fire Ch 7, that round Col Hogan picked up at random, would have landed short, possibly killing some of our own troops! When other charges are to be fired, the gun crews pull out unneeded charges, slap the projo into the shellcase, shove the complete round in the tube, close the breech and get ready to fire. When CH7 is to be fired, no charges are rejected, and the projectile is then shoved into the shellcase. So, there was only one thing to do. We did it. All my gun crews spent most of the afternoon checking each and every round of ammo offloaded as well as those still on the trucks to insure each had all seven charges intact. The result: ALL rounds were complete. Col Hogan, with Irish luck, picked up the ONLY round in the battery that was not a complete round. As he departed, I thanked the Bn CO for his alertness.(Sure I did!). To wind up a perfect day, the battery, at 2130 hours, feasted on———cold C-rations. We all should have known better. What radio AFRS says seldom pertains to the lives of troops at the front. We were stripped down,—howitzers, prime movers, and M10 ammo trailers. Mess, motor and supply sections were well to the rear. Another case of "Hope springs eternal in the breasts of the stupid." ————But we could shoot! We had heard about the butchering of the 1st Cavalry Division at UNSAN on 1-2 December far to our north as we went thru Pyongyang, the capital of North Korea and on thru SUKCHON, across the CHONGCHONG RIVER thru KUNURI,...finally stopping at YONGBYON, south of UNSAN See Map p.162. We wondered if the enemy that had been stopped by our forces, extricating the 1st Cav, had increased its numbers. Things were mighty quiet and, getting closer to Manchuria, the temperature was getting down to minus 40, and lower. We never knew what the wind chill factor was, a new measurement to us, but that factor brought the misery of the cold to extremes. When that bitterly cold wind from China's hinterland swept across us troops, BRRR Many caught frostbite and worse, pneumonia. There was NO relief. Fingers froze to rifle butts, canteens and all metals. We had to start all vehicles every half-hour when not moving to avoid frozen engines. The flash-light batteries powering the lights on FA aiming posts so guns could be layed at night had to be removed after fire missions and kept warm under the clothing or bedrolls of cannoneers. When a fire mission was called, the cannoneers had to stumble around in the dark to replace the lights on their APs. No flashlights were permitted with the enemy close to our lines. When I layed the guns, I had to remove one hand from my mittens to manipulate the scales on the aiming circle. I had to strain to pull my fingers off the freezingly cold scale as I layed each piece. I was sure I was leaving meat on the scales or reticules. I was amazed when I found out later,—my finger prints remained distinct and unchanged. Men handling the sights at the guns (#1 men and gunners) suffered in similar fashion but they had their gunshields to protect them from the icey wind, if even that helped. It was miserable for everybody. I found out much later, maybe at Sasebo enroute home, my men would wonder how I, standing in the cold, howling wind, could pull back with my bare hands the truck tarps removed from trucks and used for ground shelter starched by the cold but protecting them from the wind to check on their condition as they tried to snuggle warm in their bedrolls on the cold, cold ground. To such queries I replied that I wondered in similar vein how they, the cannoneers, could stand sleeping atop the exposed shellcases and projos as the men rolled in their prime movers along the MSR at night when the wind blew even harder. This is how soldiers and officers bond under brutal conditions such as we endured in this Manchurian "vacationland".

BACK TO HEROTODUS:

24 NOV 50

0725 LnO 3 sent in Opns O and overlay of 3rd Bn. 1000 Attack jumped off; no preparation fired. 1035 Air OP reported road blocks at (YE351201), (YE369209) and (YE373208). Notified D/A, 8th FA and Rgt. 1045 LnO 2 reported E/35 as 3/4 of the way to their obj. 1050 Air strike on ridge vicinity of (YE3933); one tank knocked out. 1055 Maj Evans, Exec O 90th FA Bn, requested a certificate of performance on 2nd Lt Osbourne while he was a member of this Org. 1055 D/A 3 informed us that the 11th ROK Rgt on our left flank was at (YE2713), (YE2515) and (YE2313); the 12th ROK Rgt on a line from (YE1806) to (YE2110). Notified 8th FO and Rgt. 1100 FO E reported leading elements of his Co on hill 325. Notified D/A, 8th FA and Rgt. 1120 LnO 3 reported the leading elements of the 3rd Bn at (YE320140), that his posn was at (YE312123). Notified D/A, 8th FA and Rgt. 1140 8th FA Air OP reported road blocks at (YE377236), (YE382205), and (YE381233). Notified D/A, 8th FA and Rgt. 1230 D/A 3 reported enemy acft in area. Notified 8th FA And Rgt. 1235 Air strike of four F-51s on UNSAN (YE3928) received ground fire from vicinity of (YE3923). 1330 Col Dick D/A 5, visited CP and conferred with Col Hogan. 1510 Maj Waddell, Bn Comm O, departed for Rgt - will act as LnO for a few days. 1540 D/A 3 informed us that TF Dolvin was on Obj W, that possibly a Btry of the 90th FA Bn would be attached to the 64th on 25 Nov. Bn S-3 informed D/A 3 that neither the 64th or 8th FA would displace today. 1545 LnO 3 reported K Co on Obj K3. Notified D/A, 8th FA and Rgt. 1555 LnO 2 reported that we should not fire at the bridge which is our BP as it is needed by the Rgt. 1618 Air strike on bldgs along the road at (YE392214). 1640 LnO 2 reported G Co on Obj Y at 1530, F Co on Obj Z at 1600. D/A,

8th FA and Rgt notified.1645 Relayed msg from 35th RCT to CG 25th Div that contact was made with the ROKs on our left at 1510. 1700 Air Strike of four F80s on IKSONDONG (YE389252) 1700 Air OP reported that the front lines were now 1000 yds S of our BP. Notified D/A, 8th FA and Rgt. 1701 D/A 3 reported 90th FA Bn registering at (YE4026). 1900 FO G gave the dispositions of 2nd Bn. LnO 2 radio was out of order. 2100 LnO 2 reported dispositions of 2nd Bn 35th and tomorrow's plan of attack. Radio repaired and now in. Weather clear and cold at end of the period. Bn expended 67 rds (total to date 42,419 rds)

NOTE: This completes my record of the 64th FA Bn in Korea as I fell and broke an elbow on the 26th and was evacuated to Japan on the 27th.

Herman R. Smith Jr
Exec Officer, 64th FA Bn, 25th Div
Aug 49 - Nov 50

CHAPTER FOUR

To the Rear, March

On that 25th of November, things moved fast. Fighting Able started firing firing missions like these, with 1 or 2 minutes in between:

FO: Fire Mission- Coordinates 456123- Inf Company in Open, VT in Effect
FDC: Roger, Wait…….. BA, ShHE, Ch7, FQ, Df2870, Site310, 6 rds, El 1245
Fire ……….. On the Way.
FO: RT50 ADD50 Over
FDC: Roger Wait FzVT, Btry 12 Rounds, El 1250 FIRE OTW
FO: Cease Fire, End of Mission, 2 Mortars destroyed, Est 45 Casualties
***.
****
FO: FM, Coord 461155, 100 Enemy in Open, Request WP in Effect
FDC: Roger Wait….. BA, ShHE, Ch7, FQ, Df2905, El 1335
Fire…………. OTW
FO: L100, DROP 100 Over
FDC: Roger Wait………Df 3005, El 1290 FIRE OTW
FO: ADD50 FFE
FDC: Roger Wait………. ShWP, Btry 15 Rounds, El 1340 FIRE OTW
FO: Roger Wait………. CFEM, Est 100 casualties
****
****
FO: FM etc etc ————CFEM————-FM————CFEM————
————FM——on and on! After an hour or so, our firing battery

moves to a new position in the rear and fires for another hour or so. That's the way it went. When ordered to CLOSE STATION, we reloaded ammo, hooked up the prime movers, moved to the rear and resumed firing ASAP. As the Chinks got closer to our supported 35th, our firing elevations kept increasing, firing high angle,—above normal elevations. The guns were cranked up to elevations above 1000 mils.(800 mils = 45 degrees). Normally, the guns, at these elevations, like any others, would fire, recoil out of battery and counter-recoil, ready to fire again. But, remember our earlier unfilled request for RECOIL OIL SPECIAL? The tubes could not return to battery but hung loose in the cradle. Our cannoneers had to, after lowering the tube to reload, manually shove the tube back into battery. Then the tube had to cranked up to the high angle of fire. All this used time that increased the casualty rate of our defending troops. Again, our tough, reliable Cacti informed us when they were forced to pull back, enabling our 105 batteries to displace safely to the rear and maintain as continuous close fire coverage as possible. But the time was approaching when we might not be able to fire higher angles safely. Like water hoses, a point is reached when the water (projos) fall back on the "hoser". Such critical elevations with guns are determined in the firing tables. (Recall that 800 mils = 45 degrees). When firing Charge 5, for example, an elevation of 771 mils will reach 8370 yards while one of 841 reaches but 8300 yards; at Charge 7, the corresponding values are 783 mils/12330 yards and 822 mils/12300 yards. Luckily, we did not have to fire below our minimum range line; we pulled back and resumed firing at lower angles, but eventually working back up to high angle as the enemy surged ever forward. When we moved, we found the MSR was jammed packed with hundreds, maybe thousands of South Korean refugees, mad with fear trying to distance themselves from the cruel Chinese hordes. They clambered aboard my howitzers, the trails and the trucks. Drivers were hardpressed to maintain forward movement. Something had to be done. My NCOs, like most normal soldiers, had no desire to kill civilians. I had to jolt them into action.

Firing High Angle

Grabbing my rifle by the stacking swivel, I flailed at the mass, forcing them off the howitzers and trucks so we could get to our next position ASAP to maintain our direct support of the heavily engaged Cacti. The NCOs, now seeing what had to be done despite the apparent pain inflicted, helped the battery continue its march. In order to keep a steady fire support of our infantry, Bn FDC would displace one or two batteries to the rear while the 3d maintained its firing. Then, in turn, when the other battery(s) would get into position, Bn would displace other batteries. This leapfrogging technique more nearly assured continuous fire support to the Cacti. Later, higher headquarters in the frantic effort to avoid wholesale retreat before the enemy hordes, ordered that FA prime movers, as soon as they got their batteries to their new firing positions, return north and drive their supported infantry units to their new positions. Riding our trucks better enabled our doughs to distance themselves enough from the Chinks so new battle lines could be accommodated. But while the firing btry began firing in its new firing position, it became a bit nervous when its prime movers pulled out! Our constant fear, that of all field artillerymen,—running out of ammo—, was fortunately, never realized. Our heroic Service Battery shuttled back and forth between ammo supply points (ASPs) at Division and higher level ASPs as ammo resupply became ever more critical. These hardworking ammo handlers and ammo truck drivers never let us down; we never ran out of ammo. That is quite a testimonial to the efficiency and dedication of ole "Circus" Battery as we used to needle them. They actually fought at their job the way our cannoneers fought at theirs. Our direct fire support was maintained without disruption, contributing to a higher morale amongst our Cacti. During all this truly heavy firing, our battery FDC got this gruesome message from our ever-on-the-road battalion commander, LtCol Arthur H Hogan:

BAILEY! STOP FIRING! YOU'RE KILLING OUR OWN TROOPS!

You do not have to be a combat veteran to judge the effect this transmission had on Able battery's FDC crew, including me in the FDC ¾ ton, in the midst of the bitter, freezing cold. Beat, no time for rations or sack for the past 60 or so hours, firing and pulling our guns. Sgt Francis and I went numb. Finding no errors in our response to FO fire missiion requests, we were completely nonplussed. Finally, just prior to our deciding to commit hari-kari on the spot (at least the mess halls in Heaven served hot chow and we would be warm), our FDC radio crackled with this announcement:

MINEWORKER TWO ONE, THIS IS MINEWORKER ONE. DISREGARD MY LAST TRANSMISSION. THOSE WERE INCOMING ROUNDS. OUT.

Never, ever, had two soldiers ever been so blessed and relieved as Able's FDC, staring at the battery firing charts, shivering in that icey ¾ -ton. It warmed our hearts if not our bodies. We rumbled on, pulling off the MSR to fire missions as they were requested. On 27 Nov, in the bright, now comparatively warm sunshine, the FO kept saying:LOST! REPEAT RANGE!" The FDC gave "CENTER, ONE ROUND "—-but to no avail. Then, to salvage the mission, I told FDC to try WP. (WP was in dire shortage throughout the theatre at this time) This did not help. What's going on? Fighting Able is above all this! Then it hit me! We were almost surrounded; our M12A1 sights on each piece did not know this. To explain, the panoramic 'scope used in the FA to lay each piece at the correct deflection is graduated, not in full 6400 mil traverse, but in 3200 mils (180 degrees). FA gunnery experts and manufacturers could foresee no requirement for FA sights to accommodate a full 360 degrees. So when 105s are laid at base deflection 2800 mils, the typical df when first layed, they are pointed at the base point that is straight ahead of the gun tube or—-directly behind! And that is what was happening on 27 November at Able battery. So I rushed to the adjusting piece and with some help—-—-the 105 weighs a few tons—-turned the "offending" howitzer 3200 mils in the opposite direction. This time when we fired, the FO shouted in delight: "R50, ADD 50, FFE." (our initial data, except for deflection and a minor site change, must have been pretty good!) Incidentally, the well trained exec always points his aiming circle in the general direction of fire to obviate gross 3200 mil errors. Typically thorough training at TAS. I do not recall Fort Sill's ever being hit despite the thousands of rounds fired on its ranges day in and day out. Firing missions steadily——-the gun crews and I didn't sleep for three days and nights—-while the Chinese played havoc with our excruciatingly outnumbered forces. We were in the midst of one furious encounter when the adjusting FO, Lt Foss, commanded : "CEASE FIRE. YOU'RE COMING TOO CLOSE!". I quickly told him I could give him "SPLASH" 2 seconds before the rounds landed so he and his men could take cover but he replied in the negative and said he was going to try for an airstrike. When I told him.—right in the clear—ALL of Korea was under attack and the USAF would concentrate on targets deep in enemy territory and his chances for getting such strike were zero, Foss was adamant. So I had to cease fire. Lt Foss, his FO party and supported doughs were all captured. (Several years later, by the way, I ran across ex-POW Lt Foss and he said he sure wished he had listened to me. In his typically brutal Chinese captivity, he was thrown into a hole 9 feet deep where he froze and starved. He was thrown a handful of rice each day and meager amounts of water. Surviving that treatment, he stubbornly refused to repeat the Communist propaganda he was fed. He stated it was his very stubborness that kept him alive.) Having rushed thru Kuni-ri prior to the enemy's bottling up the ill-fated 2d Infantry Division, the 25th crossed the CHONGCHON RIVER. When "A" Btry crossed, an MP directed us to turn right. We barrelled down the road but finally came to a narrow portion going uphill. Checking with battalion via radio, I learned we should have turned LEFT when crossing the river. So, again, as mentioned on an earlier day, I had to do a 180 with six towed hows, 9 two-and-half tons, 3 M10 ammo trailers, two ¾ Ts and my jeep. When I passed the errant MP, I chastised him thoroughly. One problem was his gabbing with others instead of concentrating on his mission of traffic control,—most important with the Chinks riding our tail.(In all fairness, I must add that was the only such dereliction I encountered with MPs. They were often posted at lonely crossroads directing traffic in proper, safe directions. All these brave MPs faced brutal death at their post, being alone and easily overcome by a savage enemy.) We headed down the MSR to a jammed up SUNCHON. Kuni-ri, as stated earlier, was clogged with overpowering numbers of the enemy, the hapless 2d Div and now the 7th Div. The marines had pulled out and were headed for WONSAN on the east coast. The four FA battalions of the 2d Division were destroyed and those in the 7th fared little better. So one escape route was via SUNCHON. Once we reached SUNCHON, we headed west toward SUKCHON, 25 miles away. Took us 24 hours. Beat, sleepy, starving doughs marched alongside our trucks, inching along the MSR. We gave the doughboys most of what rations, cigarettes and water we had. We were all miserable but at least we Redlegs were mounted. All of a sudden, during this bedraggled trip, we saw a fighter plane bearing down on us. We crawled under our trucks and tucked ourselves in our helmets as it swooped upon us. But it suddenly banked steeply to our left, smashing into rice paddies, breaking into three parts,—nose, cockpit, and empennage, a toughly built aircraft.

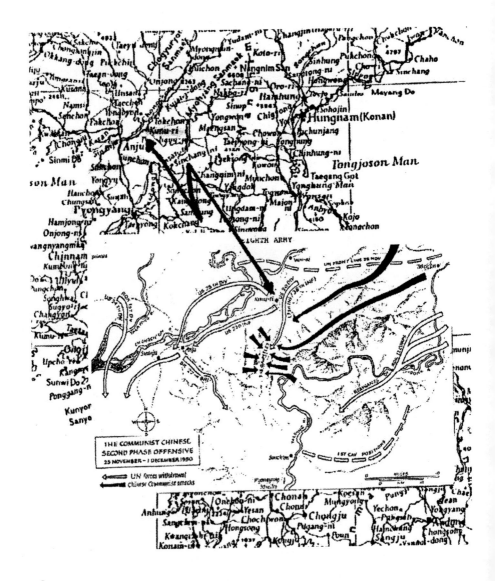

We saw it was one of our F80s and we rued the certain death of the pilot But no, 30 minutes later, here streaks by a litter jeep with a big pilot's helmet setting on the front seat with the thankfully alive pilot on the litter. We cheered as Lucky Pierre of US AIR choggied by. While bringing up this encounter with an Air Force type, I felt that coverage of USAF support in Korea in THE GRAYBEARDS magazine dated Jul-Aug 01 might be of interest to readers of this book. The USAF helped to evacuate the X Corps from NE KOREA during the perilous times in December. As reported by our "Herodotus", Major Herman Smith, the 64th FA Bn Exec, USAF TACPs(tactical air control parties) served us well during our fighting on the ground. The USAF also airlifted Eighth Army personnel, equipment and supplies. Between 1 and 4 December, Combat Command evacuated combat echelons of fighter-bomber wings from PYONGYANG and PYONGGANG airfields to SEOUL and SUWON in S KOREA. Using C46s and C47s, it flew emergency evacuations of UN forces They transported thousands of WIAs from KOREA to JAPAN. As the CCF approached SEOUL, 12 C54 Skymasters from the 61st TCG air evacuated more than 800 children from KIMPO AIRFIELD to CHEJU DO, an island off the S Korean coast. This operation was called: "OPERATION KIDLIFT" At year's end, UN Forces, as already discussed, were withdrawing into northern South KOREA, hoping to stop the Chinese and NKs before they reached PUSAN. Airlift continued to play a major role in the war, even after it became a war of little movement. In the crucial months of 1950, airlift had already demonstrated its ability to influence the outcomes of battles and, some say, shape the war itself. Without airlift, American civilians would have been captured at SEOUL in June. Perhaps the US Forces would not have been able to enter the war as early as July. Without airlift, UN Forces could not have hoped to advance as rapidly as it did from PUSAN to INCHON on into N Korea. Many more casualties would have occurred, surrounded by the Chinese as we were. In 1950 airlift contributed significantly to the success of the defense of S KOREA and to the escape of UN forces from North Korea. As much as did strategic bombing, interdiction and reconnaissance and close air support, airlift demonstrated its powerful influence on the Korean War in its critical first year, it must be noted that although all these operations were used in WWII and the Berlin Airlift, airlift itself matured in KOREA.

Not part of THE GRAYBEARD article, the information I now relate are my personal observations of close air support provided by the USAF during the fighting I saw in Korea. Good as were airlifts mentioned earlier, not so with close air support. To hit targets close to the front lines, pilots must know exactly where our troops are located. Front lines were often traced in treacherous, mountainous terrain and required the utmost attention to a detailed map to engage close-in targets. Whereas Army pilots flew almost every day including during heavy attacks and used the same maps used by all those fighting in ground units, i.e. 1:25,000 topographical maps, and became acquainted with the constant shifting of troop locations, the USAF pilot had not these important advantages. The typical USAF pilot used the same maps to spot troops as he used to navigate his jet,— aeronautical charts with very small scales. One of these charts would cover Japan and half of Korea while the Army pilots' map covered about 1/40th the area of an aeronautical chart. Sorties were flown by many USAF pilots across the entire front. Later herein, you will see the best close air support was derived from close cooperation and coordination with Army-USAF pilots working together via VHF radio. It worked so well that by General Murphy's Regulations, this type operation was scrapped. Read on.

F-82 Twin Mustang

Top Speed: 482 mph - Range: 2200 mi - Armament: 6 .50-cal machine guns, 25 5-in rockets and 4,000 lbs of bombs.
The F-82 was the last propeller-driven fighter acquired in quantity by the USAF. Its twin-fuselage design accommodated both a pilot and a pilot/navigator in order to reduce fatigue on long-range bomber missions. During the Korean Conflict, Japan-based F-82s were among the first USAF aircraft to operate over Korea. On 27 June 1950, all-weather F-82G interceptors shot down the first three North Korean airplanes destroyed by U.S. forces.

B-26B Invader

Top Speed: 322 mph - Range: 2850 mi - Cruise: 214 mph - Ceiling: 21,700 ft.
The B-26 Invader was originally designated as the A-26 Invader, a World War II attack bomber. In the Korean Conflict, B-26s served as night intruders, bombing North Korean supply lines. The Invader was removed from service in 1958, but was recalled in 1961 for use as a tactical bomber in Southeast Asia. The aging B-26s were again retired in 1964, but were resurrected, modified, and rebuilt before being returned to Southeast Asia until 1969.

KOREAN WAR 1950-1953

F-80C Shooting Star

Top Speed: 580 mph - Cruise: 437 mph - Range: 1090 mi - Ceiling: 46,800 ft. Armament: 6 .50-cal machine guns and 8 5-in rockets or 2000 lbs of bombs.
The Shooting Star was the first USAF aircraft to exceed 500 mph in level flight and the first USAF jet to be used in combat. Although designed to be a high-altitude interceptor, the F-80C was used extensively as a fighter-bomber in the Korean War, primarily for low-level rocket, bomb and napalm attacks against ground targets. On 8 November 1950, an F-80C flown by Lt. Russell J. Brown shot down a Russian-built MIG-15 in the world's first all-jet fighter air battle.

F-86 Sabre

Top Speed: 685 mph - Cruise: 540 mph - Range: 1200 mi - Ceiling: 49,000 ft. Armament: 6 .50-cal machine guns and 8 5-in rockets or 2,000 lbs of bombs.
The F-86 was the USAF's first swept wing jet fighter. Originally designed as a high-altitude day-fighter, it was later redesigned into an all-weather interceptor (F-86D), a fighter-bomber (F-86H) and a reconnaissance airplane (the little-known RF-86). In the Korean Conflict F-86As, Es and Fs engaged Russian-built MIG-15s. By the end of hostilities, they had shot down 792 MIGs at a loss of only 76 Sabres, a victory ratio of 10 to 1.

C-119 Flying Boxcar

Top Speed: 281 mph - Cruise: 186 mph - Range: 1630 mi - Ceiling: 21,580 ft – Capacity: 32,000 lbs or 62 troops.
The C-119 featured a twin-boom tail. During the Korean War, C-119s flew from Japan, airdropping supplies to United Nations ground forces. The Flying Boxcar's large capacity made it the transport of choice for dropping paratroopers during major assault and for delivering cargo into combat areas. In the 1950s C-119s ferried supplies to the Arctic for construction of the Distant Early Warning (DEW) Line radar sites.

C-47 Skytrain

Top Speed: 230 mph - Cruise: 175 mph - Range: 1600 mi - Ceiling: 24,000 ft – Capacity: 10,000 lbs or 27 troops.
One of the few U.S. aircraft to span several wars. C-47s flew in every combat area of World War II and dropped paratroopers during major invasions-Sicily, Burma and Normandy. In the Korean Conflict, C-47s hauled supplies, dropped paratroopers and evacuated the wounded. They served again as transports in Southeast Asia and modified versions used as "gunships" for attacking ground targets and as electronic reconnaissance aircraft.

C-54 Skymaster

Top Speed: 265 mph - Cruise: 245 mph - Range: 3900 mi - Ceiling: 22,000 ft – Capacity, 25,000 lbs or 50 troops.
This long-range heavy transport became famous in World War II, the Berlin Airlift and the Korean War. Originally developed for the airlines, the first batch was commandeered off the assembly line in 1942 to serve as a trans-oceanic cargo and troop transport. C-54s flew the "Hump" airlift over the Himalayas in the China-Burma-India Theater during World War II. More than 300 took part in the Berlin Airlift, supplying food and coal to West Berlin during 1948-49 in defiance of the Soviet blockade. A specially designated VC-54C became the first Presidential aircraft.

C-46 Commando

Top Speed: 245 mph - Cruise: 175 mph - Range: 1200 mi - Ceiling: 27,600 ft . In World War II, more than 3100 C-46s were used to haul cargo and personnel and to tow gliders. The aircraft gained its greatest fame by flying the treacherous "Hump" airlift; it transported war material over the Himalayas from India to China after the Japanese closed the Burma Road. In Europe, C-46s dropped paratroopers during the aerial crossing of the Rhine in March 1945. During the Korean War C-46s were used extensively to resupply combat forces and drop Army paratroopers into combat areas.

(I may have missed a few. We did the best we could. Editor)

F-82 Twin Mustang

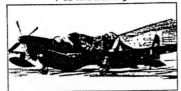

Top Speed: 482 mph - Range: 2200 mi - Armament: 6 .50-cal machine guns, 25 5-in rockets and 4,000 lbs of bombs.
The F-82 was the last propeller-driven fighter acquired in quantity by the USAF. Its twin-fuselage design accommodated both a pilot and a pilot/navigator in order to reduce fatigue on long-range bomber missions. During the Korean Conflict, Japan-based F-82s were among the first USAF aircraft to operate over Korea. On 27 June 1950, all-weather F-82G interceptors shot down the first three North Korean airplanes destroyed by U.S. forces.

B-26B Invader

Top Speed: 322 mph - Range: 2850 mi - Cruise: 214 mph - Ceiling: 21,700 ft. The B-26 Invader was originally designated as the A-26 Invader, a World War II attack bomber. In the Korean Conflict, B-26s served as night intruders, bombing North Korean supply lines. The Invader was removed from service in 1958, but was recalled in 1961 for use as a tactical bomber in Southeast Asia. The aging B-26s were again retired in 1964, but were resurrected, modified, and rebuilt before being returned to Southeast Asia until 1969.

As we wended our way into Pyongyang, we saw all manner of abandoned and destroyed equipment, e.g. an overturned Turk truck with its deceased gun crew laid out under blankets, a 155 gun burned and deserted, the same mortar ammo we had seen lying alongside the MSR when we were driving northward. We entered the North Korean capital and saw lots of new equipment such as tanks, RR cars loaded with FA and small arms ammo. I wandered around the railroad cars and noted one was crammed with 105mm WP rounds. I quickly contacted our Bn CO and begged him to let me load up as much WP as I could load on my trucks. But the colonel was concerned about possible uses higher headquarters had for this ammo. We moved out without all those precious Willy Peter rounds. Tough pill to swallow; WP was the most effective ammo we had to drive the Chinese out of their holes and caves so we could annihilate them with HE and FzVT. For the next few days we just kept marching on down the MSR through SARIWON, KAESONG, and MUNSAN-NI on the IMJIN RIVER. Fighting Able went into position on a tip of land that jutted out into the IMJIN like an infantry outpost. The CO of the 35th Infantry passed by and said: "All you people need are bayonets on your tubes". We were that far ahead of the infantry's MLR. To top it all off, a British 26-pounder FA outfit set up to our rear, fired their basic load all afternoon, then bugged to the rear while we caught all the "incoming mail"(enemy rounds). Here a few days, we did a thorough maintenance on all howitzers and other equipment. Gun crews, showing typical GI ingenuity, built small huts out of discarded ammo boxes. We looked like the Raleigh North Hilton. I fired a 105mm round with Sgt Cummins' howitzer whose projectile was inscribed in chalk: "TO WU FROM TOMMYE LOU". Thus my wife blessed the round that hopefully landed on the skull of Gen Wu, commander of the CCF or at least landed in his rice soup.

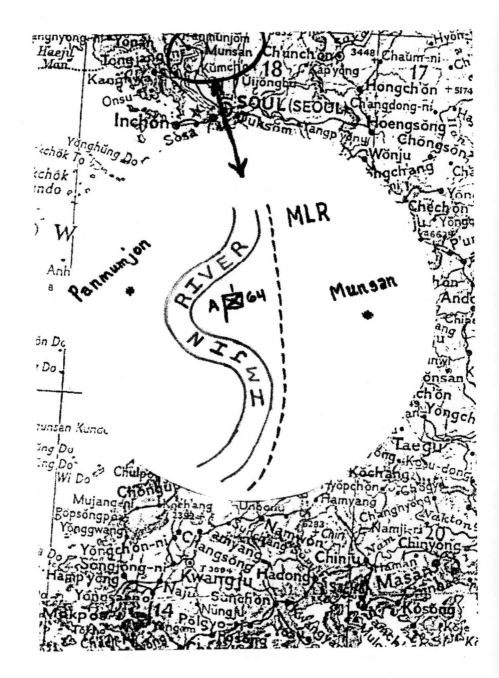

168

Raleigh North Hilton-on-the-Imjin. Admission: see Recruiting O and get free ticket!!! On next two pages, see C/FB Rufus Cole, the btry's Able FDC crew, i.e. Nisei Cpl chart op, Sgt Carl Francis, FDC Chief, and Cpl McDonald, cmptr. On 2d are Gunner Col Gentry and me, and on second photo are C/S Cummins with me ready to load one round WP for Wu.

SGT TIMMIS, ANOTHER EXAMPLE OF LANCER ABLE'S
FAULTLESSLY ATTIRED OUTSTANDING CANNONEERS

On 15 December, Eighth Army set up a defense line north of SEOUL at the Imjin. But the Chinks were pressing. We crossed the Han River on 1 January and the 64th set up just north of Kimpo Airfield. We could see the flames shooting up in the sky to the north while in the south we heard UN troops blowing up tons of ammo to prevent its capture. These events vividly pointed out the senselessness and waste in war. Kimpo was a first class airfield,——long runways that accommodated jets, well designed traffic towers and facilities for passengers, maintenance of aircraft,————the works. But Here we were blasting it all to Kingdom Come, only to rebuild it from scratch when, as all felt we would, we returned, driving the enemy back from whence he came.

Sgt Gousey, Motor Sgt

From 1-15 January, the Chinese, now numbering 500K, pushed us 50 miles south of the 38th parallel, recapturing SEOUL. This was the lowest point of our morale. Some thought of PUSAN and evac to JAPAN. But most of us felt we would turn things around. America always had, right? Well, a change in Eighth Army command did just that. Read on, patiently. The 64th left Kimpo on 2 Jan marching through SWAN-MI, IPCHANG, SINPO (10 miles SW of OSAN), PYONG-NI, TONGARI, PARAJANG, CHANG-DUNG, SUCHON and MIRUK-TONG (3 miles S of SUWON.) We pulled off the road, fired a few hours and moved on again. One of the missions I had was firing on Hill 300 near ANYANG. Col Dolvin, leading TF DOLVIN, shelled SEOUL as soon as it came within range. Using his tanks in an indirect fire role with observers giving commands to place projos on targets enhanced the role and killing power of tanks firing as artillery.

The CCF had heavily reinforced their troops ocupying Hill 300. We fired tons of ammo in support missions but could not dislodge the enemy. Later, when I departed A-64FA as explained in due course, Hill 300 was seized on 7 February with the help of a frenzied bayonet charge led by Captain Lewis Millet, CO, Co"E", 27th Infantry. For this Millet was awarded a Medal of Honor. Amazingly, the previous commander of this same rifle company, Co "E", Captain Desiderio, also won, but posthumously, an MOH. We did not need General MacArthur's planning wisdom going into Inchon this time. Another of the 25th Division's regiments dashed overland this time and secured the city. The enemy was nowhere to be seen. One GI stated: "When they bug out, they bug out BIG!" With the piers battered and broken, the city was all but destroyed. Barbed wire and twisted metal were stacked 15 feet high. By 10Feb, SEOUL was half-surrounded. Altho there was no military reason to retake SEOUL now, any more than before, it was yet a political plum to be plucked by the driving ROKs. On 11 Feb, the First ROK Division probed across the bridgeless HAN to find the city fully defended by fanatical Chinese. Came the counterattack! Just before midnight, 50,000 Chinese and NKs launched a crushing blow against the X Corps in the central mountains. They drove a large wedge in the littered road junction of HOENGSONG. They apparently hoped to make a solid breach of UN lines to outflank UN forces along the HAN. One night during this drive, the USAF had a surprise of its own. Instead of dropping rockets, bombs and napalm, they dropped over 3.5 million ROOFING NAILS on Chinese supply roads. Next day, the USAF bragged they had destroyed more trucks than ever before, like 65. They claimed they strafed columns of troops to a halt in daylight, then stopped them again at night, disrupting their supply lines. Nothing can stop the Army Air Corps, or in modern vernacular,——the USAF! As the main body of UN troops approached the HAN RIVER, the enemy pulled back into the rugged central mountains north of SEOUL to face IXth and Xth Corps. February the tenth became the most satisfying, glorious day for UN forces since the breakout from the Perimeter with the INCHON landing on 15 September 1950. The Cacti secured YONGDONGPO, across the HAN from SEOUL. This suburb was an industrial and railroad complex but was captured without the Cacti's having to fire a shot. The rubble-covered streets were awash with

Chinese and Russian hammer and sickle flags. Blackened buildings bore banners reading: "Cement the iron-clad unity of China and Korea. Make friends with your brothers who are carrying on in the people's war for independence." Of the city's normal population of 80,000, only a scant number of ragged children were on hand to wave the same dirty paper South Korean flags that they had waved when they were first liberated last September.

The grimy, tired Cacti raised a new flag over the bombed-out city square : "The 35th Infantry Welcomes You!" Now entering Kimpo, Task Force DOLVIN swept the runways and found no Chinese. The TF, consisting of a 25th Division regiment and a British Brigade found that nothing in sight was of use or had been used. Back to the ranch, with the 64th FA in position in MIRUK-TONG, Corps phoned down to the Bn with the message: "You have a man down there named BAILEY. He's wearing wings. Get his (posterior) back to the airstrip or have him turn in his wings." LtCol Williams, now battalion commander, asked me what I wanted to do. I said I would certainly miss my battery and battalion friends but I would like to get in some combat flying. So I reported to the Div Arty Air Officer, Captain Michael Magri, at the Division Airstrip on 5 February 1951. Prior to reading on to the next chapter, two matters must be addressed,——one, the careful reader will note that I have described events on the ground that I could not have known about after I joined the Div Air Section. However, to preserve continuity in my reporting, I recently enlisted the help of Jack Dodson, one of my cannoneers who had been in "A" Btry. He generously fed me pertinent info obtained thru reading newsletters of the KOREAN WAR VETERANS ASSOCIATION of Hernando County, Florida, in which he is a hard-working member,—— two, before going into my operations as a liaison pilot, I feel an explanation about how adjusting FA fire from the ground by the field artillery FO differs from that by an air observer. This facet of FA firing is covered in APPENDIX "D". As the reader has discovered in reading so far, tanks have a secondary mission of firing as artillery. For those interested, I have dwelled on this aspect of gunnery in APPENDIX"E", "Tanks as Artillery."

Able FO, Lt. Edwards

Another ABLE FO
Lt Jackson Showalter

The two sets of aiming posts for the 105mm howitzer are emplaced either to the left rear of the howitzer or the right front at 50 and 100 yards, depending on congestion of any sort around the how, e.g. natural obstructions, expected gun crew activity that will block viewing the APs with the panoramic scope, etc.

The APs will be lined up at 45 degrees to the axis of the gun tube and in line with the scope. They are painted in alternating red and white stripes for good visibility. A battery-powered night light is provided for attachment to the APs for sighting at night or under other conditions of poor visibility. Cannoneers pay close attention to the alignment of these APs at all times. The accuracy of fire is highly dependent on their accurate alignment.

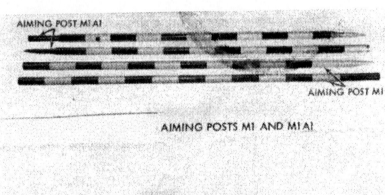

AIMING POSTS M1 AND M1A1

AIMING POST LIGHT M14

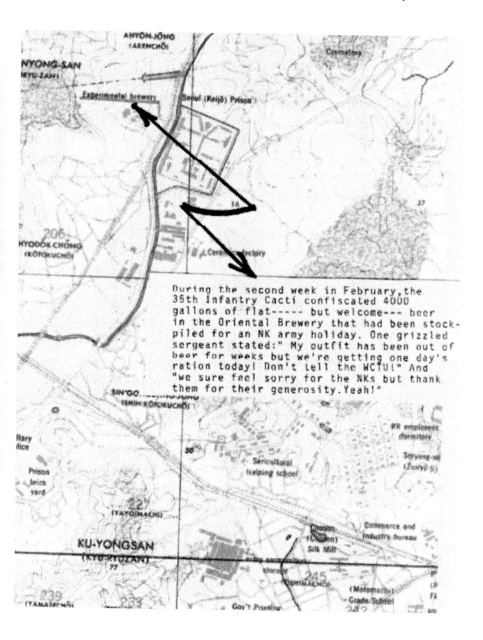

During the second week in February, the
35th Infantry Cacti confiscated 4000
gallons of flat----- but welcome--- beer
in the Oriental Brewery that had been stockpiled for an NK army holiday. One grizzled
sergeant stated:" My outfit has been out of
beer for weeks but we're getting one day's
ration today! Don't tell the WCTU!" And
"we sure feel sorry for the NKs but thank
them for their generosity.Yeah!"

Kincheon H (Bert) Bailey

THE KOREAN WAR VETERANS ASSOCIATION
NATURE COAST CHAPTER #174
of
HERNANDO COUNTY, FLORIDA

Florida Nature Coast #174 - Spring Hill, Florida   AUGUST   SEPTEMBER 2000
NEWSLETTER

182

CHAPTER FIVE

Firing from the Air

From the AOPA magazine dated Dec55, these remarks are a good way to introduce the kind of man who flew Army aircraft in Korea: "The Army has been AOPA's (Aircraft and Owners Pilot Association) most valuable ally among all armed forces aviation on its own. Be sure you understand one basic point: this is the Army, not the Air Force. These are the walking soldiers,—the artillerymen, the walking soldiers, the ground forces—but they are using aviation with such imaginative abandon that we are flabbergasted. To the Army, there's little of the old-fashioned starry-eyed aeronautical romance about airplanes and flying. A flying machine to these hard-bitten characters is just another vehicle, like a jeep, half-track, or an amphibious tank. An airplane—or any vehicle—that will make the Army more mobile is precisely what they want, and they've got no time for folklore. It's that attitude that is behind some of the controversy between the Army and Air Force which fears the Army is trying to set up an air force of its own. Army Aviation thinks, talks and acts like private flyers. As a matter of fact, they're private pilots in uniform. Their problems are much like ours. They don't buy the concept that the majority of the air space belongs to the high speed, instrument flying professionals. They insist on flying low and slow, anywhere, at any time. They want the kind of safety and reliability we want." On my brief visits to the Div Arty airstrip(s) during my primary duty with "A" battery, I became acquainted with the two 64th FA Bn pilots, Lt "Bull" Reese of California and Lt Chastain of Oklahoma. Ole "Bull" was one laid-back individual, friendly and most agreeable; he did not let much upset him. He was a baseball pro, a pitcher, and with my love of the game, we had that much in common. I never got over his indifferent outlook on life. For example, I had never even seen an L4, much less flown one. I had flown L5s,

L16s, L17s and the USAF's T-6 during instrument training at Waco AFB in Texas. In each I was given a thorough checkout before climbing into the cockpit. So one day, in between fire missions, I came to the Div strip to get some flying in. The only aircraft available at that time was our L4. I asked"Bull", lying in his sack reading a Western to check me out on the L4. He drawled: "It's like all the rest,——got a stick, rudder, needle, ball and airspeed. Just fly it like all the others. No problem." Well, I thought to myself, he's probably right but this type checkout was a new approach to me. I recalled at least one USMA classmate of mine, a USAF pilot, who died, spinning in with a "puddlejumper" L5. The old saying was: "You just barely get killed in a light aircraft." Dismissing these morbid reminders, I hustled out to the L4. The first problem I noted was the fuel gage,——a rod sticking out in front of the windshield that apparently floated in the fuel tank. There was a prop, a stick and the basic instruments needed for basic flying. After my preflight check, I clambered aboard and took off. I told myself: "If Bull can do it, so can I!" No crash on takeoff with a stiff crosswind but I did get a bit disoriented with the sameness of all the hills, dark roads, brown zig-zagging paths up thru the mountains and other rugged terrain. I knew I would have to orient myself more quickly and accurately if I wanted to adjust artillery from the air.

Flying theL4

Standing by the L5

As I flew in the general direction of north to get to the combat zone, with mountains all around, I almost got lost. At altitude, I could see no enemy. And that's the way it was. It actually took 2 or 3 days for an air observer to actually detect live targets. The enemy wore drab, dark OD uniforms hard to spot in the dark brown terrain. It seemed that the enemy popped into view from the air only when one's eyes became accustomed to detecting movement, the greatest tipoff, from the air, to enemy presence. New leadership in the Eighth Army really raised the morale of the UN. General Matthew Ridgway, an old Airborne type, took over Army on 26Dec and immediately gave an ABOUT FACE to all troops. He announced OPERATION THUNDERBOLT, a counteroffensive against the driving CCF. This operation lasted from 26Jan thru 28Feb. We have already read about some of the prevalence of the attack mode,—Hill 300, retaking SEOUL, etc. General Ridgway installed new commanders at many levels, all of whom shared his philosophy of "Take not counsel of your fears; be not timid or afraid. ATTACK! Do not constantly worry about being beaten.

CHARGE!"

Gen Ridgway, a great believer in the efficacy of field artillery, obtained an increase of 5 to 10 battalions to include 155 guns,8"hows and an increase in general support 105 and 155how battalions. Many NG units contributed to this massive increase in firepower. It was not long before we became inured to the loud crack and 30 foot sheets of flame belching forth from tubes of medium and heavy FA in "Artillery Valley" just south of the Iron Triangle, all firing in GS(general support) of Army, Corps and division units. It was awesome and restored the confidence of all UN troops. "This man wants to fight and so do we" became the battle spirit of the entire UN forces in Korea. As General Ridgway's WWII airborne troops would shout: "AIRBORNE ALL THE WAY!", we added: "TO THE YALU!" Maybe we never got that far but that had zilch to do with us fighting men. Any remote thoughts of we gung PUSAN; we gung be evacuated, exploded in thin air. Adjusting the bigger guns was a lesson in probable errors(PEs), as was adjusting a gun more accurate than the ubiquitous 105. The first time I adjusted a 155 gun, I gave the command: "DROP 200". I got back: "DROP 200, WAIT" Then: "BTRY 5 ROUNDS, FIRING FOR EFFECT!" I excitedly asked the FDC what the heck they were doing but the FDC was busy with other missions. When I got back to the airstrip, the 64th FDC clued me in. The 105 can accurately split a 100 yard bracket and enter FFE because it has a PE of about 25 yards, insuring, within mathematical limits, a bracket of 50 yards, in range, about the target. The bigger 155G, however, within its normal firing range, has PEs much greater than the 105's 25 yards. They enter FFE when they split a much larger bracket. Trying to split lesser brackets could result in as many rounds falling "out of the box" as "in." Conversely, the unbelievably accurate 8" how frequently goes into FFE not until after splitting a 10 or 20 yard bracket! It is disturbing to adjust the 8 incher and not enter FFE until splitting a 20 yard bracket, i.e. "DROP 10, FFE!" Again, the USA FA is the best in the world. It can shoot, march and communicate, putting more rounds on more targets faster than any other FA on the planet. Over hill, over dale.........!!!!! The arrival of these larger guns really befuddled the enemy. They used to take great delight in setting up their defenses just out of 105/155H range. They did not need firing tables; they just observed where the closest rounds landed and camped just beyond. Now I always got airborne at near first light when weather and assigned missions permitted.

Both are 8"H SP

189

Top is 155H SP; bottom is 8"G SP

One early morn, I spotted an enemy soldier sitting out in the open cleaning his weapon. He glanced up at me, ignoring my presence. His learning he was out of range of what we had to offer, behaving with utter nonchalance toward our great US Army, did not set well with me. I had no other target at the moment so I peeled off and dove down right at him, my L5 prop just behind his quivering butt. Chased back into his foxhole, streaking all the way, he dove headfirst into his hole, abandoning his filthy AK47. This episode made my day and ruined the morning sunshine for one swaggering enemy, an erstwhile rifleman. If only an 8" How were available! (Of course I would then wait for the diver's buddies to assemble just beyond the range of the 105, forming a worthy target.) On 11 Feb, as we went after the Chinese in SEOUL, I received my first burp gun (AK47) blast on my L5. From our strip location in SUWON, we moved on 18 Feb to a new one at KUMYANGJANG-ni. On a mission on 4 Mar, firing 4 and 5 battalions of artillery with my observer, Lt "Rock" Campbell, on hundreds of enemy retreating across the HAN RIVER, we headed home before runnng out of fuel. Now if we just had a couple of USAF tankers.......... Flying home at about 200 feet to escape twisting winds, I flew into some type of type of cabling stretching across my flight path. The cable snapped my propeller without, thank the Lord, smashing the nose section or flipping me end-over-end. Noting that dead ahead were a squad of men loading ammo aboard trucks, I resolved to avoid crashing into them. So, sans any power, I banked sharply to the right and levelled out to the left, heading for a rice paddy enbankment. With my airspeed dying out, I touched down and tried to maintain a straight course. But with a cross-wind from my left, I could not maintain control and slowly slid down the enbankment for a perfect three-point landing,——two wheels and the nose! Then, all of a sudden, "Rock" leaned over from the back seat and—kissed me! First time ever by a non-female! But he was one happy lieutenant because when the engine quit after hitting that cable, he prayed hard to escape with no broken bones or even dying. That was my first and last forced landing. Sgt Moore and Cpl Youts (later becoming an L-pilot himself) jeeped to the site in PABALMAK and determined the L4 was a total loss, unreparable. This loss actually delighted Lts Reese and Chastain. They had been trying for months to get rid of the L4 with its limited range and crude instrumentation. Photos of the illfated L4 are shown on pages following. We were issued an L19 replacement. This was quite a step up. The L19 handled well, with cabin heat,—which neither the L4 or L5 had—ample room for both occupants and greater range with its increased fuel capacity. However, as luck would have it, with summer approaching, we had no need for heat. We even had to take the doors off the 19 when we flew to avoid burning up. Ironically, when we really needed heat in the Korean winter, we had zilch. Glancing up at the L5's outside air temp gage, I read many times temperatures near and below -50 degrees. Big flying boots were of scant help.

Standing by my ill-fated L4

Bn Air Mechs Sgt Moore and Cpl Youts

L19 taxiing in the mud

I would land the L5 with little feeling in my feet, kicking the rudders right and left to maintain direction on short dirt runways. There was a big difference flying the L5 and the L19. The L5 Stinson Voyager had a heavy empennage(tail section). On takeoffs, one instinctively shoved the stick forward immediately to lift that big tail off the runway. As soon as you poured the coal to the L19 on takeoff, it leaped off the runway, whereas you had to practically jerk the L5 off the runway. The mechanics loved us as we soon learned after landing to taxi to our parking slot amongst many gas cans and mechanics' tool kits, give the L5 full throttle and lift that heavy tail over all the cans and settle down, parked perpendicular to the runway, ready for maintenance and the next mission. Do that to any other aircraft and you shove the nose into the ground. But not with that heavy L5 tail! With OPERATION THUNDERBOLT extending from 25Jan thru 20 Feb, and OPERATION KILLER lasting from 21Feb to 7Mar, we drove the CCF back across the HAN and kept up the pursuit. Got some most lucrative targets, killing in excess of 200 Chinese on one mission. With so many targets and attack missions, the air space got congested at times. Early one morning I was intently adjusting fire on a mountaintop target. The way I operated was to give my fire command to the FDC and immediately turn full-circle to position myself to see the next round. This time, as I banked my L5, I was staring right into the eyeballs of a marine pilot in his F4U Corsair about 100 feet below me! I'm sure he was as agitated as I and that we both offered prayer to that Master Architect of the Universe. Spared again. It is impossible for all arms to transmit timely reports on exactly where people are in the sky—and on the ground for that matter—and advise where their bombs, rounds, or other niceties are dropping or landing. Another example similar to this last hairy circumstance occurred when I was asked to check cordinates 456122. Flying there on the deck to comply, my L5 rocked sideways. fore and aft, as I was buffeted by concentrations fired by several FA battalions. Made one feel unappreciated or maybe even unwanted. I saw the same thing happen to one of our Turk pilots. Luckily I was not too close to that concentration. We commiserated on our joint miseries after landing at our airstrip. A few times I returned to our strip, only to encounter heavy ground fog that rendered any landing impossible. So I would radio Bn and request they seal off a length of road in their area so I could land. Being near lunchtime, I hoped for an invite to break bread with the Bn staff. With the troops clearing the road running thru Bn Hq, I would land and partake of a fine repast with my fellow officers in the 64th. While we ate and disscussed the progress of the war and when we might rotate home, troops were flocking about my L5, amazed that such frail craft could destroy so many of the enemy. They could now relate to us since they had heard fire missions being conducted over our radios. Those working in FDC were, of course, intimately familiar with the routine of conducting fire missions via liaison aircraft communications. So we all enjoyed these happy interludes and, thanks to the savoir faire of our dedicated troops in Bn Hq, I never had to worry about landing or taking off strips improvised by them. Such affairs as these tied all us troops together, and helped to relieve some of the strain of daily combat. Changing the subject to USAF aircraft, I must comment on our dealings with them. Early on, when four USAF jets, a sortie I believe, were unable to release their ordnance,——targets socked in or otherwise no longer feasible to attack—they, as they flew back to their home base, would contact us Army types via our VHF radios for local target info. I would identify one or more juicy targets either beyond the range of our artillery or perhaps bigger than what we could handle. When the jets identified my target, they radioed: "OK, Army, get out of the way, we're coming in!" I would comply with alacrity and watch the target disappear in clouds of smoke and dust. The jets were happy because they would not have to jettison their bombs out in the boonies somewhere. We, as a team, went thru such drills from time to time, but the USAF hiked their commo up to UHF. We did not have UHF in our aircraft. So, during the few times thereafter when jets wanted targets, they would wag their wings, I would return the greeting and dive on a juicy target, wag my wings back as I climbed up and out. It was great to have the USAF help us annihilate our mutual enemy. Captain Michael Magri was the Div Arty Air Officer at the Division strip. He coordinated missions among us FA battalion pilots. We were an amiable group and enjoyed such pleasantries as warm cots beneath pyramidal tents, three hot meals a day and time at night to do some reading, meditation, plan next day's activities and bitch about slow rotation. We Div Arty types flew almost all the C21 missions, those over the enemy, whom we delightedly destroyed. Div pilots flew most of the C27 or administrative missions involving flying personnel to and from the rear, recon for S2-G2 staffs and others. From photos on the next page, note the happy poses of Captain Mike's motley crew, i.e. both types of pilots. We FA pilots conducted fire missions from the air. As stated earlier, the FO on the ground had limited vision, compared with the L-pilot. We would spot large concentrations of troops or materiel and the Bn FDC and those from higher levels like Division, Corps or Army could give us beaucoup de battalions to adjust on these more lucrative targets. This advantage of greater firepower enabled us pilots to amass multiple battalions. Div Arty had two Turkish pilots in its Air Section. I struck up a friendship with one, Sam Sabunju. We visted a Turk firing btry. The Turk BC was constantly fanned by his orderly as the BC welcomed us to his tent.

Captain Mike Magri, DivArtyAirO

Lts Chastain and Reese w/AO Capt Hoffman

Clowns Jim Lawrence and "Bull" Reese

Lt Jim Lawrence, 8th FA Bn pilot

Reminded me of Persian satraps I had read about. The btry area was well policed and there was evidence of firm discipline. The Chinese dodged these Turks whenever they could. When Turks ran out of ammo, no problem. They would stand fast and throw large rocks. I saw such acts several times during missions. One time I passed on to Sam that his Turkish brigade had received 200 new replacements. Sam said: "Yah,200 new bayonets!" The vets traded their dull bayonets with those of the new arrivals. Again, I say, those Turks were tough and a great body to have on our side. As seen on next photo, Sam and I renewed our friendship years later in Germany. Receiving a letter recently from Andrew Tomaro, one of our top cannoneers, now retired in Pahrump, NV, relating a story about when he served with "C" Battery. He almost killed a Turk ally in combat. It seems matters got a bit out of control one night around the btry area and Andy thought a Turk soldier penetrating the battery perimeter was Chinese. Andy jabbed his bayonet into him but stopped short when he saw he was a member of the adjacent Turkish Brigade. The Turk luckily realized it was an unfortunate mistake and both clasped hands in friendship as staunch allies. The wound was not serious; a tragedy was thus happily averted. As stated, Turks were one tough outfit. To understand how they came to be so proficient working with US troops in combat, I have added an an APPENDIX "F" that deals with the joint schooling and training shared by our troops.

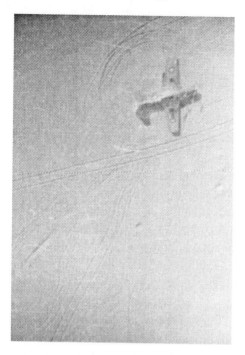

Grounded P51 South African AF

Sam Sabunju and I reuniting in Germany

The data is taken from a fine writeup by Gen (then Col) Thomas E de Shazo, an old, well-known Redleg, appearing in an issue of the old classic: THE FIELD ARTILLERY JOURNAL.

On 12 March, I flew one mission for 3hrs 5min. The fuel capacity for the L5 is 3hrs and 30min. That's cutting it pretty close. It was too easy when firing 4, 5 or 6 battalions to lose track of time and such matters as how much fuel is left. On several other targets, watching my fuel more closely, I noted the target on which I was adjusting sometimes became funtime for a Chinese outfit on an adjacent hill, who strained their heads and eyeballs to watch the show, their buddies getting killed. This aggravated me even though they were just more of the enemy. So after I commanded "DROP 50, FFE!" and reporting the target destroyed, I gave the command: "L1000, REPEAT RANGE, FFE!" That target, located exactly 1000 yards west of the first, aided in the destruction of the second, joy-watching"target". From 28Mar to 5Apr, I flew 55 hours. For these 9 days that's an average of 6 hours per day. This shows the intensity of the fighting undergone by the troops in the field and the splendid support they were getting from the the proverbial GREATEST KILLERS ON THE BATTLEFIELD, THE FIELD ARTILLERY! Flying 28 out of the 31 days in March, my daily average was 4 hours 20min. These figures, developed thru bad weather when flying was limited, point up the dedication of Div Arty's Air Section. Examples of the days of maximum hours I flew were (6h10m) on 9 and 15Mar, (9h20m) on 28Mar and (6+35m) on 30Mar. Remember, these were the days of OPERATION RIPPER resulting in the recapture of SEOUL. April was a big month for battles. On 5-15 Apr, OPERATION RUGGED secured LINE KANSAS (the 38th parallel). The CCF were heavily fortified in the "IRON TRIANGLE" formed by the towns of KUMWHA, CHORWON, and PYONGGANG.(See map on page 228). On 5 April, after 2 or 3 days of trying to locate a 120mm mortar that had been harassing our 35th Cacti, I was flying my mission and noted a flutter of leaves below. Unlike an artillery round, a mortar round is noiseless as it leaves the tube with a small pop. One never knows such round has been fired until in lands. With no noise what else could cause that flutter but a mortar? I told my observer, TJ Sexton, to get some fire on that mortar, probably the one we were looking for. His crass reply,"Aw, there ain't nothing down there"really ticked me off. With my experience adjusting from the air and his limited knowledge of aerial observation, there was no way I was going to miss this opportunity to help our doughs get that mortar.

Bridge crossing the PUKHAN
at SOKCHONG-NI to CHINCHO
(MASOGU-RI) NW of YANGYONG

Rolling over in a steep bank, I dived toward the target, killing my airspeed enough to dump flaps. Slow flying over the expected target so even Sexton could see it, I saw the startled crew from an altitude of less than 60 feet. Immediately lifting flaps, and so losing a bit of altitude, I climbed up out of there. The NKs fired 3 or 4 bursts, leading me like duckhunters. That is what saved me, their leading me along the predicted path of my climbout. When flaps are raised, an aircraft loses altitude. So their rounds missed me but not by much. The first hit my engine, the second bent the aileron turnbuckle one foot above my skull, bending the turnbuckle 45 degrees and the third went between me and Sexton. (See photo on second page following). Hollering to Sexton to get some fire on that "ain't none" mortar, I looked back; he was out of it, completely useless. I grabbed his map and called in a fire mission, requesting: "ALL AVAILABLE" on a 120mm mortar, its crew and protecting infantry. Heavy weapons were priceless to the Chinese; they would protect them at all costs. And the 120 was one of their deadliest weapons. The battalion FDCs all knew that and gave me all I wanted and more. I adjusted 4 battalions on that conglomeration for about 45 minutes. The 120mm mortar and rifle company were destroyed, but completely. My commands ran something like these:

"CLAMSHELL RIGHT 50, DROP 50, FFE!" "BOXCAR, LEFT 100. DROP 100" "POWERHOUSE. ADD 200" "CLAMSHELL, RIGHT 100, ADD 100" winding up with coupe de gras like these: "CLAMSHELL, REPEAT RANGE, REPEAT FFE" "BOXCAR, ADD 50, FFE" "POWERHOUSE, DROP 100" Then "ADD 50, FFE" "CLAMSHELL, LEFT 50, DROP 50, FFE" Each callsign was that of an FA Bn, including, as I recall, 2 105 bns and 2 155s which included some Corps artillery. Overkill? No way. As I started firing I could see the woods crawling with Chinese and NKs. Firing up and down a river next to the mortar brought out more than 150 enemy who never saw the light of another day. In the last week of April, as we maintained steady pressure on the fleeing enemy, we set up our airstrip on a SEOUL UNIVERSITY racetrack. We felt as tho we should be wearing cleats as we took off and landed. As we flew in and out of this strip, we could see the great damage done to SEOUL, including its university. See photos on the second page following. Some time prior to this, when we operated off an airfield in YONGDUNGPO, across the HAN from SEOUL, we shared the field one day with elements of the Fifth Air Force. The runway was too short for F51s. Apparently, time-to-target and fuel requirements were a problem in striking juicy targets deep in NORTH KOREA. One hundred F51s were parked at the airfield one day. On the next day at noon, 100 of them, heavily armed, roared down the short runway, The pilots would yank the stick back, bouncing up to get airborne, repeating if necessary until clearing the runway.

Aiileron turnbuckle hit by AK 47 during dive on mortar.
Fingers point out holes made in canopy.

HOURS I FLEW DURING APRIL				
1Apr	5h10m	15Apr	5h15m	
2	5	15	17	6	5
3	5	50	18	5	30
6	5	55	20	6	25
7	5	10	21	6	31
8	5	05	22	5	40
9	5	10	23	5	10

The **SEOUL UNIVERSITY** racetrack shown above was used during the last week in April. At the left below is shown the capitol building. At the right is a rare shot I took of bomb craters made in the outfield of the university's ballpark. Looks like 5 runs (passes), 5 hits and one error (missed home plate!)

Most of those who did this succeeded in getting airborne. All went well until the last pilot, #100,—he didn't make it. He crashed at the end of the runway. We rushed to his aid, his aircraft smoldering, and reached him as he fumbled for a cigarette. We lit one for him as he trembled. He was certainly glad to be alive. But it was quite a show, 100 F51s tearing down that short runway and 99 of them setting sail for their rendezvous point. OPERATION DAUNTLESS secured Phase Line UTAH. General Ridgway was certainly invigorating his Army. Then came a real shocker——General-of-the-Armies Douglas MacArthur was summarily dismissed from command of the Far East Command. General Ridgway learned of this most surprising command change late on 11Apr51. The next day he flew to Tokyo, where he found General MacArthur amazed by the President's action in relieving him. He did not, however, appear bitter or resentful. He briefed Ridgway on some of the key problems of the command, then wished Ridgway the best in his new assignment. I remember well when over 20 helicopters dropped in on our airstrip as General Ridgway went on a tour of all the units he could to simmer things down and introduce himself as the new commander of the Far East Command. The loss of the hero of WWII and other wars, General MacArthur, was a shock but we all respected his combat-hardened successor. General Ridgway had already made an impact on us all for his brilliant offensive attitude and his instilling in us all a fervor for winning this cotton-picking war. General Ridgway did not take command immediately but returned to Korea and directed Eighth Army operations until Gen. James Van Fleet, scheduled to arrive on 14Apr, could take charge. In winding up affairs on 13Apr, Ridgway finalized plans developed during his term of command for rotating Army troops. An eligible soldier could leave Korea only after his replacement joined his unit. More than 70,000 troops were already eligible. Since replacements exceeded losses at this time by more than 50%, Ridgway wanted the rotation begun before the end of April. Three defense lines were established: DELTA, the first line in the south, stretched from coast to coast, centering on and running almost due east and west from CHUNCHON. NEVADA, the deepest line, also ran from coast to coast, following the lowest bank of the HAN RIVER in the west, then sloping northeastward to the YANGYANG area.

F-51s

8"G Towed

155G Towed

8"H Towed

YULTO, on Han R across from SEOUL, on which Lt "Rock" Campbell and I fired tons of VT and WP — getting beaucoup de unfriendly rifle and MG fire right back. We obliterated them, yea man !!

WP on Chinks in hills on N bank of
HAN R just E of intersection of HAN
and PUKHAN Rivers

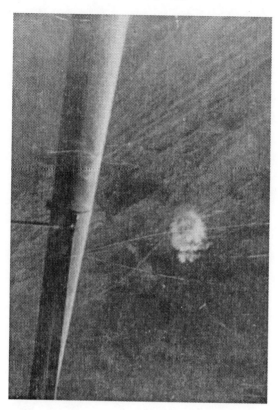

WP on hill E of CHANGO-RI

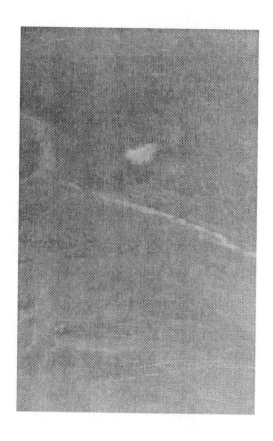

Gen Matthew B Ridgway

The defense of Seoul, if successful, would eliminate the need for a withdrawal to NEVADA in the west. Line GOLDEN looped above the city from a point on the HAN six miles west of the city to a juncture with NEVADA near the town of YONGPYONG to the east. But the war pressed on. The 22d-29th of April saw the CCF's First Spring Offensive. It included the largest single battle of the war. On 21 Apr, at dusk, I flew over three large hills forming a "W", each showing a massing of about 1500 men for a total of an estimated Chinese regiment. I excitedly reported the locations, hoping for an airstrike or heavy Corps Artillery massed fires. It was distinctly eerie. Nobody fired at me. Div Arty and Division did not appear surprised. Apparently their intelligence sources had informed them of this massive buildup. I was "out of the loop" but happy the huge assembly did not consider me a worthwhile target. They were after much bigger game. That was the largest-sized target I had ever called in to any FDC. 27 Chinese divisions pushed forward the next day. This mammoth onslaught was met with renewed spirit and confidence by UN forces. While flying a mission during this time, my observer was reluctant to fire on what appeared to be wounded carried on stretchers along a mountain trail. They appeared to me to be carrying a much heavier load than pintsized Chinese wounded along that trail. Using my mike, I called in a fire mission. With the second round in adjustment I hit one of the stretchers. Wounded jumping up and crawling or running?? On the contrary,—-the stretcher EXPLODED. Those supposed medics were toting AMMO! My observer finished the mission while I looked for more stretchers.

Shown below is the Army Mutual Aid Association 1951 calendar notebook I carried in my sweatstained left breast pocket while touring Korea in '51. Only God knows what happened to my 1950 book. At the right is the inside front cover. The dates encircled are those on which I received letters from my devoted wife. As has been said a thousand times: "There is no greater thrill in combat than MAIL CALL." (There was no "Dear John" from my beauty, thank God.) In mid-April, I was really surprised to see an old friend of mine who appeared at the airstrip. He and I attended the same L-Pilot class. He, Lew Neville, had not yet gotten a flying slot so I grabbed him as my observer. We, at the first chance, leaped off into the wild blue yonder. The best target were two companies of infantry marching down a mountain pass in parade-like formation and parallel to our front lines. This plus their being at our maximum FA range dictated our flying on the enemy side of the front.

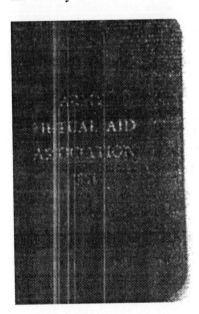
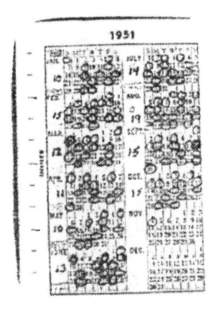

CENTER ONE ROUND, WP,
ALONG E BANK OF
THE PUKHAN

REPEAT FFE

L100, RR, REPEAT FFE

LT LEW NEVILLE

The only problem was in case of a forced landing we would be at the mercy of the enemy. But we would have less chance of being hit by our own FA. During our adjustment of two battalions on the columns, the NKs panicked, abandoning their parade precision. We were really clobbering them. Wildly tossing aside their rifles and bayonets they slid down the mountain to escape our projos——HE with Fuze VT and WP. However, our firing was all of a sudden forgotten,—our engine was sputtering! I had forgotten to switch tanks. In missions over one hour, gas tanks must be switched. If the belly tank gets hit, switch to the wing tanks, or vice versa. Relying on but one tank can, as now noted, be frustrating or worse! Now Lew and I had gone to school together; both knew our stuff. But I was more recently in the act. So my left hand was wrapped around the fuel tank switch to my left rear one millisecond before Lew's hand squeezed the same switch. Lucky we, the engine began purring like a kitten and we both traded mikes furiously to mass those two, now three, FA battalions on the panicstricken Chinks. Wisely, we ceased firing before we coughed up our last drop of gas, and landed safely back on the Division strip. As an old Fort Sill gunnery instructor would say: "Mission accomplished in a satisfactory manner." This latest CCF drive evoked a maximum response from all resources but, as ever, none delivered more iron on enemy skulls than the Greatest Killer on the Battlefield—the ubiquitous, ever-alert Redlegged Field Artillery. And we Army aviators guided many of the projectiles onto juicy targets. We Div Arty types flew lots of missions. My contribution, for example, for the month of April was flying 28 of the 31 flyable days in the month, totalling 136 hrs 03 min, averaging 4hrs 20 min per day. The maximum hours I flew during April have already been chronicled. During 17-22 May, the CCF launched its 2d Spring Offensive. Also, during the period 20May-8 Jun, Operation DETONATE was kicked off to regain LINE KANSAS. On the 18th we were being pushed back and I flew well ahead of our lines, beyond the range of our artillery, to locate targets for other means of attack. I flew into a valley with three surrounding hills and met several bursts that appeared to be from cal .50 type MGs. As these rounds zinged by my L19, discernible by tracers as well as sharp cracks, I climbed up in a hurry and called in a fire mission in desperation knowing they were no doubt out of range of our FA. So I also requested an airstrike since the Chinese heavily guarded their few heavy weapons. The next day, 19 May, I flew back out to this area and saw little evidence of any air attack having been made. I called Div Arty FDC and, somewhat heatedly, asked: "How come no airstrike?" Their reply: "Air-strikes were for other targets." I then replied: "Roger. I will not risk my life getting targets for you if you are not going to engage them, OUT!" Immediately I was called: "SHOVEL ONE SIX, report to Div Arty S3 when your mission is over. OUT!" Wow, I was in for it now! And where the devil was the Div Arty FDC? I contacted another pilot on another frequency and he gave me usable data. I landed on a road near the FDC and entered the D/A FDC. A tall, lean colonel came over to me, Colonel Cathrae, and asked if I knew how my terse remark sounded over the fire command channel with all his personnel listening? I replied I had not thought about that. I just wanted to destroy a target that could endanger our troops. The colonel then said he and everybody else appreciated my efforts but I must yet adhere to established military discipline. I told Colonel Cathrae I appreciated his handling of this matter and would confine my remarks to fire commands in the future. We both saluted and I returned to my L19 with a great sigh of relief and a determination to abide by what I had just said. On the 24th the airstrip moved to KWANGJU and on the 28th to CHONGSON. This Second CCF Offensive was nothing like the first. Gen Ridgway's efforts were paying off. Morale was high and we had hopes of crushing the enemy and driving them back across the YALU from whence they crept. But matters were out of the hands of battlefield commanders. Politicians, per usual, were to rule the roost. For the month of May, Div Arty kept up a blistering attack on all targets discovered. Bn was visited one day by several USN pilots working in the FSCC aboard the USS El Dorado off the nearby Korean coast. Their work being aboard ship, they could not fly and thus were losing flight pay. So the 64th FA sent them to our airstrip to rack up C21 flying time with our "puddlejumpers". This was a lot of fun for us. We pilots would fly back-seat with them and let them try to conduct some fire missions. One frantically called to get some fire on "all those Chinese squatting down in their foxholes with fixed bayonets!" I tactfully pointed out to the USN types that what they saw were C-ration cans reflecting the sunlight. (Commanders were forever chewing out GIs for not disposing of these cans properly.) But the Navy and Marine pilots had a ball, appreciating our help and inviting us to their flagship, the USS El Dorado. We spent the night aboard their ship and what a treat! We dined in a luxurious messhall, replete with juicy steak. mashed potatoes, salad and ICE CREAM. After this reenlistment chow, fancily dressed stewards passed out aromatic cigars and poured us some Stateside whiskey. Wow! We were ecstatic! Next,— real, live hot showers and warm, comfortable bunks added to our supreme enjoyment. The only major problem was we kept bumping our heads on the low passageways. Should have kept our helmets. We boarded a motor launch next morning for shore, rewired for another six months of frontline combat in the boonies. We all rejoiced in this bit of interservice camaraderie and roundly thanked our gracious hosts.

TWO OF THE PILOTS STANDING WITH ME AT THE DIVARTY STRIP: COLONEL NEWLANDS, USMC, AND CAPTAIN ECCLEFIELD, USN

In the month of May, I flew 29 days of a total of 31 in the month. Total hours were 122 plus 50 minutes for an average 5 hours 15 minutes per day with the heaviest days listed below:

3May 5h20m	18May	5h00m	
6	5h10m	19	6h45m
9	5h25m		

On 3-12 Jun, Operation PILEDRIVER was initiated to secure LINE WYOMING and the "Iron Triangle" shown on the following maps. On 1Jun the Div Airstrip was moved to WONGTON. Once I

started recording the number of bullet holes I picked up on flying missions, I counted 21. But there were more. I was just happy to avoid the Purple Heart, especially those posthumous issues. The Chinese I understood were under under orders not to fire on our liaison aircraft. They found out that when they did, our retaliation was certain and deadly. But I found they would fire on us as we flew away from them, on another mission or just establishing a new flight path, their figuring we would not be able to pinpoint their position. In any case, Div Arty pilots flew at lower altitudes than the other pilots and so picked up more lead. One of our pilots was killed while covering the movement of a task force of our 89th Tank Bn. He was hit by a round ricocheting off a rocky hilltop. On the 8th, I was the beneficiary of two large holes in the tail of my L19. These were not rounds from AK47s but from weapons more like our Cal.50s.

TOWN OF KUMWHA
In August or July, when I
returned as BC"A", I
raced my hows over the
the bridge shown, one by
one at top speed, to a-
void enemy interdiction
fire, to take up firing
psn on N side of river

AIRSTRIKE ON KUMWHA

HILL 604

THE IRON TRIANGLE
Kumwha, Chorwon, Pyonggang

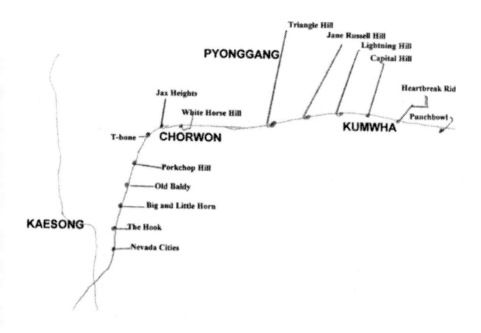

Cal..50 AA batteries fighting with infantry--
not many air attacks for normal AA msns

Luckily, none of the many controls in the L19's tail was severed. If they had been, control of the aircraft is wellnigh hopeless. Then, on the 15th, a Sunday as I recall, my L19 was blasted by a really big 'un. Must have been the size of one of our 37mm AT guns. But, lucky again, the large round hit no cables. I landed at a forward strip to check the damage. The Div Arty XO, Colonel Dick, was there on another flight. He looked at the damage and just shook his head as if to say: "What fools these L-pilots be!" Overall, June was a a good month for me. I went on R&R to FUKUOKA, Japan, 13-19 Jun. That was the first stop; I bailed out to maximize my free R&R time. Others flew on to Tokyo for bigger things, but wasting more time flying. I was in a hot tub as they drooled over the big metropolis, ichiban TOKYO. But not for me. See us happy warriors as we assembled at our chosen spots of delight on the next page. I ascertained that FUKUOKA, but a small village in the hinterlands of Japan, was yet the Headquarters of the Fifth Air Force! Ran up a small fortune, at $20 per three minutes, talking with my beloved in San Antonio. Man, it was pure torture to hang up! Enjoyed at least a dozen more hot baths, outstanding rations at the swank USAF headquarters O-Club. While all the Air Force officers wore their dress or regular uniforms to the club, I was dressed in the fatigues I wore in Korea. Quite a contrast! But everyone was nice to me and I really pigged out out at the supper table. The little Japanese waitresses giggled as I ordered juicy steak after juicy steak, and wallowed in quarts of ice cream for dessert as if these were my last meals. The visit was all too short.

The photo on next page shows some of those who spent their R&R in Tokyo. Leftmost is Lt. Jackson Showalter, "A" Btry FO, Lt Hoffman of the 1st Ob and Capt Bonnell, 1st Bn, 35th. Insert shows me in FUKUOKA, clutching the telephone bill for my phonecall to my wife on hour earlier.

As I clambered aboard that C47 for Korea, I regaled my self in pleasant nostalgia and thought of a dozen places I would rather be. But back in full swing the next day, 20Jun, I was trying to adjust 105mm rounds on a target on the reverse slope of a mountain harboring at least a platoon of Chinese. Try as I might, I could not adjust on the target. When rounds hit the top of the mountain and I increased range, those rounds flew right on over those Chinks. I could not adjust from the other side of the mountain without becoming THEIR target. So, in utter frustration, I banked my L19 close to the enemy and fired, not 105s, but my cal.45 pistol. I reported to FDC: "SEVEN ROUNDS CAL.45 EXPENDED ON TARGET. ZERO CASUALTIES BUT LOTS OF HEADACHES. OUT." This transmission was, per usual, overheard by doughs listening to the FO's radio. Months later, rotating home, some Cactis heard I was that air pistol shooter and I was kidded by all. On another day, when bad weather precluded flying normal fire support missions, I took off with the ceiling under 1500 feet, enough "vis" to fly safely around the lower mountains. There were times when such flights could help stalled columns, roadblocks, and knocked out bridges ahead. I spotted our infantry carrying wounded down a trail to medical rescue. I could not establish commo, their not being my directsupported troops. I flew around them several times in rolling clouds and they waved. I waved back, not seeing any signs of attack or emergency, just what appeared routine evac of wounded or sick. So, wagging my wings, I headed for the ranch. I learned months later, rotating home at SASEBO in JAPAN, these troops were heavily engaged on the other side of the mountain from where I flew and they were carrying out the wounded on the side I was flying around. But I was told I yet saved the day because the Chinese broke off their attack, expecting me to bring down our deadly artillery. Little did I realize at the time how my routine excursion on a cloudy day was so beneficial, actually lifesaving, to our beleagered doughs engaged in some fierce fighting. The Good Lord looked after us all!

When the 3d Infantry Divison arrived in Korea, my brother-in-law, then Captain Wallace C Magathan, Jr, (pure Scotch), USMA June'43, was S2 of the 10th FA Bn. Our Divisions shared the same airstrip. So I got to fly Wallace about the target area; he got a good feel for the terrain and the problems our troops faced. He eventually moved up to the G2 Section, spending much of the time at the front collecting intelligence on enemy activities. He went right up the ladder after Korea, earning a PhD at Princeton University, commanding the 553d FA Bn (8"H) at Fort Sill, progressive assignments at high level staffs and finally retiring as a Brigadier General. He and my sister Margaret(others call her "Peggy") now live in Charleston, SC, where, in 2001, we all celebrated Wallace's 80th birthday. My old friend, Captain Walter B Thompson from Fort Sill and more recently, the Perimeter, and in the First FA Obsn Bn, motored out to the airstrip around this time and we took off in my L19 to spot all his flash and sound bases to render more accurate data to locate enemy gun positions and other inimical positions. Based on such flight I recommended years later at "exit interviews" at Fort Sill that Obsn Bns have assigned aircraft or easy access to such so that data like Tommy got that day would be more readily available. As the war became less tense, I had more occasion to observe the proficiency of individual battalions in their firing. I could not help but notice the falling off of my old battery's efforts. When I conducted their base point registrations (now called "registraton point"), I saw their proficiency had deteriorated. 100 mil errors, crossed sheafs, and other carelessness were hard to overlook. Such erratic performance was most disappointing to me and costly to the efforts of our FA to bring accurate, timely fire on the enemy. Later, when I took over command of my old battery, I found some of the reasons for this decrease in performance by "A" Battery.

Capt Wallace
Magathan

Lt Walter B
Thompson

**HARD TO SEE BUT THIS WAS OUR
LANDING STRIP IN MUNAM WHERE
THE 25TH DIV REINFORCED THE 3D DIV,
SHARING THIS SAME AIRFIELD. MET
WALLACE HERE IN JUNE AND FLEW
HIM AROUND THE COMBAT ZONE
WHERE HE GOT A GOOD FEEL FOR
WHAT WE WERE ALL UP AGAINST.**

25TH DIVISION AIRSTRIP
IN CHONGSONG

I flew 23 of the 30 days in the month of June. The average mission consumed 3 hours and 30minutes. Coming into July the war had really simmered down. But not completely. I flew one mission that was right out of the FAS at Fort Sill except the "school troops" were the enemy! Scouting out targets one day, I spotted a Chinese 75mm battery that looked just like one of our batteries. Their exec held his hand aloft just like at Fort Sill as his cannoneers loaded their guns and, when all were ready to fire, the exec dropped his arm and the battery fired. Instinctively, I gave an ON THE WAY to MY FDC! Recovering, I prayed our guns did not hit me. (Hard to do with me in the air. Maybe Fuze Time!), In short order I pulverized that 75mm battery and headed for home. In the excitement of flying this most unusual mission, I had not noticed the oncoming darkness. It was a bit hairy flying below the mountain tops in ever increasing blackness. I radioed the airstrip to put some lights on the runway to keep me oriented. Landed without mishap and regaled my fellow pilots with, my encounter with enemy firing right out of FM 6-40 Field Artillery Gunnery. Four months later I had my driver, taking me to the Division Replacement Company for the first step in my rotation home, drive me to the point where I fired this mission and I took a picture of one of the 75s I KO'd. It was quite a thrill getting a picture of one of the hundreds of targets I had destroyed and this one in particular was extremely gratifying to me. By the tenth of the month, battle lines had stabilized near the 38th parallel and negotiatons for a rumored peace being discussed in KAESONG. The Division strip moved to TONGDO on the 16th but returned to WONTONG on the 31st of July. On this last day of July, the CO 64th FA Bn, LtCol Williams, came out to the airstrip and asked if I wanted to take over my old battery. I thought about this long and hard. Flying was becoming a real bore. Very few targets presented themselves; the war was definitely winding down. Yet we still had to maintain a constant patrol across the front. I was mildly rebuked for doing acrobatics in the target area. One time I landed on a road and took up some South Korean kids for the thrill of their lives. They were brave little youngsters. Although fear was in their eyes they possessed childlike admiration for all their American "saviours". One little 12 year old girl climbed into the back seat with her little brother in her lap and, as

I strapped them into their seat, their eyes widened with both a little fear but lots of excitement. I had done this same type thing during Christmas in 1945 with the Army of Occupation while serving in "B" Btry, 82d FA Bn of the 1st Cav Division, with a jeepload of little excited Japanese kids. Both groups of little ones, I am sure, remember these rides with a warm nostalgic feeling toward friendly Americano GI's. I reminisced on my days of flying, reminding myself of the hard-working aircraft mechanics who maintained our aircraft in such top shape in weather both hot and freezing,———-Sergeants Moore and Gorman and Cpl Youts, air observers like Lts "Rock" Campbell, Griffith, Kelly, Neville, my old 1st Sgt and others——-and counted my blessings, thanking the Lord for helping me serve my country and sparing me from many close encounters with GRIM SIX. For a listing of my total hours flown, see APPENDIX "G"

The best accolade I received for my flying was in my ER submitted by LtCol Williams who wrote: "This officer has demonstrated a tenacity for seeking out and destroying the enemy." I did feel a tiger 's eagerness in wiping out all the enemy I possibly could but that was certainly coupled with the tremendous support I got from all the battlion and higher level FDCs with whom I conducted fire missions. When I called for "ALL AVAILABLE", I invariably got all the fire I could handle. This type of interworking between highly trained field artilleryman produced a maximum amount of dead NKs and Chinese on the battlefields. After this much thought and deliberation, I decided to quit flying and resume a career with the foot soldiers with whom I had trained for the better part of my career up to this time. I also felt my old Able Battery needed help. So, on 31 Jul 51, I left the Division Airstrip and reported to the Bn Commander, LtCol Williams of Auburn, Ga, as CO, Btry "A", 105mmH. It was a move I never regretted.

"And where e'er we go
You will always know..."

CHAPTER SIX

Able Battery Commander

The previous BC, Captain "Red" Milliren, coming off FO duty, went to work on administration and enabled many topnotch NCOs to receive their authorized TO&E grades that had been dormant during the heavy fighting in the Perimeter and on up thru the fighting to the Yalu. Administrative justice was put in place. Gunnery-wise, I noted several areas that needed improvement. The FDC tent was sometimes occupied by personnel not part of the FDC. The close attention that must be paid to conducting fire missions just does not permit any but a bonafide FDC team to be filling the FDC tent. Months earlier, when I was the battery exec, the BC sat down in my FDC and started kibitzing with and harassing the FDC crew. Such action, understandably, caused them to make errors in plotting and sending commands to the guns. The BC was treating the FDC like the mess or motor sections whose duties do not require such apt attention to detail under fire. The captain apparently did not realize the seriousness of the situation, but I surely did. I called the BC outside the tent and told him either to stay out of my FDC tent or get himself a new exec. He saw the light and promptly apologized; never entered the tent again while fire missions were being conducted. That's the way it must be if sound gunnery techniques are to be applied and maintained. Without these parameters, no direct support mission can be properly sustained. About this time, all units in Korea were reminded by AFRS(Armed Forces Radio Service) and the STARS AND STRIPES newspaper of the importance of the Army Emergency Relief (AER) Association to all members of the Regular Army, particularly to us soldiers and officers in Korea. The AER was established in 1876, after the massacre at Little Big Horn. Many of the widowed and their families were in extreme financial stress. The Regular Army set about establishing a fund to assist the sufferers in this tragedy. This was the start of the AER ; it yet assists in similar ways today. I gave a talk one pay day to all the men and officers in my battery on this history and its importance to each of us fighting in Korea and our families. One Nisei corporal donated all his pay. But I advised him his response was most thoughtful and generous but he needed some money to buy necessities from the PX truck that visited us every so often. He agreed to a lesser amount and we were both happier. This type spirit was one of the distinguishing characteristics of this firing battery. Now the STARS AND STRIPES, published for the entire Far East Command, like the ones in Europe and other theatres in which our troops serve, cover the entire spectrum of their areas. So it was a very warming feeling for us Able Battery types to read a small article in our STARS AND STRIPES stating, quoting from memory: "The soldiers of "A" Battery of the 64th FA Bn, 25th Infantry Division, may not be millionnaires, but the battery contributed an average of $4.01 per man to the AER drive." Remember that most soldiers in combat send home the bulk of their pay to their families back home, so what's left, if four bucks, is a lot of dough. At any rate it did merit theatre-wide acclaim in our "local"blurb. About a week after assuming command, I was awakened at 0400 hours by a loud CRACK of an exploding projectile to our immediate front. Leaping out of my tent, I noted the projo had landed atop a hill directly in front of the howitzers. I queried the C/S and he said his ME was X mils. But X was much too low, I knew from experience, considering terrain. I asked Lt Galloway, now my XO, how he came by such a low figure. He stated that was the elevation to the highest hill. I was thunderstruck. "Where is the pad of my precalculated MEs I gave you when I left for the Air Section?" I asked. Galloway said he was told by the BC to throw the pad away; it was not required for any useful purpose and to simply use the highest boresighted elevation reported by the chiefs of section. Wow! For one thing, we were lucky nobody was killed atop that hill and for another, calculating MEs is vital to accurate fires by the btry. It protects friendly troops in front of the guns from being hit by their own artillery. When I was a young firing battery exec at Fort Sill, I studied a little red pamphlet I had purchased from the bookstore, "HOW TO PRODUCE AN EFFICIENT FIRING BATTERY." It was written by two young officers Handy and Burger, who later became general officers during WWII. This little "FA Bible" described in detail how to compile one's own table of MEs instead of having to "discover the birth of the FA" every time one pulled into a new firing position. By listing in a column those ranges most likely to be encountered when moving into position, depending on the local terrain and adding the 4 parameters taken from the firing table to each listed range, the most tedious and time consuming work has already been done. All that remains is to add the highest of the six elevations to the highest mask as measured and reported by the six chiefs of section. Such computations are shown in in APPENDIX "H". Yet a third major error in sound gunnery techniques occurred during the first week of my command. While shaving out of my helmet one morning within earshot of the FDC, I heard the FO command, during a base point registration: "ADD 1000." I was alarmed! Still in the same firing position with no weather change over the past few days, a 1000 yards range during registration approaches transfer limits for a 105. Such a range change had to be due to gross manual error somewhere. The complete nonchalance of the FDC chief, and the gun crew firing the mission for that matter, was aggravating. They should all have been, at the least, highly embarrassed and seeking reasons for such a large change in computed range and corresponding elevation. This is one way to seriously endanger our own supported troops. Without waiting to discuss the matter with the Btry XO, —-fast action was mandatory—- I took action to replace the FDC Chief, the gunner and #1 man at the howitzer firing the errant round, with three other men pulling FO duty.

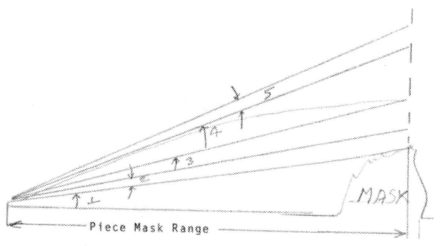

Piece Mask Range

1. Angle of Site to Mask
2. 5 yards vertical clearance at mask
3. Comp Site
4. Elevation to piece mask range
5. 2 Forks

GENERAL THOMAS T. HANDY

**TENT FROM WHICH
I LEAPED**

241

The former would thus have time to reflect on why their round was so much in error, becoming better Redlegs when they would eventually get back to their firing battery. The latter, under the leadership of capable, dedicated men remaining in the FDC and gun crews would soon develop into seasoned, dependable Redlegs delivering accurate fire in all fire missions. New attitudes were acquired and noted by all. For example, I noted no 100 mil errors or crossed sheafs during the remainder of my command tenure. The major credit here goes to our outstanding XO, Lt Galloway and, after his rotation Stateside, his successor, Lt Keeling. On 5 Aug, the battery moved to HATODONG, about 5 miles east of KUMWHA and 15 miles south of PYONGGANG, two of the towns forming the well known IRON TRIANGLE, the central location of the CCF on the eastern half of KOREA. The following moves were made by "A" Btry: 7Aug to CHOOPSULMAK 8 back to HATODONG 10 back to HAKTORI 18 to position 1.5 miles SW of KUMWHA It was in this time frame I ran across 2d LIEUTENANT Chauncey E Schick. He was as proud as a peacock wearing those gold bars, as well he should. We reminisced about our days together in the Perimeter. He had been transferred from my battery to "C" Battery. When I called the Bn CO, he said he felt it was not good for EM making officer grade to remain in the same unit. When I reminded him of the 2 FOs already in "C" Btry who remained there after receiving their commissions, the colonel was adamant in his decision. I had lost a good soldier and friend, Lt CE Schick. The worst was yet to come. My men came to me on 18 Aug with the news that Lt Schick, while serving as FO with "C" Btry was KIA. His body was found, when dawn broke, spread out on the ground, his pistol arm extended to full length, all seven calibre.45 rounds having been expended and six dead Chinese at his feet. I vividly remember Chauncey back at the Perimeter, as we repelled that bloody NK attack. Hit in the shoulder, Chauncey was evacuated to Japan the next day and returned on the first plane back to rejoin his comrades in Fighting Able. I disappeared into my tent to compose myself. It was a most bitter episode. I ordered a dozen roses from a Stateside vendor to be sent to to the crushed parents of Chauncey in Hawthorne, Pa, in the name of all members of his battery to their best soldier. Not surprisingly from the family of such offspring, we got a letter back, amidst all their grief, thanking us for our remembrance and our determined pursuit of victory for the free world in fighting communism. All efforts to obtain a Division bugler failed. We of the battery sang Taps at our own funeral for our hero Chauncey Schick. It was with heavy hearts that Battery "A" resumed normal duties. None was heavier than mine. We had lost our best fighter/soldier. Not long after I had returned to "A", a new Div Arty commander took over. A colonel, he was yet certain of making general; he brought with him a young lieutenant to pin on his stars and be his aide. The colonel apparently was paranoid about his FA eating three hot meals a day while the doughs were lucky to partake of daily cold C-rations. His try to limit his FA to one hot a day was nullified by "cooler" heads up the chain. Then he, or somebody became obsessed with the FA units being in one position for so long. So one cold, rainy evening, we were march-ordered to a new forward position. In the driving rain, our hows got stuck in the mud around a turn in the road. As the prime mover drivers gunned and gunned their engines, the cannoneers sitting in the trucks tried to inch the hows forward with "body English." But I jumped out of my jeep, put shoulders to gunshield and tried to muck the beast forward. This galvanized the troops to action, as I was sure it would, and we finally "overhilled and overdaled" our stuck hows. As we slaved away in the driving raindrops, we saw doughboys passing by, lugging their heavy baseplates and tubes of their 4.2" mortars. Ears twitched and jaws went agape. Thoughts were "What the h——are we doing up here with infantry MORTARS???" When we finally slid and slithered into position at the break of dawn, we noted we were a few hundred yards behind these mortars and our position plotted less than 1000 yards from our 105mm how minimum range line! All but useless for direct support, a travesty of our mission. We soon got orders to return to our old position that we had occupied 12 hours earlier. What a sense of accomplishment! (Cannot print our comments or conversations.) When we settled into our old position, I salled forth with my driver to check on my FOs. One was Lt Duke from Dallas, TX. He was barefooted, no boots. When queried, he said his feet were temporarily swollen and he could not put on his boots. I gently chastised him and told him to return to the battery until he could put on his boots; I would replace him with my exec or me. But the stubborn, conscientious young man said "No thanks",——he liked it with the infantry and, with the weather warming, he said he would be fine by nightfall. This is the type dedication we commanders encountered with our young officers and NCOs. A distinct thrill to lead. While visting my doughboy friends and FOs. I received a landline. Div Arty wanted our FOs to have and use BC scopes. FOs normally used their small, shoulder-slung M13 binoculars to adjust fire. BC scopes are big and heavy, designed for static warfare and training FOs on the hills at the firing ranges of the TAS at Fort Sill. They are designed to be used in foxholes with only the "periscope" visible to the enemy. In Korea. we could never bet on any situation becoming static. With rapid displacements, keeping up with the supported infantry, the FO has all he can do to evacuate himself with but M13s, map(s) and radio. So,——I ignored the request for BC scope issuance. I paid for this later! As it got dark, my driver and I headed back to the ranch. One does not roam about infantry front lines unless that is one's natural habitat and one is known by the doughs. The infantry has an unnerving habit of drilling ANYBODY moving after dark. When we got back to the battery, I was asked if I had delivered the BC scope. I called the Bn CO and explained the idiocy of giving our FOs BC scopes. Lt Col Williams did agree but stated that was a decision made by Div Arty. Well, since it was my fault, I could not with a clear conscience detail the mission to another, so after we ate (hot) supper, my driver and I, lugging the heavy scope and tripod, climbed into my jeep and headed for Able FO. As we lugged the two bulky, heavy components up the ever, ever steep hills (what else in Big K?) under cold, blackout conditions, I heard the distinct click of a rifle bolt closing and the muted word "CIGAR!". With clammy hands and tightened throat, I thought furiously and whispered back: "SMOKE!" The dough guard checked us out and told us where the CP was. Our lives had been spared because I remembered the password of the day. Had I replied to the challenge with any OTHER word, my driver and I would have been added to the list of KIAs for the night. Disciplined recording of such 24-hour passwords was an absolute ritual for all but especially for those expecting to be with the infantry at night. However, I did not visit the doughs that much; so my recalling the password was not a given. I recorded such data in my little USAMA calendar book mentioned earlier.

**BC
SCOPE**

Sweatstained, kept in my left pocket, it proved several times to be a virtual life saver. Incidentally, that BC scope was abandoned by the FO when his supported infantry company was forced to pull back. He decided his life and that of his sergeant were worth more than the price of that cumbersome scope; he abandoned it, escaping with his M13s, maps and radio. I wonder if the Chinese used that scope, as light as they travel? (Note that little jewel book below.) On 30 Aug, the battery moved back to HAKTORI. On the 31st, we moved to a position 1.5 miles SW of KUMWHA. On 18 Sep, it was a position 2 miles east of K-town, a position used earlier by the 8th FA Bn.

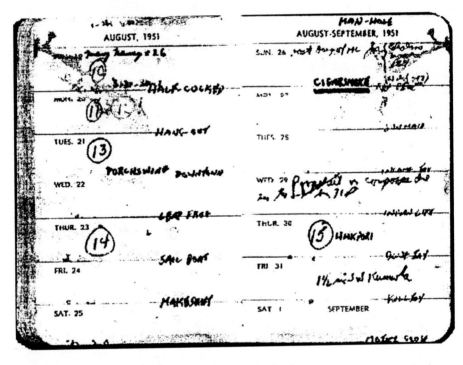

As I travelled along the MSR, I noted a small sign posted along the side of the road near one of the 8th field's old firing positions, saying: 8th FA. THE WOLFHOUNDS BARK. I tired of the marine-like publicity given every day and more to the 27th Infantry ("Wuz you in da Alley?") and its supporting 8th. Despite all this rah, rah, I did know some fine officers in this 8th Field. They were three of my USMA'45 classmates, Robert C Burgess, Robert E Dingeman and Edmund G Heilbrunner. I decided to prick this bubble in its infancy.

Querying my NCOs, I sought a gregarious, likeable, go-getter on whom we could count on to carry out a mission that might involve a trip as far south as PUSAN if necessary. The NCOs selected their man,—- a live-wire Corporal whom they felt would cut the mustard. Given some slush funding, a 3/4 T, and hopeful bon voyage, little Napoleon set forth on a critical mission. Within two days, he really delivered! He came back with a 6'X4' sign finished in beautiful readable colors that proclaimed our "A" Battery was:

FIGHTING ABLE————THE LEOPARD'S ROAR

From pictures following, note that the 1st Bn, 35th Infantry, also erected a sign at a crossroad stating,(in also rebutting the 8th FA's dwarfish credo), that the Cacti were ALL BITE, NO BARK. Our battery personnel, as well as all others who went by our battery entrance, were entranced with our Corporal's accomplishment, both envying and respecting the unit pride reflected in such displays However, our Bn CO, stating the sign was indeed a work of art and congratulating the battery on its initiative, competitive spirit and unit pride, BUT——— the sign had to come down. LtCol Williams said "We do not want to start a sign warfare". This broke some hearts but we got in the last words: "Yes Sir". Now ——————back to the war. Battalion Hq had set up its CP just 50 yards west of our battery just outside KUMWHA. This was the first exposure of "A" Btry to Bn's being so near. We envied their portable, manmade shower unit. Some of the Bn staff paid their first visit to a firing battery since entering KOREA. The Bn adjutant, a major from Texas, paid us a visit one night. When he finally reached my hq, i.e. where I stood, he slammed his helmet to the ground, angrily exclaiming : "How would you like it if at every 25 yards, someone said: 'Halt! Who goes there?' It took me 1/2 hour to get here just 50 yards away." I informed the major he was in KOREA and security this close to the front has got to be tight, especially in any unit I command. For his information I advised walking in the REAR of any unit at the front just may be safer than cutting across its FRONT. Thinking hard, he felt he could not argue my point; he learned an important survival lesson that night. On 13 Oct, Hq and Able were shelled, the first undergone by Bn since the war started. It really shook 'em up. The volleys were few and random. I figured the Chinese had fired their allotment for the year. But the next day, Bn S3, Major Ned Burr USMA '44, sent me out to check some coordinates for a new FP (firing position) about 3 miles to the rear. I reconnoitered the area and found it dangerous, utterly useless for a firing battery. High hills close in front and dense tree mass throughout the position rendered it unsuited to emplace any FA pieces. Hurrying back to report to the S3, I was set back by the sight of my battery closing station preparing for a move to the rear, i.e. the

Lt Robert C Burgess, Firing Btry CO. 8th FA Bn

THE CACTI WITH
US ALL THE WAY!!

area I had just left. I asked my exec, Lt Keeling: "How come? I tell this outfit when to move." He said Bn S3 had given the order. Most irritated, I dashed to Bn Hq 100 yards to the left flank of my battery and talked with LtCol Williams, explaining about the proposed new FP's being hopeless for emplacing a firing battery. He listened most intently and no doubt thought about the S3's recent arrival in the theatre and my being a seasoned veteran of the fighting in KOREA. He told me to remain where I was. This was a most gratifying reply, considering the fact I could not even begin to accomplish my mission in a veritable jungle. We, by the way, as I expected, received no "incoming" in our position for the rest of my tour.

Pfc Jay H Randie, my always cheerful driver who wheeled me all over the Land of the Morning Calm and never got lost —and that was hard to do !

"A"s Mess Tent

FIGHTING ABLE
THE LEOPARD'S
ROAR ALONGSIDE
MSR BELOW

Hill on our W flank shelled heavily
in October.Bn Hq and C Btry
moved to rear.Fighting Able stood
fast No more incoming !

Road leading to "A" Btry's
1 howitzer in gun position
5 miles from KUMWHA

251

Our Battalion Commander, LtCol Williams, had graduated fom Auburn University and was a most capable CO. Knew his stuff and was a good leader. Affable, he bet on all Auburn's football games. Checking the records for the '51 football season will reveal its unparalleld success that year. We officers scoffed at little ole Auburn's team and lost our rear ends that season. The good colonel cleaned up! But alas! He rotated on 20 October; we lost a top CO. Col Williams' successor visited my battery shortly after assuming command and wondered why we were digging in our ammo two feet deeper. My reply: "Sir, somebody at your FDC told us an hour ago to do this." The colonel just nodded his head and continued his inspection. One thing learned from combat is it is normally easier to obey orders, regardless of your agreement or not, than to wrangle or procrastinate. There are, of course, exceptions, e.g. my rebuttal of that last new proposed FP. On the other hand, my dilatoriness in delivering that BC scope came close to causing my own demise. In any case, my prompt response to orders from his staff impressed our new CO to the extent he entered on my abbreviated ER: "Although I have known this officer but a short time, I have been well impressed by his strong leadership." While in position at this time, I finally came to the conclusion that our Battery 1st Sergeant was better fitted for higher headquarters with his experience at such levels being in demand at the time. I visited some new arrivals,—replacements, at Bn Hq. Checking out a 6'6" first sergeant from Texas, I asked him if he were a good first sergeant. He, drawing himself up to his full height, replied: "I wouldn't be here if I weren't!" That was my man! (After I rotated home, I received several letters from my men thanking me for my wise decision and giving ole Able a real firing battery top-sergeant. This made me feel real good, contributing to the success of "A" Btry even in my absence). On 15Oct, I learned I was eligible for a 2d R&R. I told Hq if I went, I would not return. The memory of my last R&R was too vivid for me to enjoy #2; I recalled how tough it was to return to Korea. The Bn adjutant saw the determination in my jaw and scratched off me off the list. (He probably thought: "All I need is another court-martial!)

Our houseby
"Kann"
with us
since Pusan

) Lt Jack
Edwards and
id driver
'c FD
illiamson

Cpl Vacuolo
and Cpl
Ernest T
Howell of
FDC.(Howell
a Bro Kappa
Sigma!)

Lt Bynum, another hard-working,
proficient Able Btry FO

Our South Korean
houseboy helping
in the kitchin

My exec, Lt
Wm C Keeling,
a good one.

Lt Edwards,
Pfc William-
son just
 after KIAing
some Korean
pheasants

Sgt Wm AA
Stokes, one
of Able's
top crew
 chiefs

Cpl Thomas
A Baillie,
gnr on #1 wh
had all the
answers for
the D/A exe
when he in-
spected "A
Battery

255

Sfc Edward
Gilliam
and I

Pfc IA Brooks
Sfc Archerd
and Cpl Hill
our supply
team

Cpl Hanes
standing.
Cpl Troy and
friend squattin

Our great
mess sgt,
Sgt Tilman
F Barker

As it turned out, not taking R&R was the best decision I ever made. On 16 Oct, first heard of impending orders to rotate home! Gave a last talk to my assembled cannoneers and my fine exec, Lt Keeling, upon receiving my rotation orders. Praising them all who gave a fine example of what good Redlegs are all about, not without a tinge of sadness at leaving such truly great, dedicated fighters, I departed my last firing position with Able Battery on 30 Oct after 16 months of frontline combat and 6 battle stars on my Korean campaign ribbon. On my way to the 25th Division Replacement Company, I had my driver stop by those coordinates where, as related earlier during my last month as a Bn pilot, I destroyed six 75mm Chinese howitzers.

It was a thrill to be able to take a picture without being captured, of one of the hundreds of targets I had KO'd as I flew 619 hours of combat missions over the front, flying for my one and only 64th FA Bn,105mm, in DS of the great 35th Infantry Regiment "Cacti" I arrived in PUSAN on 5Nov. Departed for Japan aboard the USS BLATCHFORD, landing at SASEBO, Japan, at 0700 hours on 6Nov. It was a tremendous relief to be "off the line" for good. Stuffing on delicious steak (what ones aren't?), ice cream and Tuborg beer, I was surprised at how many Cacti recognized me from my flying. Heard for the first time how I saved a rifle company from heavy casualties that day I flew around them on a mountainside in the fog, those seven .45 rounds I "expended on the target", dropping hand grenades from a practised altitude so they would explode at enemy skull height and the Chink I chased into his foxhole with my L5 prop twirling right behind him. The Good Lord was, over all, foremost in our hearts as we gave thanks for His saving us and accepting our less fortunate within His Gates. So mote it be! We gleefully boarded the USN AIKEN VICTORY for our trip home but the ship had a huge gash in its port bow. So, as pictured on the following page, we put into

YOKOSUKA, a repair facility just SE of TOKYO, for repairs. We were not too unhappy—we WERE HEADED HOME, our next port had to be SAN FRANCISCO! After surviving KOREA, we could wait if need be. And sure enough, on 2 Dec, we gazed enraptured at the beautiful sight of the GOLDEN GATE BRIDGE. What an ecstatic feeling!!

Boarded USN AIKEN VICTORY for the
ZI but we put in to YOKOSUKA for
repair to the AIKEN'S bow on 19Nov

USN AIKEN

Crane used to repair bow
in YOKOSUKA, Japan

We waited patiently as the pilotboat motored its way to our VICTORY, a sloop anchored nearby, —aptly named for us! "It won't be long now" we all chorused. But alas! The pilot boat capsized in the rough seas. The pilot, seen to be up in years, flailed about in the icy November waters and was rescued by the sloop. There was no replacement aboard and the hapless pilot had to get back to hospital. So, we would have to wait another day. Not to worry, still patient, we enjoyed the bright lights of SAN FRANCISCO from the deck of our anchored AIKEN VICTORY.

The next day, 3 Dec, we sailed under THE BRIDGE and disembarked at FORT MASON. That night began at THE TOP OF THE MARK as we imbibed a bit, made most important phone calls, finalizing transportation plans for flights, trains, etc, to our families and other friends, bubbling over with excitement at the thought of joyful reunions on the morn or soon thereafter. Let there be no doubt that each and every one of us truly fortunates gave fervent thanks to the Great Architect of the Universe for our survival and blessed so feelingly those fine soldiers and friends who fought like us but died on the battlefield. Can America ever forget? We hope not. After all this has been said and done, who are the real military heroes?? Our WIVES! And last, but by no means least, praise those brave South Koreans. May God, in His infinite wisdom, preserve SOUTH KOREA as a free country forever.

25th Infantry "Tropic Lightning" Division at a
reunion in Schofield Barracks, TH—oops! Hawaii!

Kincheon H (Bert) Bailey

APPENDIX "A"

ADJUSTING FIELD ARTILLERY FIRING

In WWII, adjusting FA fire was a job best done by well trained field artillery FOs. The bulk of the adjusting was done by the FO. His location was not important to the Fire Direction Center (FDC) doing the firing. The FO had to keep all rounds fired on the Gun-Target (GT) line. From tabular or graphical firing tables he had to determine, at the range being fired by the guns, the number of mils required for a 100 yard shift in deflection AT THE GUNS, or "C" factor, the same for range, the "D" factor, the value of "C/D" and what the angle"T" was (the angle at the target between the gun position and the FO's location). How these factors were used to achieve Fire-for-Effect (FFE) is not important to this book. It merely illustrates two things about adjusting the Field Artillery in WWII, (1) It was difficult; only well trained FOs could bring fire on the target quickly and accurately; and (2) There had to be better way. Again the illimitable guru of US field artillery gunnery, the FA School at Fort Sill, came up with a simpler method of getting FFE on targets. It placed the onus of relatively complex computations where it belonged, at the FDC. It devised the target grid system.(See next page). The FO location Is still unimportant to the mission. He merely transmits to the FDC the azimuth from his location to the target, and the target coordinates. During the adjustment phase, the FO simply reports each shift required to move the the last round fired to the target, using his reported azimuth to target as his FO-Tgt line.

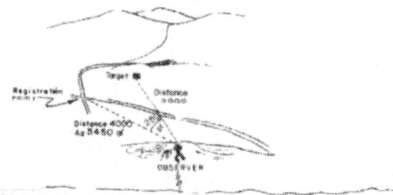

BANNER 9, THIS IS BANNER 31, FIRE MISSION, FROM REGISTRATION POINT 1, AZIMUTH 5700, RIGHT 1000, DROP 2000, PLATOON IN OPEN FUZE VT, WILL ADJUST

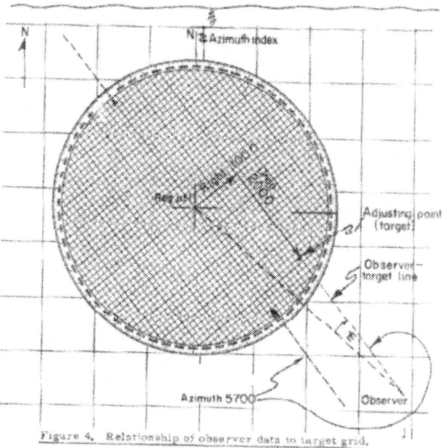

Figure 4. Relationship of observer data to target grid.

The FDC converts the FO's shifts to the GT line, sends commands to the guns and it's "ON THE WAY", continuing thru the FO's final command: "CEASE FIRE! END OF MISSION! ENEMY CP DESTROYED! This procedure may still be a bit difficult for one who has little experience with adjusting artillery fire. To illustrate, when I was G3Air of the 2d Armored Division in Bad Kreuznach Germany, in 1954-57, the Assistant Division Commander, General Johnson, asked me to explain why the FA did not have to know where the observer was located when firing on targets. At 0730 the next morning, I brought appropriate equipment to Division Headquarters and explained to the general why such was true. I probably got a bit basic for a general but I used this opportunity to help ensure the Division could carry out its secondary mission of direct artillery support. General Johnson thanked me and was appreciative of my efforts. Not too long thereafter, the S3 of the 67th Tank Battalion in CCA at Bad Kreuznach learned more about his secondary mission of fire support when I, on a G3 inspection team, flunked the battalion on its inability to accomplish this mission in training. He learned a lot. So it can be seen that the use of the target grid and the simplified requirements for the observer result in far simpler and, most times, greater accuracy in putting rounds on the target. Had I, or anyone else, tried to teach keeping rounds on the GT line from an OP to armored or any other non-FA branches, the instruction would most assuredly have taken days rather than hours.

FDC SENSINGS IN PRECISION FIRE FOR EFFECT

	Observer Sensings	Fire-Direction Center Sensings		
		100-799 m	800-1399 m	1400-1600 m
Guns on left Observer on right	? Right	+ ?	+ ?	+ ?
	? Left	- ?	- ?	- ?
	+ Line	+ Left	- Left	- Left
	+ Right	+ ?	- ?	- Left
	+ Left	+ Left	? Left	- Left
	- Line	- Right	- Right	- Right
	- Right	- Right	? Right	+ Right
	- Left	- ?	- ?	- Right
Guns on right Observer on left	? Right	- ?	- ?	- ?
	? Left	+ ?	+ ?	+ ?
	+ Line	+ Right	+ Right	- Right
	- Right	- Right	? Right	- Right
	+ Left	+ ?	+ ?	+ Right
	- Line	- Left	- Left	- Left
	- Right	- ?	- ?	- Left
	- Left	- Left	? Left	+ Left

For angles T less than 100 mils, fire-direction center sensings coincide with observer sensings.

Kincheon H (Bert) Bailey

Brig Gen Johnson

ADC

2d Armored Division

Bad Kreuznach, Germany

1956

APPENDIX "B"

CASUALTIES IN "A" BATTERY 3 SEP 50

Kincheon H (Bert) Bailey

CASUALTIES SUFFERED BY 'A' BTRY ON 3SEP50 <u>KIA</u> SGT JOSEPH R PURSELEY TN WILSON COUNTY SGT HERBERT L RAWLS NC EDGECOMB COUNTY PFC JAMES CARROLL WV KANAWA COUNTY PFC WALTER D ROWATT IL LA SALLE COUNTY PFC ALAN S SNOUFFER MD BALTIMORE CITY COUNTY PVT RICHARD FLEISCHER CA HUMBOLDT COUNTY PVT CARLSON E WALLACE MI PRESQUE ISLE COUNTY <u>WIA</u> CPL VICTOR A BAUDER NY CORTLAND COUNTY CPL WALLIS L BENTON AZ YUMA COUNTY CPL HAROLD E CAMPBELL MA BARBSTABLE COUNTY CPL JOHN R MORGAN ME OXFORD COUNTY PFC BILLY C ASHFORD TX HUTCHINSON COUNTY PFC HENRY E BAKER AR BENTON COUNTY PFC HAROLD D BARKER IL KANKAKEE COUNTY PFC FRED N CAMPBELL TN SHELBY COUNTY PFC REUBEN E CAMPBELL KS LINCOLN COUNTY PFC THOMAS A CASTELLO UNK PFC BERNARD P FAGAN OH SUMMIT COUNTY PFC CEBERT T HOOD KY CLARK COUNTY PFC JOHN R McMAINS OH HAMILTON COUNTY PFC SANFORD B MOORE UNK PFC CHAUNCEY E SHICK PA CLARION COUNTY PVT BOBBY L RIGGS TN KNOX COUNTY (DOW)

APPENDIX "C"

REGISTERING FIELD ARTILLERY

REGISTRATION

Registering the firing battery is a necessity because firing table data are prepared for ideal conditions and many factors besides non-ideal weather (wx) and ammunition affect a projectile's trajectory. The factors considered are listed following this paragraph. No artillery projectile will land at the precise coordinates desired. But it behooves all who fire in support of our infantry to minimize all errors to the maximum extent possible. When a gun is registered at a set of coordinates, careful evaluation of the "should-hit" and "did-hit" data must be made. This did hit data is recorded. With GFTs, the line on the GFT slide is placed over the range at which the gun was fired and then, with ruler and pencil, lines are drawn over the "did-hit" elevation, time (if using FzTi), and any other fired-in values, if any. This then becomes the GFT setting. If the only factors affecting the trajectory were weather and gun-ammo variations, the FA could relax and never worry again. But, we are not out of the woods yet. Whenever possible, like always, we receive a concurrent wx message by CW over our radios. Saving this info, we next compare the DIFFERENCE between the wx effects when we last registered and those of the current wx msg. We then adjust our GFT settings accordingly, i.e. K =(TOTAL CORRECTION made per registration - Correction for wx at registration) plus or minus the (difference in the two wx effects recorded) For practical purposes, we say our firing error equals "VE plus wx". This is, of course. not 100% correct but it is the formula that has been proven to be "good enough" for the FA with "perfection" actually unobtainble, particularly in combat. So the FA registers at least once per day, more when feasible. Some of the more important variables dealt with by the FA are listed below: 1. Gun VE. Each gun developes its own velocity. The lands and grooves in each piece cannot be identical. This means more or less gas will escape past the projectile fired from different tubes. Eventually Ordnance will have to replace worn-out tubes. 2. Propellant. This is made in lots, e.g. Lot COP1325 is made at a certain powder factory at the same time, temperature and physical location. The FA tries to conduct all missions with the same powder lot, especially during registrations. One does not have to be a veteran Redleg to see how impossible it is to do this. The closest we come to meeting this requirement is at Fort Sill which has a priority at the powder plants.(Recall that the USS IOWA that blew up in April 1989 was using "ancient"powder manufactured in WWII, a gross violation of sound gunnery technique. 47 sailors were killed because of this tragic error.) 3. Temperature. Firing tables are based on STP whichs seldom exists in the real world. The temperature of the powder at the time of firing should be measured and applied to weather messages(MIFMIF). 4. Tube condition. As more rounds are fired, the lands begin to erode. This affects MV and so, range. Each Chief of Section maintains a gun book that shows the number of full service rounds that his gun has fired. With the 105 Charge 7 is a full service round. Charge 6 is 0.5, etc. The battery exec checks these data and rotates the base piece(the gun used to register) to even out the rounds fired per piece. 5. Weather. Firing in different kinds of weather obviously changes the range that rounds will reach, hence the procedures just discussed to obtain accurate GFT settings or replot data. These wx messages (MIFMIFs), by the way, contain weather conditions existing at over each of over 15 levels above the ground at 1000 foot intervals. Ground conditions at the source of the data are also recorded. 6. Battery personnel training. Poor training cannot be tolerated in the FA. Too much is at stake. The proverbial "short round" is the Redleg's nightmare. Mastering all aspects of gunnery techniques around the guns and in the FDC goes a long way towards insuring FA rounds land where the supported doughboys need them. 'Nuff said!

Kincheon H (Bert) Bailey

APPENDIX "D"

ADJUSTING FIELD ARTILLERY FROM THE GROUND AND FROM THE AIR

ADJUSTING FA FROM THE GROUND AND FROM THE AIR

The ground observer, generally an FO, oversees that part of the battle area for which his supported infantry company is responsible. Typical frontages vary between 500 and 1000 yards. But they can vary greatly under extreme conditions such as diverse terrain, enemy front, location of adjacent units and their proficiency under fire, disposition of supporting artillery, future plans, etc. In any case, the areas that the FO controls with his FA are limited to the infantry's zones of action. He may not be able to adjust artillery in all of his area for such reasons as heavy forests, hill crests, vegetation, valleys, etc. Because of his relatively limited area of responsibility and varying degrees of his being able to view or sight his entire area, he is at many times, at a disadvantage. With a limited range of vision, the FO cannot normally acquire targets larger than infantry platoons or companies He can seldom, if ever, see the enemy artillery firing at him. Not often will the FO engage targets that require more than a battery or battalion to destroy or neutralize. The FO can call for fire support at any time but he is generally limited to those targets that threaten his supported infantry. Now the air observer has much more vision over the entire sector of his supported infantry but he does not face the restrictions common to most FOs. The AO sees the complete battlefield and is normally available to fire on ANY target he sees or that FDCs of higher headquarters request be fired on. Proper coordination between FA battalions involved is made by the headquarters requesting such missions. The AO may also report to the FDC(s) any bits of intelligence he discerns from his flying in the area, e.g. enemy units assembling in areas that spell trouble for friendly troops. He reports real or likely activity in areas difficult to be seen from the ground. Many ambushes have been averted by such timely reports. The AO can spot troop buildups or artillery positions, requesting additional artillery to cope with the larger targets. Conducting registrations are a most important function of the AO. He can register all the battalions he can handle in minimum time, a blessing for the S3 trying to complete each battery registration before dark or bad weather sets in. He has an advantage the FO does not always have,—a base or registration point in the center of the battalion zone of action that he can easily identify for both himself and the FDC using map coordinates. Since target location poses no problem; he frequently completes a registration firing but 7 or 8 rounds. He can also easily orient himself along the GT line, and send commands that require no corrections for being "off line". A more mundane advantage for the AO is he is stationed at the Division Airstrip and does not have to dog the footsteps of an infantry company CO. Each day he flies over the same terrain and gets to know the area well. The FO must constantly relocate himself—frequently advising the doughboy CO where he's at—and in a moving situation, in enemy territory, he must keep abreast of the situation constantly. The Airstrip does not have to displace as often; the pilots thereby get to know the terrain intimately, greatly enhancing their abiity to bring accurate fire down on the enemy wherever he is seen and regardless of which infantry sector he is flying in. He is yet primarily concerned with his own battalion's threats. At the same time he can be available to attack the enemy anywhere on the front if additional help is required. The FDC coordinates most of this type "shuffling" across the front. These are the more important differences between adjusting artillery from the ground and from the air. Like the USAF socked in by the weather at their home base, the Army aviators, being closer to the front, may or may not be able to fly missions. But, making the Field Artillery the Greatest Killer on the Battlefield, the groundpounding FO can adjust fire every hour in all kinds of weather and any other adverse conditions. If the infantry is fighting, the FOs can shoot.

Kincheon H (Bert) Bailey

APPENDIX "E"

TANKS AS FIELD ARTILLERY

Sherman Tanks
in Korea

TANK GUNS AS ARTILLERY

The fire power of tank

guns, firing indirectly

can give added

oomph to artillery

Lieutenant Colonel

Dean E. Painter

UNDER certain circumstances, the tanks in an armored division can be used to reinforce the artillery fire of their own division. In the defense of a river line, for example, direct fire of tanks usually cannot be brought to bear on the enemy until he approaches the banks of the river or actually crosses it. But tank guns, using indirect fire, can supplement regular artillery in the destruction, harassing, and interdiction of enemy troops beyond the range of direct fire.

No variation from standard field artillery observer procedure is required. Regularly assigned artillery observers may observe and adjust the fire of the tanks, or tankers themselves may be trained to observe and adjust the indirect fire of tanks.

Tank guns have a higher muzzle velocity, flatter trajectory, greater range dispersion, and shorter time of flight than field artillery weapons. Ammunition designed for tanks is likely to have special characteristics, and ammunition supply should be the subject of careful planning. To insure smooth functioning of tank cannon used to augment artillery fires, an SOP should be established. Ammunition should be stockpiled in the position area so that the tank's basic load of ammunition does not have to be used for this mission.

INDIRECT firing of tanks is very similar to field artillery battery procedure. In laying a tank for direction, establish the 0-3200 line of the aiming circle in the direction of fire, and command: AIMING POINT THIS INSTRUMENT. At this command, the gunner traverses the turret until the vertical hair of the M12 range finder (M47 tank) or T156E1 direct-fire telescope (M48 tank) is centered on the center column of the aiming circle. The gunner sets his azimuth indicator at zero by turning the resetter knob, until the top and middle pointers coincide. He then depresses the knob and rotates it until both pointers are at the zero position. The vertical hair of the aiming circle is laid on the left objective lens of the M12 range finder (the reticle of the range finder is in the left lens) and deflections are read to each piece. This procedure is covered in paragraph 106, FM 6-140. The M20 or M20A1 periscope present on both M47 and M48 tanks may also be used for laying the gun for direction.

Upon receiving a deflection, each gunner traverses his turret until the announced deflection appears on his azimuth indicator. The guns are now laid parallel. The tank commander has aiming posts placed and lined in with the M12 or T156E1. The purpose of the aiming posts is to check displacement in firing all subsequent shifts are made through use of the azimuth indicator.

Then each gunner, without moving his turret, sets his azimuth indicator to read 2600 mils—deflection used by armored field artillery for emplacement of aiming posts. Before the initial shift on any mission, the gunner sights on his aiming posts through the M12 or T156E1 and makes sure that his azimuth indicator reads 2600 mils. The tank is laid for range by using either the elevation quadrant or the gunner's quadrant.

THE 90mm tank gun is rarely fired at its maximum range of approximately 19,500 yards, but when it is, FDCs need 26,000 yard range deflection fans. In this case the necessary elevation must be obtained by placing the tank on a natural slope or by digging an inclined ramp. When the long axis of the tank is approximately level, the maximum elevation of the 90mm gun is 338 mils and the maximum range approximately 14,500 yards. The defilade of positions must be checked to insure that minimum ranges desired can actually be fired. The artillery FDC will need graphical firing tables for the 90mm gun.

For accurate firing, the horizontal axis of the weapon must be level within practicable tolerances. The level can be checked by placing a gunner's quadrant crossways on the breechblock, with the elevation arm and micrometer of the quadrant set at zero.

A platoon or company of tanks using indirect fire may be controlled by an artillery FDC

If the piece is out of lateral level by 100 mils or more, the tank should be moved slightly, or one track can be dug in to correct for excessive cant.

The indirect fire of tanks can be controlled in five ways: by attaching a tank platoon to an artillery battery; by adding one computer for each platoon to the artillery FDC; by setting up a FDC separate from, but adjacent to, the artillery FDC; by using the men and fire-direction equipment organic to the tank battalion to form a FDC with artillery assistance; or by having each tank battalion handle its own indirect fire missions from prearranged data sheets.

If a medium-tank company is attached to an artillery battalion, each of its three platoons may be further attached to a battery. The field artillery battery would then be responsible for survey, communications, and fire control of its attached platoon, and some fire commands might originate in the battery FDC. Commands would normally originate in the artillery battalion FDC and merely be transmitted to the tank platoon through the artillery battery. The ability of the battery to control the tank platoon effectively will decrease as the distance between the platoon and the battery increases, so this distance should not exceed 500 yards.

ATTACHMENT would neither relieve the parent tank battalion from responsibility for supply and administration nor prevent it from breaking off the attachment should the responsible commander decide that the primary mission of direct fire should take precedence over the indirect-fire mission.

The addition of one computer per platoon to the artillery battalion FDC should be the normal procedure when only one platoon of tanks is attached. This platoon would then form, in effect, a fourth battery.

When a tank platoon or company is attached to the artillery, setting up a separate FDC wastes manpower. But if the terrain makes it necessary to emplace the tanks at some distance from the artillery, a separate FDC must be set up in the vicinity of the

When tank guns are used for indirect fire, an observer is needed. Tankers can be trained as observers.

tank-company or tank-platoon headquarters. Equipment and men should be furnished by the artillery.

Fire-control equipment in the tank battalion is limited. Lack of trained fire-direction personnel within the tank battalion usually precludes the tank units assuming total responsibility for the conduct of indirect fire. However, tank units can be trained to perform the indirect-fire mission independently, with the aid only of an artillery liaison officer.

A CALCULATED proportion of the tanks are usually placed well forward in concealed positions awaiting the opportune moment to strike with direct fire. These would seldom be used as indirect-fire weapons. But the tanks in the rear may be used in the artillery role. They may contribute to victory by knocking out the enemy's antitank capabilities and otherwise clearing the way for direct-combat tanks.

Although tanks may be used effectively as artillery, such use must be subordinated to the purposes for which tanks are designed. Tank cannon should be made available as artillery only when this auxiliary reinforcement of fires does not jeopardize the primary mission.

Kincheon H (Bert) Bailey

APPENDIX "F"

AID TO TURKEY

AID TO TURKEY

By Col. Thomas E. de Shazo, FA

EARLY in 1947 The Truman Doctrine was announced by the President, in which military aid was provided to certain countries whose independence was threatened by communistic expansion. It is distinct from the later Marshall Plan. Under the provisions of The Truman Doctrine, Congress appropriated one hundred million dollars for fiscal year 1948 for aid to Turkey. Additional funds have since been appropriated. A joint survey made by the State and War Departments in June 1947 determined that the first needs of Turkey were for military aid in order to modernize and to increase the effectiveness of her fighting forces, and that the greatest portion of the initial funds should be applied towards this end.

In August 1947 the Mission for Aid to Turkey was created, with temporary headquarters in Washington, and was made up of Army, Navy, and Air Force Groups. Major General Horace L. McBride, the head of the Army Group, by virtue of seniority, is also coordinator of the joint mission. The Army Group is titled "Turkish United States Army Group" and abbreviated "TUSAG." It is organized under the conventional United States staff organization of general and special staff sections, to include the Arms and Services. The scope of this article will be confined to the activities and experiences of the Artillery Section of TUSAG. It is regrettable that for security reasons many interesting details cannot be published in an open article.

The first mission of the Artillery Section before departure from the United States was to determine itemized lists of artillery equipment required for a tentative troop strength for the Turkish Army, and the second mission was the preparation of plans for instruction of key personnel of Turkish units in the reception, operation, and maintenance of American equipment. Study of the report made by the original survey group (OLIVER REPORT —Maj. General Lundsford Oliver) supplied information about the Turkish Army, its organization, and its installations. When the location and physical facilities of the Turkish Artillery School were learned, it was decided that the most practical and effective method of conducting indoctrination and technical courses of instruction would be to fully exploit the facilities of the school. It was early apparent

that artillery material would con a generous portion of the aid ment. Much equipment was obt from surplus war stocks at about of cost price.

By extreme good fortune the A can personnel of the Artillery S. were selected directly from instr: of Departments of Instruction at Sill and Fort Bliss. By November the advanced echelon had arriv Turkey and by February 1948 al sonnel had closed in Ankara. Al riving was a large shipment of con copies of Programs of Instruction son Plans, Instructor Notes, and instructional material used for courses at Sill and Bliss; duplica Training Aids; American training and film strips; and of course cop American field and technical man

Continuous conferences were s with the Turkish Chief of Ar. with the Commandant and Facu. the School, and with the General It was apparent that the activit: the Artillery Section would lie i fields: in instruction at the Ar School and in an advisory capac tactical units, with the first re ment becoming the main effort. for security reasons the field force not be discussed, except to say dealings with them are in the nat: follow-up visits, to insure that de and technique as taught in the is being correctly disseminated a assist with training problems.

105mm how btry on the road at the School

288

I must pause to say that the reception of American personnel by the Turkish Government, the Army, and the people has been hearty and open-handed. From the beginning there have been frank, straightforward, and direct dealings on both sides. Far-reaching good will and important understanding has resulted, since neither the Turks nor the Americans are subject to thin-skinned sensibilities.

Out of the conferences there evolved a plan to introduce initially into the school, under the guidance of U. S. instructors, special courses of instruction, and at a future date to level off into a long-range military educational program. The Chief of Staff of the Turkish Army having announced the decision that American tactical doctrine and technique was adopted by the Turkish Army, the way was cleared for the American personnel to make detailed plans. Among the first things that had to be done were: preparation of new T/O & E's; blocking out and preparing courses for the school, including the voluminous work of writing lesson plans; and the great task of translation into Turkish the adapted instructional material and the field and technical manuals to be used as texts.

T/O & E's were based on those of similar-type units and calibers in the United States Army, with some adaptation and modifications. Loading charts ere prepared as a check against the T/O and E's and to be used as a training aid to quickly disseminate detailed understanding of the T/O & E's. Except for uniform differences, although there is a striking similarity between the newly adopted Turkish and the American uniforms, an American artilleryman would have to look sharply to distinguish between the new Turkish and an American artillery unit on the march, in firing position, or in camp or bivouac.

The first courses at the School were designed to indoctrinate key officers and soldiers in American technique and to teach them mechanical operation and maintenance of equipment, in order to reorganize, under new T/O & E's, to receive, operate, and maintain equipment arriving from the United States. Graduates returned to their units and conducted unit schools. Thereafter courses at the school were patterned after the war-time short courses at Bliss and Sill, with the aim of providing quickly sufficient numbers of qualified graduates to fill key and specialist T/O positions in troop units. There are also special basic and advanced courses for junior and senior officers. At a later date the school program will level off into annual and semi-annual courses.

Translations presented a problem of large proportions as to volume and numbers of translators required. The Turkish General Staff rounded up all the English-speaking officers it could lay its hands on and supplemented these with civilians. Enough were assembled so that, by 1 May 1948, courses were in full operation at the school. The best working plan developed was that the Americans would write out subject matter in longhand, pass it on to translators who turned it into Turkish longhand. From there it went to Turkish typists who cut mimeograph stencils, with draftsmen reproducing drawings, sketches, etc.

Translation introduced many new technical terms and phrases into the Turkish language. A dictionary of military terms was prepared by a board of American and Turkish officers, which was invaluable in translations. Realizing that errors and foggy translations would occur as a result of haste and newness of terms, no effort was made to print manuals until after the mimeograph copies had been tested as texts for one or more courses in the school. Students and instructors were charged to be alert and errors were discovered and rapidly reduced.

Another problem was to assemble course instructors. English-speaking Turkish officers who had worked as translators formed a nucleus and additional students were added to each course from which future instructors were chosen. To tag the top students as instructors is a pernicious practice, condemned by the Turkish as stoutly as by the American tactical units, but necessary if high standards are to be established and maintained at the schools. A longer-range program of

---

sending English-speaking Turkish officers to courses in the American artillery schools was instituted.

Sound-tape recorders were brought over with the training aids. The English-narrative sound tracks on training films were translated into Turkish and recorded. It is simple to synchronize the recorder and projector, and American training films are effectively used in instruction.

Concurrently with the introduction of new courses, the school-troops units were increased, reorganized under new T/O & E's, equipped, and trained. A plan for the reorganization of the school to provide an adequate staff and faculty was drawn and approved. Instructional departments were reorganized or newly created. A building program was initiated to provide increased housing for students, instruction, troops, gun and motor sheds, maintenance, and storage facilities. Firing ranges and training areas were greatly increased. The Turkish Army has or is rapidly acquiring the facilities for a completely modern artillery school capable of turning out graduates as well trained as those of any army, and in sufficient numbers to fill full mobilization tables of organization spaces with a reservoir of trained replacements. While an artillery training center is not independently set up, the school at any time could be separated into a school and training center.

Unabashedly the Turkish Artillery School is patterned in detail after its American counterpart. A current cliché among the American personnel is that should an instructor from Sill be transported to Turkey overnight he would find his class and could continue his instruction without pause. This is a slight exaggeration. A visitor from Sill, however, would find a duplicate of every instructional department and the air full of cub planes. The local terrain is a duplicate of West Range, Ft. Sill.

While many difficulties do arise, American personnel have found this a most interesting and challenging assignment. All armies are bound by regulations and red tape to about the same degree. We have found the Turk to be a forthright person. He is very serious and intent in his undertakings. As a student he compares favorably with American students. The average soldier does not possess the same mechanical or educational background, but earnestness of purpose goes a long way in making up the difference. He grasps and retains what he has been taught. Since Turkey has universal military training, considerable numbers of trained automobile mechanics, drivers, radio mechanics, operators, instrument operators, clerks, and typists will annually return to civilian life. This will be an important boost to the national economy.

The Staff College and other branch and service schools have been operating in the same manner as the Artillery School with about the same experiences.

The post-war American Army is operating some twenty military missions to aid foreign countries, and the chances are that this number may be increased. It probably will not [be] common for most officers soon later to be assigned to this ty[pe] duty. For this reason details a[re in]cluded in this article which othe[rwise] would be of no particular interest[.]

The Turks have traditionally [been] rugged combat men. There is toda[y] intense national spirit. No such t[hing] as a potential fifth column exists. [An] American moralist could no d[oubt] make criticisms of individual free[dom] and an economist could criticize [mo]nopolies, but the country is on a mo[bili]zation footing, and security and [eco]nomic controls are necessarily tight.

The discipline of the Army is [out]standing. Outside of the unkn[own] quantity of Russia they have the b[est] army in Europe today. Modern equ[ip]ment being supplied under the aid p[ro]gram, skillfully employed on natura[l] strong defensive terrain, will make th[em] a formidable opponent indeed. Th[ere] is no doubt about their ability or w[ill] to put up effective and stubborn res[is]tance if their country is attacked.

The United States has a long-ran[ge] stake in Turkey. The geographic[al] location in Asia Minor and across th[e] Bosphorus in Thrace places it on th[e] flank of a possible communist advanc[e] through the Balkans to the Mediterra[-]nean, or through Iran, Irak, Syria, an[d] Palestine to Africa. Full value i[s] realized for every American militar[y] dollar spent in strengthening Turke[y.] This is a critical area where effective measures, if continued and exploited, can be placed in opposition to the expansion of communism.

Demonstration at the School — Occupation of position by 105mm how btry

APPENDIX "G"

MY TOTAL FLYING HOURS IN KOREA

FLYING HOURS IN KOREA 1950 – 1951

Type Msn*	L4	L5	L19	TOTALS
C21	20h 30m	152h 20m	422h 20m	595h 10m
C27	6h 30m	20h 20m	28h 05m	54h 55m
TOTALS:	27:00	172:40	450:25	650:05

*C21 missions are those flown over the front lines
*C27 mission are administrative flights in rear areas

MONTHLY RUNDOWN

Month	Hours Flown	Days Flown/Flyable Days	Avg hours/day
Aug. 1950 ⎫	36:05		
Jan. 1951 ⎭			
Feb.	51:50	17/26	3:00
March	126:30	28/31	4:30
Apr	137:00	30/30	4:20
May	122:50	29/31	4:15 6
June	75:40	23/30**	3:30 **days R&R
July	100:10	28/31	3:35
TOTAL:	650:05		3:52 (avg. for 6 months)
C21 Time	595:10		
C27	54:55		

Avg hours flown/day during heaviest fighting:

28Mar-5Apr 55 hrs 9 days 6 hrs/day (Operation RUGGED-Retaking Ln KANSAS,
                                           38th Parallel)

20-27 Apr 32   8   4   (CCF first Offensive – Largest single battle of the
                                           Korean War)

22-25 May 23   4   6   (CCF Second Spring Offensive)

N. B. This is a lot of flying. The USAF certainly puts in much, much more flying, but remember, much of that time is spent just getting to the target area and, hopefully, returning safely. When our "Puddlejumpers take off," we are firing missions in a matter of minutes.

APPENDIX "H"

COMPUTATION OF MINIMUM ELEVATIONS FOR

THE FIRING BATTERY

COMPUTATION OF MEs FOR THE FIRING BATTERY When one boresights on obstructing terrain to the front of the battery firing position, one cannot simply measure the elevation, or quadrant (which includes site, or vertical interval between level and that highest point divided by range), and fire without serious effects on troops to the front. The howitzer, rather than a gun, is used in direct support because it can fire at higher angles to clear high ground and still drop its projectiles in the target area. But when a projo leaves the tube, it is naive, even for a non-Redleg, to assume it will follow a straight line path or trajectory. When the projo leaves the tube, spinning from the rifling in the tube, it immediately follows a hypocycloidal path, and then when such wobbling ceases, it remains subject to forces that further disrupts straight line flight. These deviations may yet allow the round to land close to the target but not exactly where the firing table intended or planned. In calculating firing table data, factors such as probable error, both in range and deflection, complementary site (compsite), VE, etc are considered. But FTs are based on actual firings of the piece and its ammo under, or correlated to a set of wx, position and materiel conditions defined or accepted as standard. Therefore they render data more accurate the closer actual firing conditions approach these standards. So far, enough has been said to emphasize the importance of accuracy in calculating the minimum elevation at each firing position. It should also become obvious that merely pointing the tube at the highest peak or crest directly in front of the howitzers, measuring the elevation and labelling it the ME is just not very bright and worse, it is dangerous. Without delving into definitions of PE's, forks, VEs and such, we can now jump to how MEs are calculated. As seen from the sketch on the fourth page of Chapter 6, four angles besides the simplistic. erroneous "boresighted" angle to the obstruction, MUST be added to that angle to insure the safety of friendly troops including those in the firing btry if they are occupying the crest concerned. Now the exec can laboriously consume important time and compute the ME for every position his battery occupies. But, once the charge to be fired is known, the only variable that deviates from the FT values for that charge and range to the obstruction before the battery is the angle of site, or "boresighted" angle. To avoid countless repetitive, time consuming calculations every time the exec pulls into a new FP, he can prepare his own table

of "canned" values such that all he has to do is to add the highest
angle of site reported to the value he already computed in his little
"pocket table for MEs." Looking at Table #1 the Work Sheet For
Elevation Table following, note the exec has listed all the parameters
required for the determination of an ME for a particular Charge at
arbitrary ranges to the mask. Next, peruse the following Table 2
Elevation Table and see the precalculated values for an ME at the
range to the mask and the charge to be fired.

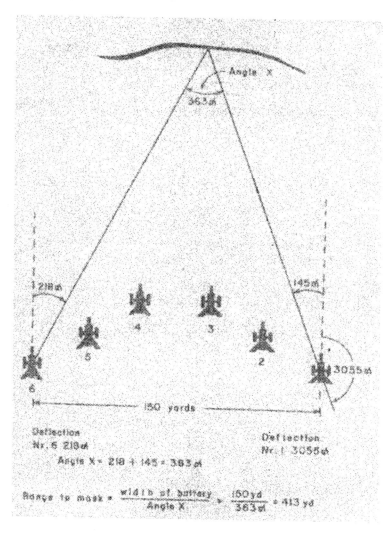

TABLE 1

WORK SHEET FOR ELEVATION TABLE

105-mm Howitzer M2, Shell HE, Charge 5, Fuze M48 and M54

Range to Mask	Elevation	Two Forks	8 Yards	Total
100	5.4	4	50	59.4
150	7.8	4	33.3	44.9
200	9.8	4	28	38.8
250	12.1	4	20	36.1
300	14.4	4	16.7	35.1
400	18.2	4	12.5	35.7
500	23.8	6	10	39.8
600	28.6	6	8.3	42.9
700	33.4	6	7.1	46.5
800	38.4	6	6.3	50.7
900	43.2	6	5.6	54.8
1000	48.2	6	5	59.2

Adding the proper value from table above to the elevation from the Firing Table at the correct range to mask, the XO has quickly gotten the ME

TABLE 2

ELEVATION TABLE

105-mm Howitzer M2, Shell HE, Fuze M48 and M54

Range (yards)	Elevation (mils)						
	Ch 1	Ch 2	Ch 3	Ch 4	Ch 5	Ch 6	Ch 7
100	60	61	60	61	60	57	56
150	48	50	47	47	45	42	40
200	46	46	42	42	39	36	33
250	48	46	43	41	37	32	29
300	51	48	44	41	36	30	26
400	58	55	47	43	36	29	24
500	70	63	53	46	40	30	24
600	81	71	59	53	43	32	24
700	94	82	66	59	47	34	25
800	108	91	78	65	51	37	27
900	118	101	83	71	56	39	28
1000	132	113	91	77	60	43	30

Note: To obtain minimum elevation, add greatest site reported by chiefs of section to appropriate elevation in table.

e.g. With piece mask rn of 600 exec adds 42.9 mils from Work Sheet above to the firing table elevation of 43 mils at range of 600 using Ch5 and FQ to get ME of 85.9 or 86 mils.

Now all the exec has to do is leap out of his jeep or FDC 3/4 ton, lay the battery, check boresighting of all pieces, if necessary, with the help of his C/S's, receive the highest angle of site from the six reported, and add that value to those precalculated from his pocket table. Note these tables shown are for a 105H firing HE and PD or time fuze. Separate tables may have to be prepared for other fuzes or different mask ranges. But, if, for example, Fz VT is to be fired, the exec's table would only require changes in Angle 2 because the clearance then becomes 80 instead of 5 yards. The ranges to mask will vary with the existing terrain and other factors. Experience will dictate any such changes in range, perhaps involving ranges in between the ones calculated or greater/lesser ranges to mask. But these are minor problems and should never bar the habit of making such useful and important time savers. Upon simple reflection, all true field artillerymen have a debt of gratitude to Generals Handy and Burger for their brilliant contribution to the efficacy of and time saving advantages given to every good firing battery executive officer, the most rewarding job in the US Army. 'Nuff said

Kincheon H (Bert) Bailey

APPENDIX "I"

MEDICAL SUPPORT FOR TROOPS IN KOREA

MEDICAL SUPPORT

Every combat soldier is well aware of the utility and outstanding bravery and medical expertise exhibited by the company medics. Many lives have been saved or the effects of wounds minimized by the work of these generally unsung saviors. In my battery in Korea, our two medics, Attikouzel and Beaton, were prime examples of what I am trying to say. You have already read about their heroics in old "A" Battery. Our losses were severe that night of 3d September but not nearly so bad had these two heroes not been on the job.

Another class of heroes amongst our medical cadre are the self-effacing members of the gentler sex,—-our nurses. These heroes are not usually heard of much. But here I have extracted from THE GRAYBEARD magazine, that outstanding organ of our Korean miasma, three articles that bring out prime examples of the work done by our nurses in various parts of Korea. The first expounds on the heart thrown into their work of saving lives in the battle area. The next two present the splendid work performed by two outstanding nurses in the field, one in several wars.

The Language of the Heart

By Janice Feagin Britton.
801st Medical Air Evacuation Unit

In 1946 the Fifth Air Force assigned twelve flight nurses to Tachikawa, an airbase thirty miles from Tokoyo. My orders assigned me to the 801st Medical Air Evacuation Unit attached to the 317th Troop Carrier Wing. Our primary mission was to move patients from the Army Hospital in Seoul, Korea to Japan. The orders were full of the unknown to me.

"We're flying where? Doing what?" I didn't know one thing about Korea. The map showed Korea a peninsular off the Asian continent east of the Sea of Japan. A fascinating discovery on my first trip was that both men and women all wore white. Clear, stark white. This seemed unbelievable because they always appeared neat and clean despite the dust and poor accessibility to water. One well served people in a settlement of thirty or so people who lived in mud-straw huts. Women squatted as they washed their clothes then carefully placed them flat on the grass to dry in the sun.

Air evacuation of patients from Korea to Japan in C-46 or c-47 planes was soon routine. At first we flew a "round robin" along with a "medical tech" from Tachikawa to Kimpo Army Air base, a two hour flight, where we spent the night and returned next day with a plane load of patients.

We had to get a weather clearance and call the hospital before the patients actually were loaded into ambulances and traveled twenty tortuous miles from the Army hospital in Seoul to the Kimpo airbase. They traveled over dusty-muddy

red clay roads across the one bridge (it was on pontoons) spanning the Han River.

Like a sponge my mind sucked up bits and pieces of their fascinating culture. These Koreans, created by God the same as me, were different and yet the same. They revered their ancestry, buried their dead standing up. Males were born into a dominant role. My mind's eye still sees the women wearing black rubber shoes with upturned toes trailing behind the men as they walked down the road.

Kimpchee, a favorite food, was a mixture of garlic, hot peppers, cabbage and onions was stored in clay crocks looking precisely like the old Alabama churn used to made butter. The troops were not allowed to eat off base. Koreans were struggling to feed themselves.

In time, a 50 bed holding hospital rose up in Kimpo near base operations. This made for smoother operations but

required the nurses to spend a month on TDY at Kimpo. Quarters in a Quonset were provided for the flight nurses, the only women on base overnight, with MP's on duty nearby to protect us.

A rosy cheeked Korean girl named Kim kept our meager quarters clean. We did not know each others languages but we communicated. One day I noticed her she was having difficulty doing her work because her forefinger was swollen. I arranged for her to have it treated at the dispensary.

After her finger was healed she arrived one morning, all smiles as usual, and handed me a foot long bundle of rice straw, round like a tube. I thought, "what a strange custom giving sheaths of rice straw." But wait, I felt something, then I saw. The straw covered five fresh eggs laid end on end. I hadn't seen a real fresh egg for eons. How good it would be to eat a fresh egg. This was a true sacrifice for her. The language of the heart has no boundaries.

Picture of H-13 showing how the patients got to the 8076th M*A*S*H for whom I flew Med. Evac. in 1951-52. The location is the town of Hwachon, Korea. I am the one with my head down, to avoid the rotor blades, in the white T-shirt. I was unloading two patients at that time. To learn more about our service the University Press of Kentucky is the publisher and Dr Apels book is titled MASH. His words are being inscribed in the National Archives and the book is now in its fifth reprinting. Ed Ziegler, Major USA

These Koreans, created by God the same as me, were different and yet the same. They revered their ancestry, buried their dead standing up.

301

8062 Mobile Army Surgical Hospital, Korea
Chapter honors Capt. Betty Burns, MASH Nurse

Capt. (ret.) Elizabeth (Betty) Burns (17598 KWVA) was honored by the Central NY Chapter and her fellow 7th Division past members to which her MASH unit was attached. Members were 17th Regt (Fred Osborne, John Reidy, Dick Houser, Pete Doyle, Henry Tisdall, Tony Spoto, Nick Bronchetti), 31st Regt (Frank Hyman, Lloyd Pittman, Jon Trembley, Richard Owens, Anthony Clavelli), 32nd Regt., Rawls, Dick Rutkowski.

Betty Burns with Papa-san hat and pipe outside her tent.

Aerial view of hospital taken from helicopter.

8063 Mash chopper takes only 2 patients, pilot and Evacuation Nurse Frank Shatlude (cousin) riding shotgun.

Capt Elizabeth "Betty" Burns with unidentified veteran comrades.

"She saved my life twice," said William E. Broader who was in Pattons 3rd ending up in the 97th Hospital (Berlin) where Betty was a nurse.

"She saved my life twice," said William E. Broader who was in Pattons 3rd ending up in the 97th Hospital (Berlin) where Betty was a nurse. The 2nd time was in Korea where Bill was with the 13th Engineers (7th Div.) wounded and treated by Betty again. I was amazed to see her again 50 years later when I joined the CNY Chapter, also was amazed that we grew up together and our family's lived 1 block away.

Betty's comments in "Back Down the Ridge" by W. Z. White were that they were at all times 4-8 miles from all battles near Wonju -- moved 33 times in 1 year -- advanced with tanks and bugged out when tanks retreated. They handled approximatley 300 casualties per day; averaging 16 hrs surgery and 4 hrs break per day. This resulted, in many burnouts of Medics, Doctors, Nurses and Chaplains who set up wounded for surgery. They provided white sheets to all wounded on both sides and the Chinese carried packets of morphine and usually had cooties, lice and maggots in their wounds, also many foot problems from their canvas shoes. All were given type "O" blood.

Tents eliminated Red Cross Logo as they were bombed by MIGS. Tents had dirt floors only and because of rats (the kind with ears) nests and mites which spread Sango (Hemorrhagic) Fever, many patients were transferred to Murphy Army Hospital, Boston.

(Thank you K. Dave Allen for a great story about a brave veteran called Betty, that helped save many lives including those named.)

Betty Burns in North Korea.

302

Parts extracted from article by Jack Tamplin in THE GRAYBEARDS THE MOST DECORATED FRONTLINE ARMY NURSE—WWII AND KOREA Col Bradley, the most decorated woman to ever serve in the Armed Forces of the US, now in her nineties, is still as spry and engaging as anyone could imagine. This 30-year old member of the Army Nurse Corps, was captured in the Philippine Islands by the Japanese in Dec 1941 and held prisoner until Feb '45.

In Jul '50, Bradley was ordered to Fort Bragg, NC, to take over as Chief Nurse of the 171st Evacuation Hospital, a unit headed for a "police action" in a cold and dusty place called Korea.

Ruby was off to war again. From Aug till Dec, the evac hospital shifted its position along the front lines, treating wave after wave of casualties. "It got to the point." Ruby remembers, "where I didn't want to see another drop of blood."

From Taegu the hospital moved to Pyongyang then up to Kongyang and just as the unit was settling in, the Chinese finally entered the fighting. Hundreds of thousands of "Chi-Com" troops joined by North Korean regulars came sweeping across the 38th parallel and the 171st Evac was right in the enemy's path.

Quickly, aircraft and ambulances started to evacuate patients and staff. Bradley sent her subordinates out with the first round of evacuees and stayed to supervise the withdrawal of the rest. "Some of the girls who came back to help could see the North Koreans going by. We were really that near the fighting. WE were right up there and by this time we didn't know how to get out."

Headquarters, meanwhile, suddenly remembered Ruby had once been a POW. "Now I didn't know this till later on," she said, "but they said, 'You get her out of this. We can't have that happen to her again. Get her out as fast as you can." As her evacuation plane taxied down the runway, Bradley could hear the sound of sniper fire just outside the aircraft door.

In 1951 she was named Chief Nurse for the Eighth Army, supervising the work of some five hundred nurses at various hospitals and aid stations across Korea. Along the way, she was promoted to Lt Col and in Jun '53, with the Korean truce talks under way at Panmujon, she was handed orders for home. The CG, Eighth Army, Gen Maxwell Taylor, decided to give her a big sendoff. He had been so impressed with her three years of combat service in Korea, he ordered a full dress military review and parade for her departure, the first time a woman in the American military had been so honored. On 4 Mar 58, Ruby Bradley became one of three women in the Army of the United States to be awarded the permanent rank of Colonel, an extraordinary achievement for any woman. In the years that followed she won more medals and more honors and finally in 1963 Colonel Ruby Bradley. 50 years old, retired from active service, the most decorated woman in American military history. So even the women serving in Korea were the best! So mote it be!

Lt. Col. Bradley

Stone marker in front of the Roane County
Courthouse in Spencer, WV to honor Ruby

APPENDIX "J"

AWARDS RECEIVED BY "A" BATTERY

The 64th FA Bn received the DISTINGUISHED UNIT CITATION for outstanding performance of duty for the period 1-5 Sep 1950 as described in General Orders 49, DA, dated 11 Jul 51.

The 64th FA Bn also received the PRESIDENTIAL UNIT CITATION for extraordinary heroism in action against enemy aggressor forces in Korea during the periods 21 to 26 April, 16 May to 30 Jun and 11 to 25 Sep 1951.

The following personnel received the Silver Star for action with "A" Battery on 3 Sep 50 while beating off an attack on the battery in Saga, Korea:

> Lt KH Bailey, Btry Exec O
> Cpl Bobby McQuitty (his 2d Silver Star), Battery Wire Team
> Unknown soldier who received the Silver Star posthumously

The following personnel received the Bronze Star for Valor, also on 3 Sep 50:

Sgt Herbert L Rawls, Jr	Wire Team Chief
Sgt Joseph R Pursley	Wire Team member
Cpl Attikouzel	Btry Medic
Cpl Beaton	Btry Medic

The Air Medal w/9 OLC awarded Lt KH Bailey for the period Feb-Jul 51

These are the only orders I have in my possession; there were others but all reflect highly on the recipients as well as all members of the battery each of whom contributed to the successes "A" Battery enjoyed under intense battle action and continuous pressure from the best the North Koreans and Chinese could hammer against vastly outnumbered UN forces.

```
GENERAL ORDERS:                    DEPARTMENT OF THE ARMY     GO 49
No. 49         :                   Washington 25, D.C. 11 July 1951     109
                                                              Section

DISTINGUISHED UNIT CITATION-Citation of units                     I
MERITORIOUS UNIT COMMENDATION-Awards                             II
```

Sect 1, para 1 and 2 extracted

3. The 35th Infantry Regiment (less Heavy Tank Company), 25th Infantry Division, and the following attached units:
    64th Field Artillery Battalion
    Company A, 8 th Medium Tank Battalion
    Battery C, 90th Field Artillery Battalion
    Company B, 65th Engineer Combat Battalion
    1st Platoon, Battery A, 25th AAA Battalion
    Tactical Air Control Party, 80th Fighter-Bomber Squadron
are cited for exceptionally outstanding performance of duty in combat against the enemy near Masan, Korea, from 1 to 4 September 1950. The regiment and attached units, deployed in a defensive position along the Nam River on a 25,000-yard front, were heavily attacked by the 7th North Korean Division and elements of the 4th, 6th, and 9th North Korean Divisions, including supporting armor and artillery. The determined and repeated assaults drove the units back on each flank of the 35th Infantry Regiment. By infiltration and flanking movements, the enemy was able to penetrate to the rear of the regiment. Under these critical conditions and in the face of fanatical frontal assaults, the gallant defenders turned back attack after attack by small-arms fire, grenades, and hand-to-hand combat. Artillery and rear echelon units were brought under direct assault by hostile infiltration and flanking attacks. Several positions were surrounded, but the men stood their ground. All elements found themselves engaged in close combat. Through ability, courage, tenacity, and indomitable fighting spirit, the enemy was contained and denied his most cherished objective, the capture of Pusan. The extraordinary heroism, steadfastness, and courageous determination of the 35th Infantry Regiment, 25th Infantry Division, and attached units reflect the highest credit on themselves and uphold the esteemed traditions of the Army of the United States.

Paragraph 4 extracted

Section 2, paragraph 1 through 25 extracted

    BY ORDER OF THE SECRETARY OF THE ARMY:

```
OFFICIAL:                          J. LAWTON COLLINS
   WM. E. BERGIN                    Chief of Staff, United States Army
   Major General, USA
   Acting The Adjutant General
```

CERTIFIED A TRUE EXTRACT COPY:

K. H. BAILEY JR.
Capt., Artillery

Kincheon H (Bert) Bailey

GENERAL ORDERS)
)
NO. 38   )

HEADQUARTERS,
DEPARTMENT OF THE ARMY
Washington 25, D. C., 30 July 1957
Section

PRESIDENTIAL UNIT CITATION (NAVY)—Award to United States Army units during
  the Korean Operations - I
NAVY UNIT COMMENDATION—Award to United States Army units during the
  Korean Operations - II

I. --PRESIDENTIAL UNIT CITATION (NAVY). The following award of the
Presidential Unit Citation (Navy) is confirmed in accordance with AR 220-315:

Units

1st Ordnance Medium Maintenance
  Company
7th Reconnaissance Company
8th Field Artillery Battalion
9th Infantry Regiment, 1st Battalion
10th Engineer Combat Battalion, Company D
15th Infantry Regiment, 1st Battalion
17th Field Artillery Battalion, Battery C
21st Anti-aircraft Artillery Automatic Weapons Battalion
31st Infantry Regiment
  Headquarters Company
  Company B, 1st Battalion
  2d Battalion (less Company E)
  Tank Company
Provisional Battalion (Detachments
  31st and 3nd Regimental Combat
  Teams)
32d Infantry Regiment, 1st Battalion
61st Engineer Company
64th Field Artillery Battalion
65th Infantry Regiment, 1st Battalion
69th Field Artillery Battalion
74th Truck Company
84th Engineer Construction Battalion
86th Engineer Searchlight Company
  3d Platoon
89th Tank Battalion
90th Field Artillery Battalion
92d Army Engineer Searchlight
  Platoon
159th Field Artillery Battalion, (155
  Howitzer)
163d Military Intelligence Service
  Detachment (Redesignated Platoon

Citation

PRESIDENTIAL UNIT CITATION (NAVY)
awarded, in the name of the President
of the United States, by the Secretary
of the Navy. The citation reads as
follows:
For extraordinary heroism in action
against enemy aggressor forces in
Korea during the periods 21 to 26
April, 16 May to 30 June, and 11 to
25 September 1951. Spearheading the
first counteroffensive in the spring
of 1951, the FIRST Marine Division,
Reinforced, engaged the enemy in the
mountainous center of Korea in a brilliant series of actions unparalleled
in the history of the Marine Corps,
destroying and routing hostile forces
with an unrelenting drive of seventy
miles north from Wonju. During the
period 21 to 26 April, the full force
of the enemy counteroffensive was met
by the Division, north of the Hwachon
Reservoir. Although major units flanking the Marine Division were destroyed
or driven back by the force of this attack, the Division held firm against
the attackers, repelling the onslaught
from three directions and preventing
the encirclement of the key center of
the lines. Following a rapid regrouping of friendly forces in close contact with the enemy, the FIRST Marine
Division, Reinforced, was committed into
the flanks of the massive enemy penetration and, from 16 May to 30 June, was
locked in a violent and crucial battle
which resulted in the enemy being driven

308

Units	Citation

Units

196th Field Artillery Battalion
204th Field Artillery Battalion, Batteries A and B
441st Counter Intelligence Corps Detachment
461st Infantry Battalion
513th Truck Company
558th Transportation Truck Company
623d Field Artillery Battalion

Citation

wounded and captured. Carrying out a series of devastating assaults, the Division succeeded in reducing the enemy's main fortified complex dominating the 38th Parallel. In the final significant offensive of the action in Korea, from 11 to 25 September 1959, the FIRST Marine Division, Reinforced, completed the destruction of the enemy forces in Eastern Korea by advancing the front against a final desperate enemy defense in the "Punch Bowl" area in heavy action which completed the liberation of South Korea in this locality. With the enemy's major defenses reduced, his forces on the central front decimated, and the advantage of terrain and the tactical initiative passing to friendly forces, he never again recovered sufficiently to resume the offensive in Korea. The outstanding courage, resourcefulness and aggressive fighting spirit of the officers and men of the FIRST Marine Division, Reinforced, reflect the highest credit upon themselves and the United States Naval Service.

* * * * * * * *

BY ORDER OF WILBER M. BRUCKER, SECRETARY OF THE ARMY:

MAXWELL D. TAYLOR,
General, United States Army,
Chief of Staff

OFFICIAL:

HERBERT M. JONES
Major General, United States Army,
The Adjutant General

A CERTIFIED TRUE COPY:

C. H. BROOKS
Secretary
Dept of Gunnery

Kincheon H (Bert) Bailey

SPECIAL ORDERS   28 October 1950
NUMBER   255   EXTRACT

    AWARD OF THE SILVER STAR. - By direction of the President, under the pro-
visions of the act of Congress approved 9 July 1918 (WD Bul 43 1918) and pur-
suant to authority in AR 600-45, the Silver Star for gallantry in action is awarded to the following-named officers and enlisted men:

    First Lieutenant KINCHEON H. BAILEY JR, 027531, Artillery, 64th Field Artillery
Battalion, United States Army. When his artillery section in the vicinity of Haman,
Korea was being attacked by numerically superior enemy forces on 2 September 1950,
Lieutenant Bailey went to a howitzer and turned it completely around to fire point
blank at the oncoming enemy. Despite the intense enemy fire he remained in the open
to relay fire commands for the mission. Lieutenant Bailey's courageous devotion to
duty and outstanding leadership were responsible for disrupting the fanatical attack
and reflect great credit upon himself and the Armed Forces. Entered the military
service from Virginia.

                *

    BY COMMAND OF MAJOR GENERAL KEAN:

OFFICIAL: JOHN W. CHILDS
                                               Colonel, GSC
                                               Chief of Staff
/s/ G. W. Master
/t/ G. W. MASTER
    Lt Colonel, AGC
    Adjutant General

A CERTIFIED TRUE EXTRACT COPY:

HAROLD J. DOUBLET
WOJG   USA
Ass't Adjutant

310

Citation

Air Medal (Ninth Bronze Oak Leaf Cluster)

Section IV General Orders Number 590
Headquarters 25th Infantry Division
4 December 1951

Captain KINGMON M. BAILEY JR., 027531,
Artillery, Headquarters and Headquarters
Battery, 64th Field Artillery Battalion,
United States Army. During the period 23
June to 18 July 1951, in Korea, Captain
BAILEY performed thirty combat missions in
support of the 25th Infantry Division. By
his accurate spotting of targets for United
Nations Forces and by obtaining valuable re-
connaissance information he contributed ma-
terially to the success of Division opera-
tions.
Entered the military service from Virginia.

Kincheon H (Bert) Bailey

APPENDIX "K"

END OF THE KOREAN WAR

C-64th FA BN
firing the last
mission of the
Korean War
0714 hours
27Jul53

Charlie Battery
dismantling Hq
bunkers on
28Jul53

2d Lt Alton Janes, watching the bunkers being dismantled

Charlie Battery, 64th FA Bn——— who else ????

Sign of Headquarters, 64th FA Bn with
service ribbons added below.

A few days before 1 May 53, Lt James and his C/FB, M/Sgt John Pheiffer of Orlando, OK, were taken to the south side of the bridge shown below. They were told that there were many 1000s of enemy troops just north of our lines and they were expected to attack on May Day as they had in the past. We were to be ready to move our guns and ammo to a spot in the rice paddies and if the attack came, we would allow all UN forces cross. Then, we were to prevent the enemy from crossing as long as we could, then destroy the bridge. They did not attack (as seen by the photo below). If they had, Lt James states – stoically, — you readers would not be perusing these notes. So mote it be!!

Lamp on next page was made by Lt William Doring out of a 105 mm shellcase that held the last projectile fired in the Korean War. It was fired by C-64th FA. A most rewarding memento of the cessation of that bitter war.

On the next page is shown a larger view of this shell with the inscription thereon written below since the picture is the best I could reproduce with my HP4400C scanner.

CHARLIE BATTERY
   64th FA Bn
LAST FOUND FIRED
   KOREA
0714 27 JULY 1953

APPENDIX "L"

KOREAN WAR STATISTICS

ALLIED FORCES CONTRIBUTIONS

KOREAN WAR MEMORIAL IN WASHINGTON, D. C.

★★

Revised U.S. Military Korean War Statistics:

(Released 2001)

Battle Dead: **33,741**

Killed in Action:	23,615
Died of Wounds	2,459
Died While Missing (MIA)	4,820
Died While Captured (POW)	2,847

Non-Battle Deaths   **2,827**

Total Deaths in Theater: **36,568**

Died Elsewhere (Worldwide during Korean War)   **17,678**

Total Deaths   **54,246**

Wounded (not mortal)   **103,284**

By Branch of Service

Total Army battle deaths	27,731
Total Air Force battle deaths	1,238
Total Marine battle deaths	4,267
Total Navy battle deaths	505

Unaccounted (Bodies not identified/bodies not recovered)   **8,064**

Prisoner of War	1,900
Killed in Action	1,572
Missing in Action	4,592

Prisoners of War   **7,286**

POWs Returned to US Control	4,418
POWs Who Died While Captured	2,847
POWs Who Refused Repatriation	21

Number who Served in Korean Theater   **1,789,000**

Number who Served Worldwide   **5,720,000**

★★

ALLIED FORCES CONTRIBUTIONS DURING THE KOREAN WAR

Country	Army	Navy*	Air Force
Australia	2 infantry battalions	9 naval vessels	1 fighter squadron
Belgium/Luxembourg	1 infantry battalion	n.a.**	n.a.
Canada	1 infantry brigade	8 naval vessels	1 transport squadron
Colombia	1 infantry battalion	6 naval vessels	n.a.
Ethiopia	1 infantry battalion	n.a.	n.a.
France	1 infantry battalion	1 naval vessel	n.a.
Greece	1 infantry battalion	n.a.	1 transport battalion
Netherlands	1 infantry battalion	6 naval vessels	n.a.
New Zealand	1 artillery regiment	4 naval vessels	n.a.
Philippines	1 battalion combat team	n.a.	n.a.
South Africa	15 soldiers attached to British ground forces	n.a.	1 fighter squadron
Thailand	1 infantry battalion	4 naval vessels	1 transport unit
Turkey	1 infantry brigade	n.a.	n.a.
United Kingdom	2 infantry brigades	50 naval vessels	n.a.

FOREIGN MEDICAL UNITS

Country/Unit Designation	Beds	Medical Staff	In-Patients
DENMARK Jutlandia Hospital Ship	360	200	15,000
INDIA 60th Field Ambulance Unit	1,000	345	20,000
ITALY Red Cross Hospital No. 68	150	131	17,041
NORWAY Mobile Army Surgical Hospital	200	106	14,755
SWEDEN Red Cross Field Hospital	450	160	900

Kincheon H (Bert) Bailey

Able Cannoneer, Jack Dodson, at the 50th Reunion
at Washington DC of the 25th Division's entering the Korean War
in June 1950

324

About the Author

Graduated from the USMA at West Point. NY 5Jun45. Graduating in the top 10% of his class in English, spelling, grammar and writing were simple chores for him. Friends came to him for help in writing resumes, book reports, etc.. With the Gunnery Department at Fort Sill, OK, he helped rewrite FM6-40 Field Artillery Gunnery. He rewrote battalion tests, improving grading techniques to more nearly assure accurate grading. Retiring from the US Army in 1966, he obtained an MS degree at Penn State in '67 and a DEd (with EE minor) at NCSU in '75. An EE technology instructor at Wake Tech CC in Raleigh for 25 years, after retiring from the US Army, wrote many technical articles for professional magazines. -

Printed in the United States
23244LVS00004B/46-279

9 781418 452803